Legal Problems and the Citizen

Legal Problems
and
the Citizen

A Study in Three London Boroughs

Brian Abel-Smith   Michael Zander

and

Rosalind Brooke

HEINEMANN

Heinemann Educational Books Ltd

LONDON   EDINBURGH   MELBOURNE   TORONTO
AUCKLAND   JOHANNESBURG   SINGAPORE
IBADAN   NAIROBI   HONG KONG   NEW DELHI

ISBN 0 435 82865 7

Published by Heinemann Educational Books Ltd
48 Charles Street, London W1X 8AH

Printed in Great Britain by C. Tinling & Co. Ltd,
London and Prescot

CONTENTS

		Page
Introduction		ix

Part I The Description

1. The Boroughs and their Advisory Services	3
2. Legal Advice Services	24
3. General Advisory Services	39

Part II The Survey of Agencies

4. The Use of Advisory Services	67
5. The Users of Advisory Services	88
6. Variations among Operational Units	95

Part III The Survey of Population

7. Concepts and Definitions	109
8. The Need for Advice	120
9. The Use of Advisers	146
10. The Failure to Take Advice	166
11. Knowledge of the Advisory Services	188
12. Opinions and Expectations	200
13. Conclusions	210

Appendix I	Method of Research for the Agency Survey	227
Appendix II	The Sample Used for the Population Survey	242
Appendix III	Attitudes to the Legal System	248
Index		258

TABLES

		Page
1.	The three new boroughs by constituent metropolitan boroughs and parliamentary constituencies	3
2.	Population 1961–76	8
3.	Population density per acre 1955–68	8
4.	Housing tenure in 1966	9
5.	Average number of persons per room by household size	10
6.	Average household size and ratio of households to dwellings, 1961 and 1966	10
7.	The age of dwelling units	11
8.	Percentage of dwelling units by length of useful life	12
9.	Local advisory agencies: hours open per week and number of staff available	16
10.	Number and percentage of visits by agency	68
11.	Number and percentage of visits by agency and by borough, and the number of visits per 1,000 of population	69
12.	Number and percentage of visits by type of problem	71
13.	Percentage of visits by type of problem and agency	72
14.	Percentage of visits by source of recommendation and agency	74
15.	Percentage of visits resulting in services by agency	75
16.	Percentage of visits leading to referral by agency	76
17.	Percentage of legal problems handled by citizens' advice bureaux	79
18.	Percentage of visits to probation service by need to consult a solicitor and type of problem	80
19.	Percentage of visits by social class of client compared with social class of residents of boroughs	89
20.	Percentage of visits by social class of client and type of problem	90
21.	Percentage of visits resulting in services by agency, by social class of client	91

Page

22. Percentage of visits leading to referral, by social class of client   92
23. Percentage of visits by type of problem and citizens' advice bureau   96
24. Percentage of visits leading to referral by citizens' advice bureau   97
25. Percentage of visits by social class of client and citizens' advice bureau   99
26. Percentage of visits by country of birth of client and citizens' advice bureau   101
27. Percentage of visits by type of problem and legal advice centre   102
28. Percentage of visits by source of recommendation and legal advice centre   104
29. Percentage reporting problem by social class   143
30. Percentage reporting problems by income   144
31. Main advisers of those in need of advice who took advice   153
32. Number and percentage of cases where advice was needed and not taken   154
33. Percentage of those needing advice who took advice by income group   155
34. Percentage of those needing advice who took advice by social class   156
35. Number in need of advice who saw a solicitor in private practice   158
36. Number and percentage who had seen a solicitor in private practice by various characteristics   159
37. Number of hearings in courts and tribunals   162
38. Number of applications for legal aid for court hearings   162
39. Representation in court hearings   164
40. Number of accident cases by whether advice taken and compensation paid   170
41. Percentage obtaining 'correct' compensation in accident cases   176
42. Percentage satisfied and disatisfied with adviser   181
43. Number and percentage thinking they knew where there was a citizens' advice bureau by borough   190
44. Percentage knowing where there is a citizens' advice bureau by income and social class and age   190
45. Percentage believing that a poor person can get free or cheap advice   195

		Page
46.	Percentage who had heard of the Legal Aid Scheme	196
47.	Percentage specifying where legal aid provided	198
48.	Percentage answering how lawyer obtained for court work under legal aid	198
49.	Number and percentage estimating charges for half an hour's advice from a solicitor	202
50.	Situations in which solicitor would be consulted	204
51.	Percentage of respondents thinking the advisory services were adequate, by borough	206
52.	Number and percentage selecting best place for legal advice	207
53.	Percentage selecting best source of legal advice by borough, income group, and social class	208

Appendix I

1.	Collection of data: agencies for which systematic information was collected	231
2.	Collection of data: agencies for which less systematic information was obtained	233
3.	Minor and major legal problems	237
4.	Comparison of work done	240

Appendix II

1.	Non-response rate by borough	244
2.	Characteristics of respondents and census population	245
3.	Income group of respondents by social class	247
4.	Income of respondents by age	247
5.	Social class by age	247

Appendix III

1.	Attitudes to the legal system	249
2.	Factor analysis	253
3.	Correlation coefficient	257

INTRODUCTION

This is a study of the facilities in three London Boroughs for people to obtain advice (particularly legal advice), of the extent of the need for such advice, and of how far and by whom that need was met.

The study arose out of the suspicion of the authors that there was a considerable amount of need for legal services which went unmet, and that unmet need was particularly likely to be found among poorer people. When the study was planned, in early 1967, there was widespread concern in the United States about the inadequacy of legal services for the poorer citizen. Under a variety of public and private programmes, special services had been developed in different States to meet these needs and a new interest had emerged among both academic and practising lawyers in the legal rights of poor persons—particularly under welfare programmes. At that time there was, however, little sign of similar concern in England.

Now this has completely changed. The view that there is considerable unmet need for legal services has been widely accepted. It has been urged amongst others by the Law Society,[1] the Society of Conservative Lawyers,[2] the Society of Labour Lawyers,[3] the National Board for Prices and Incomes,[4] the Lord Chancellor's Legal Aid Advisory Committee,[5] and by

[1] Law Society, *Legal Advice and Assistance*, February 1968 and July 1969.
[2] *Rough Justice*, 1968.
[3] *Justice For All*, Fabian Research Series, No. 273, 1968.
[4] *Remuneration of Solicitors*, Report No. 54, Cmnd. 3529, 1968, para. 39.
[5] See especially the Committee's special report on the problem: *Report of the Advisory Committee on the Better Provision of Legal Advice and Assistance*, 1970, Cmnd. 4249.

a wide range of journals, both lay and legal, and by politicians of all political parties.[1] What has hitherto been lacking is quantitative data covering the whole range of legal needs. We therefore decided to ask a sample of the population about their legal problems and to attempt to assess their experience against the availability and use of advisory services in a selected area.

The Choice of Area

We decided to undertake the study in the less prosperous part of a densely populated urban centre. This decision was not taken out of any conviction that there was more unmet need in urban areas than in less heavily populated areas. There may be less *demand* for legal services in the country than in the cities but this could be because of a lower level of awareness of legal rights, less willingness to assert them, and fewer lawyers and others to provide them. We chose London for this study primarily for our own convenience. A study of this kind posed formidable methodological problems. We wanted to be able to keep the fieldwork under close supervision and we were not in a position to spend long periods far from the capital. We hope that sometime in the future a larger enquiry will be conducted on a national basis which will make it possible to make comparisons of needs and of the extent to which they are met in different types of area.

Compared with, for example, medical needs or educational needs, legal needs are relatively rare and a fully satisfactory examination of the problem would require a sample of large size. But it would have been wrong to have attempted a large survey until we had established and demonstrated a survey method from which useful results could be obtained. We decided to concentrate our work in the three boroughs of London which would be likely to have the highest proportion of poor persons. We chose three boroughs rather than one because of the additional material and variety of experience that would thereby be available to us. The different facilities available for poorer persons to obtain advice are not evenly

[1] See especially the Rt Hon. Edward Heath, *Solicitors' Journal*, 7 July 1967, p. 534.

distributed. We appreciated that by concentrating resources wholly in relatively poor boroughs we would not obtain sufficient numbers of persons in the higher social classes and income groups for really useful comparisons to be made. But at least we would obtain information about the use made of advisory services by the lower social and economic groups about whom there is naturally the most concern. A future survey could usefully be designed to compare the legal needs of the higher and lower social classes.

The data available from which we could select the three boroughs likely to have the highest proportion of poor persons was far from adequate. As the results of the 1966 sample census were not available at the time at which we had to make our selection, we extracted from the 1961 Census of the population information about terminal education age, the proportion of those aged over 65, and the social class of males who were economically active.[1] We finally decided that the best indication of the highest proportion of the poor was to select the three new Inner London boroughs which had the highest proportion of semi-skilled and unskilled economically active males (social classes IV and V). These were Islington, Southwark, and Tower Hamlets.

Method of Research
To obtain the maximum amount of data out of our limited resources, we decided to approach the problem in two ways. Unmet need could be ascertained by interviewing a sample of the population in the three boroughs. We decided for several reasons also to look at the different types of agency from which information and advice may be obtained. Firstly, the aggregate number of each type of legal problem, even in our population sample, was likely to be fairly small, and so information obtained from a population sample would be unlikely to tell us enough about the demands made on individuals and agencies for different types of advice. Secondly, these agencies

[1] The decision to work on the basis of new boroughs made it necessary to adjust the data in the 1961 census to the new boundaries. In the case of those new boroughs whose boundaries did not follow old borough boundaries we had to make assumptions about the characteristics of the proportion of old borough populations that formed part of the new boroughs.

may play an important role either in referring to lawyers or act as substitutes if demand for legal services cannot be met. We therefore decided to undertake also a study of the use made of the various advisory agencies in the three boroughs. While this second survey could only give us information on demand rather than need and had to cover visits rather than cases, we thought that it would be a valuable complement to our survey of individuals.

This study therefore falls into three parts. In the first part we describe the three boroughs and their advisory services. In the second we give the results of our survey of the work done by the advisory services in the three boroughs. The third covers the needs for legal services, the use of advisory facilities, the know-ledge of local facilities, and the attitudes to the legal system of a sample of about 1,700 persons drawn from the electoral register. Part II of this book describes the first survey and Part III the second. In a final section we relate the two surveys and attempt to draw some general conclusions.

Acknowledgements

This study was made possible by a grant of $25,000 from the Ford Foundation. We are extremely grateful to the trustees for enabling us to undertake research in England in a field in which the Ford Foundation has promoted so much pioneering work in the United States.

In the course of the study we have had help from many of our colleagues at the London School of Economics and Political Science. Dr John Westergaard, Reader in Sociology, was our adviser on the selection of the boroughs. Mr Wyn Lewis, then Lecturer in Social Statistics, gave us invaluable help with many statistical problems including those involved in the drawing of the sample. Dr A. P. E. L. Sealy, Lecturer in Social Psychology, devoted an immense amount of his time to the preparation and the analysis of the attitude questions. Miss Susannah A. Brown of the Statistics Research Division undertook the significance tests of the material especially that in Appendix III relating to attitude questions.

An immense debt of gratitude is owed to the Computer Unit of the School under the direction of Dr F. F. Land. Our study provided the computer services with a considerable volume of work over an extended period and this was handled with great patience and skill in turn by Mr Colin Taylor, Mr David Dalby, Mr Michael Houghton, and finally by the indefatigable Miss Hazel O'Hare.

The background data on the three boroughs presented in Chapter 1 was collected by Mr Richard Balfe. The maps were drawn by Mrs V. Wilson. The population survey was organized by Mrs Mariyam Harris, who undertook the heavy administrative labour of managing the interview schedules and over forty interviewers. Mrs Doris Urquhart assisted both on the pilot stages of the questionnaire and on the investigation of the advisory services in the three boroughs. The coding of social class was done by Mr Alan Deacon. The rest of the coding of the population survey questionnaires was done mainly by Mrs Harris and Miss Phyllis McMahon.

The task of typing the many drafts of the questionnaires and of this book fell to a number of secretaries. The work was difficult and painstaking. We are grateful to all the secretaries for coping so well and in particular to Mrs Betty Johnston, Mrs Irene Hunter, Mrs Vivienne Gilby, and Mrs Jean Shepherd.

Our final acknowledgements are to those who made the book possible by cooperating in the two surveys—starting with the 1,651 members of the public who allowed themselves to be interviewed on our forty-three-page questionnaire which on average took some forty-five minutes to administer. We also had a great deal of help and assistance from all the official bodies we approached for help. The Lord Chancellor, the Right Honourable Lord Gardiner, was kind enough to give his personal approval to the study and to allow us to use the fact of his approval in approaching those concerned. The Law Society itself and two local Law Societies approved our approach to the solicitors in the survey area. We also had the fullest cooperation and help from the town clerks and their staffs in the three boroughs. We greatly appreciated their kindness in assisting us. Our thanks are due to all the organizations mainly in the three boroughs which permitted us to trouble them with questions about their work and in many cases with recording schedules which they were good enough to complete. In this connection we owe a special debt of gratitude to the Citizens' Advice Bureaux and the Inner London Probation Authority.

Much valued help was received by way of criticism of drafts of the population survey questionnaire, in particular from Mr R. E. K. Thesiger of the Lord Chancellor's Department, Mr A. F. Seton Pollock of the Law Society, Mr Sproule Boulton then of the General Council of the Bar, Professor Terence Ison of Queen's University, Ontario, and Mr Geoffrey Bindman, a partner in the firm of Lawford & Co., Solicitors. A partner in a leading firm of solicitors reviewed the accident cases described in Chapter 10 and gave his expert opinion on the result of the cases and the amounts of compensation awarded.

Naturally the authors take full responsibility for all errors and shortcomings this work may have. We are conscious that it has taken much longer to produce than we had originally hoped. The report on the survey of agencies carried out by Rosalind Brooke was completed in early 1969 and the description of the agencies is as at December 1968. The report on the population survey took much longer to complete. The delay was due to many reasons of which the most important is that the analysis and interpretation turned out to be even more complex and difficult than we had anticipated.

Though the period of gestation has been long, so far as we are aware, at least at the date of completing the manuscript, it is still the first study of its kind on either side of the Atlantic. We offer it in the hope that it will provide a start to the more precise delineation of a most elusive concept—the need for advice and legal services—and that it will enable others to improve on our first attempt.

B. A-S.
M.Z.
R.B.

London School of Economics
and Political Science,
1972.

PART ONE

The Description

CHAPTER 1

The Boroughs and their Advisory Services

The History of the Boroughs

The three Boroughs covered by this survey were created by the London Government Act of 1963. They were formed out of the Metropolitan Boroughs, as shown in Table 1, and they started to operate on 1 April 1965, although their first councillors were elected in May 1964. The year before they took power was spent in arranging the hand-over and appointing new chief officers.

TABLE I THE THREE NEW BOROUGHS BY CONSTITUENT METROPOLITAN BOROUGHS AND PARLIAMENTARY CONSTITUENCIES*

New boroughs	Former metropolitan boroughs	Parliamentary constituencies
Islington	Islington	Islington East
	Finsbury	Islington North
		Islington South West
		Shoreditch and part of Finsbury
Tower Hamlets	Bethnal Green	Bethnal Green
	Poplar	Poplar
	Stepney	Stepney
Southwark	Southwark	Bermondsey
	Bermondsey	Southwark
	Camberwell	Peckham
		Dulwich

* Under the proposed redistribution of parliamentary constituencies, which will come into effect at the next election, Southwark will be reduced to three constituencies and Islington and Tower Hamlets to two apiece.

The historical development of each of the boroughs is briefly described below.

Islington

Before the coming of the Romans under Aulus Plautius in A.D. 43, Islington and its vicinity for miles around was part of the Great Forest of Middlesex, which now only survives in Ken Wood and parts of Queen's Wood, Highgate. In the Anglo-Saxon Charters the name Islington appears as Gislandune, signifying the 'hill or down of Gisla'; in the Domesday Book it is written as Iseldone and Isendone. Between the Norman Conquest and the thirteenth century the manorial system flourished. Names like Prebend, Barnsbury, Canonbury, Highbury, and Tollington commemorate these historic associations. In the Tudor period, 'Merrie Islington' was celebrated for its pleasure resorts, its pure and salubrious air, its cakes and cream, its archery, and its duck-hunting.

Following the Great Fire of London in 1666, when temporary shelters for the homeless (encamped in the fields around Finsburn and Islington) were rebult in permanent form, the area developed from its rural state to a more urban community.

In 1683 medicinal waters were discovered in the grounds of Sadler's Music House and shortly afterwards at various nearby sites. Like Islington, Clerkenwell from then on became celebrated for its pleasure resorts such as Islington Spa, Dobney's Tea Gardens, the London Spa, and, of course, Sadler's Wells, the most famous of all. With the development of education and communications, on the site of the Clerkenwell House of Detention were built the Hugh Myddelton Schools; where the grim Coldbath Fields Prison once stood Mount Pleasant Post Office was erected.

Finsbury was once celebrated as a centre of the clock- and watch-making industry. While this has declined it has still at least one world-famous firm of clockmakers and is also the home of the British Horological Institute.

The growth of public transport led to a large increase in population in the nineteenth century which reached a high point of 435,454 in 1901 when the two metropolitan boroughs of Islington and Shoreditch and Finsbury were established. The population has fallen steadily during this century and when the new London Borough of Islington was formed in 1964 the population was estimated at 254,580.

Southwark

Southwark was the earliest of the three London Boroughs in our study to be developed. From Roman times onwards the focal point has been where the roads from the Channel Ports and the South Coast came together to cross the Thames. Development started immediately across the river from the city and spread southwards gradually. The constituent parts of the present borough have tended to develop separately. Southwark, Walworth, Camberwell, Peckham, Dulwich and Bermondsey grew up with different traditions and landowners.

Bermondsey Abbey became one of the great ecclesiastical centres in the eleventh–fourteenth centuries and rivalled Westminster in importance. The monks from Bermondsey were given the estate of Dulwich and held it until the Reformation. Meanwhile Camberwell and Peckham developed as food-producing centres and grew corn, vegetables, and fruit for the city. In the parish of Southwark in the fourteenth century iron smelting, baking, and glassmaking became established trades. The next century saw the growth of tanning, gun-making, hatmaking, and a host of other cottage industries to serve the city of London. But despite this growth of industry the area was still very much a collection of small densely populated villages connected by open fields.

The arrival of the Huguenots and other Flemish refugees in the sixteenth century brought new trades to the area. Throughout the next 200 years Camberwell, Peckham, and Dulwich grew in status as favoured residential areas but as yet contained little heavily concentrated industry or population. Well into the eighteenth century Camberwell was considered to be a beauty spot and Dulwich and Bermondsey were famous for their spas.

Urbanization proceeded as the nineteenth century developed. The construction of the docks consolidated the area as a major industrial centre and the area map of 1851 shows that while all the inner areas (Southwark, Walworth, Newington, and Bermondsey) were built up, the southern part of the Borough retained its country-town atmosphere and areas of open space. By the end of the century only Dulwich still retained—as it does today—a village atmosphere.

In 1900, when the three Metropolitan Boroughs of South-wark, Bermondsey, and Camberwell were established, the combined population was 572,299. The population of Bermondsey declined from then onwards and that of Southwark increased slightly for a decade and then also declined. The population of Camberwell did not start to decline until much later. The population of the new borough of Southwark was 295,900 in 1966, slightly over half of the 1900 total.

Tower Hamlets
The name Tower Hamlets has been in use since Norman times when the Hamlets to the east of the Tower of London were governed by the Chief Constable of the Tower. At the time of the Domesday survey the area of the Tower Hamlets which was within the Manor of Stepney had a population of 800. The population of the area covered by the Borough today rose to reach a high point of 568,000 in 1899 when the Metropolitan Boroughs of Bethnal Green, Poplar, and Stepney were formed. In 1971, six years after the amalgamation of these Boroughs to form the new Borough of Tower Hamlets, the population stands at 190,000 and is slowly declining.

Within Tower Hamlets there are not just the three Metro-politan Boroughs but within them a collection of once separate Hamlets which retain their individuality and whose names are world famous—Whitechapel, Spitalfields, Mile End, Wapping, Shadwell, Limehouse, Millwall, Blackwall, Cubitt Town, Bow, Bromley, Old Ford, and the Isle of Dogs. The process which united these Hamlets into a continuous urban sprawl was not completed until the middle of the last century. The impetus came from continuous immigration, first from Ireland in the wake of the potato famine and later from Poland and Russia. During the latter part of the century the borough became overcrowded on an appalling scale. In 1899 there were approxi-mately nine persons per house.

Immigration has played an important part in the Borough's development. The proximity of the City of London has always made the area a natural one for the establishment of workshops to service the richer part of London. In Elizabeth I's time, a number of continental emigrés settled in the Spitalfields area and built up the silk weaving industry. There was a further influx of Protestants after the revocation of the Edict of Nantes in 1685. In the eighteenth century a china industry as well as scarlet dyeing and calico printing industries were developed. The Jewish communities in the nineteenth century established the East End clothing industry on a large scale and later on branched out into subsidiary shipping industries as the docks gained in importance.

The docks in Tower Hamlets date back to Norman times but it was not until the expansion in world trade during the nineteenth century that they came to dominate the lives of many people in the Borough. The largest building boom was during the 1840s and 1850s. Many of the Irish immigrants found employment as labourers and later stayed on to work in the shipping industry. Following the building of the docks, shipyards developed and for many years Tower Hamlets was a thriving industrial area and many famous vessels were built in its shipyards. By the 1870s the main social and economic structure of the Borough had been established and it is significant that this was one of the first of the London Boroughs to begin losing population (from the 1901 census onwards).

The devastation of the two world wars speeded the population decline and brought new planning opportunities. Today the population is two-thirds smaller than at the turn of the century. In 1970 Tower Hamlets was still the ninth most densely populated of the twelve Inner London Boroughs but the population is likely to fall even more in the years to come.

The Boroughs at the Time of the Survey
The Boroughs vary greatly in size. Southwark is the largest with 7,117 acres, Tower Hamlets next with 4,876 acres, and Islington the smallest with 3,679 acres. The population in the Boroughs has been declining for many years, and as will be seen from Table 2 continued to decline during the 1960s. Recent G.L.C. estimates predict a further decline of about 1 per cent per annum for the next few years in all of the boroughs. Although this prediction has been challenged in some quarters no alternative forecast has been offered.

TABLE 2 POPULATION, 1961–76

Year	Islington	Southwark	Tower Hamlets
1961*	261,232	313,413	205,682
1966†	235,340	295,900	196,830
1968‡	241,890	293,120	192,250
1976§ Estimate	221,000	260,000	182,000

* Census 1961.
† Sample Census 1966.
‡ G.L.C. Estimate.
§ Standing Working Party on London Housing needs.

In Table 3 we show the population density per acre. In 1968 Islington, Southwark, and Tower Hamlets were respectively the second, seventh, and ninth most densely populated boroughs in Inner London. The overall fall in density is associated with the general decline in London's population but the rate of decline has been slowing down. Density in Islington actually increased between 1966 and 1968. The building of new municipal housing units at a lower density than the houses which they replace is being counterbalanced by increasing overcrowding in what remains of the private sector.

TABLE 3 POPULATION DENSITY PER ACRE, 1955–68*

Year	Islington	Southwark	Tower Hamlets	Inner London
1955	71·7	45·3	45·6	44·0
1960	69·8	44·6	42·0	42·6
1964	70·4	43·7	42·3	42·5
1966	64·0	41·6	40·4	40·0
1968	65·2	41·2	39·4	40·3

* G.L.C. Estimates.

As shown in Table 4, the percentage of owner-occupiers in the three boroughs is far below the Greater London average, and extremely low in Tower Hamlets. The housing market was once dominated by the private landlord who in recent years has been slowly declining at the expense of the local authorities which have been acquiring land for the construction of municipal housing. But a considerable proportion of the population, at least 42 per cent in each borough, still depends on a private landlord for their home. This is nearly 5 per cent above the London average and in the case of Islington over 20 per cent higher.

TABLE 4   HOUSING TENURE IN 1966*

	Owner-Occupied	Rented from a local authority or a new town Corporation	Rented unfurnished from a private person or company	Rented furnished from a private person or company	Other Tenures and not stated
Islington	13·63	20·40	47·23	16·08	2·63
Tower Hamlets	3·37	51·73	38·50	3·19	3·19
Southwark	11·94	40·08	40·34	5·31	2·31
Inner London	17·07	27·04	39·09	13·59	3·21
Greater London	38·54	21·61	28·49	8·56	2·78

* 1966 Sample Census.

In 1966 the average household had 2·6 rooms in Islington, 4·2 rooms in Southwark, and 4·1 rooms in Tower Hamlets. This compares with an Inner London average of 4·1 rooms and a Greater London average of 4·75 rooms per household. Average household size in the three boroughs is about the same as the Inner London average. But the density of persons per room is higher in the three boroughs than in Inner London as a whole. This variation by household size is shown in Table 5.

The average number of persons per household, shown in Table 6, registered a slight drop between 1961 and 1966. This is in line with the trend towards smaller households: family units are being replaced by bed-sitters and single person's flats. The average number of households per dwelling has remained

TABLE 5 AVERAGE NUMBER OF PERSONS PER ROOM BY HOUSEHOLD SIZE

Size of household	Islington	Southwark	Tower Hamlets	Greater London
1	0·39	0·32	0·33	0·29
2	0·58	0·49	0·52	0·44
3	0·77	0·67	0·70	0·59
4	0·93	0·85	0·88	0·74
5	1·11	0·98	1·07	0·88
6	1·27	1·22	12·90	1·10

fairly static but the average conceals considerable changes. The replacement of multi-occupied houses by municipal accommodation causes a drop in the number of households per dwelling, as only exceptionally does a council dwelling contain more than one household. But this has been counterbalanced by an increase in the sharing of dwellings in the private sector (in Islington and Southwark but not in Tower Hamlets).

Islington has the highest percentage of persons sharing a dwelling in any London borough. The large increase in

TABLE 6 AVERAGE HOUSEHOLD SIZE AND RATIO OF HOUSEHOLDS TO DWELLINGS, 1961 AND 1966*

Borough	Persons per household		Households per dwelling	
	1961	1966	1961	1966
Islington	2·73	2·70	1·54	1·54
Southwark	2·89	2·85	1·12	1·21
Tower Hamlets	2·92	2·91	1·12	1·12
Inner London	2·70	2·66	1·19	1·26
Greater London	2·90	2·84	1·12	1·15

*Source: 1961 Census and 1966 Sample Census.

sharing in Southwark during the early sixties is partly due to the growth of bed-sitters and flats in the borough. Demolition is proceeding faster than population decline. Until an effective way of increasing population movement can be found, the number of persons sharing will continue to increase.

The age structure of the dwelling units in the three Boroughs and in Inner and Greater London as a whole is shown in Table 7. Nearly half the dwellings in Islington were built before 1875. The proportion of dwellings built in Southwark and Tower Hamlets after the First World War is about the same as for Inner London as a whole but substantially lower than the Greater London average.

TABLE 7   THE AGE OF DWELLING UNITS

	Before 1875		1875–1919		1920–39		After 1939	
	Number	%	Number	%	Number	%	Number	%
Islington	26,300	47	11,400	21	5,200	9	13,000	23
South-wark	8,800	10	37,700	43	13,400	16	26,700	31
Tower Hamlets	6,200	11	19,600	34	7,800	13	24,000	42
Inner London	129,600	14	468,400	49	157,100	16	201,300	21
Greater London	170,000	7	846,200	36	866,600	36	492,600	21

Source: G.L.C., The Condition of London's Housing, London 1970.

An estimate of the useful life of the dwellings in each borough is shown in Table 8. There is still a considerable backlog of unfit housing to be cleared in the Boroughs even allowing, as the figures do, for conversions and renovations to prolong the useful life of the dwellings. Southwark has 17 per cent of dwellings with a useful life of less than eight years compared to 6 per cent in Inner London as a whole and 3 per cent in Greater London. Despite the high proportion of old dwellings in Islington, the proportion with a short period of useful life is no greater than in Inner London as a whole.

TABLE 8 PERCENTAGE OF DWELLING UNITS BY LENGTH OF USEFUL LIFE

	Less than 8 years	8–15 years	16–25 years	26 years and more
Islington	6	8	23	63
Southwark	17	10	11	62
Tower Hamlets	10	18	15	57
Inner London	6	10	21	63
Greater London	3	6	15	76

Source: G.L.C., *The Condition of London Housing*, London, 1970.

The recent report of the standing working party on London housing[1] estimated that there was a deficit of 24,000 housing units in Islington, 8,200 in Tower Hamlets, and 15,700 in Southwark. These figures were calculated by taking the total stock of houses and comparing them with the number of potential households plus a vacancy reserve. It was also estimated that the number of existing dwellings which were in an unsatisfactory condition and in need of demolition was 18,200 for Islington, 22,800 for Tower Hamlets, and 28,000 for Southwark. Even on the basis of the optimistic forecast of the working party, there would still remain in 1974 a total of 13,600 unsatisfactory dwellings in Islington, 14,200 in Tower Hamlets, and 16,100 in Southwark. This forecast did not take into account the number of dwellings which would be reclassified as unsatisfactory between 1966 and 1974.

The Milner Holland Report[2] studied the problems resulting from poor social living conditions such as over-crowding and multi-occupation of dwellings and identified 'stress areas'. The G.L.C. has since made a detailed analysis of the 1961 Census and the 1966 sample census. As a result a composite housing index has been produced by combining seven indices of housing stress for each enumeration district for the 1961 census and for each ward for the 1966 census. The 10 per cent of wards

[1] Ministry of Housing and Local Government, *London's Housing Needs up to 1974*, H.M.S.O. 1970.
[2] *Report of the Committee on Housing in Greater London*, 1965, Cmnd. 2605, H.M.S.O.

with the highest indices have been identified as 'stress areas'. A large number of these stress areas are in the three boroughs. The major cause of housing stress is overcrowding in Islington and the physical condition of the housing in Southwark and Tower Hamlets. It is arguable that a potential ghetto situation such as exists in Islington is more serious than a purely physical stress problem such as exists in Tower Hamlets. Whereas in Tower Hamlets there is the opportunity to rehouse a static community, the transient nature of the Islington population requires a type of tenure different to that normally offered in council accommodation.

Facilities for children in the Boroughs are poor compared to the London average. There is substantially less parkland and open space per 1,000 population than in either Greater London or Inner London and such space as there is is unevenly distributed. There is also a shortage of nursery schools and day nurseries, and of most of the external services which can help alleviate the pressures caused by overcrowded and unsatisfactory home conditions. The Boroughs are above the Greater London average for children in care and below the average for most recreational facilities, restaurants, cinemas, recreation grounds, etc.

For many years the Boroughs have traditionally been Labour Party strongholds. With the one exception of the election of a Conservative Council in the Islington Municipal Elections of 1968, all the councils under the former Metropolitan Borough Councils have been under Labour control since the war. All three Boroughs return Labour Councillors to County Hall and all ten Parliamentary Constituencies are represented by Labour M.P.s.

In spite of the long history of working class agitation associated with all three Boroughs, the level of political activity as expressed by percentage of people voting in borough, Greater London Council, and national elections is consistently lower than in London as a whole. The only exception was in the 1966 parliamentary election for the Dulwich Constituency which has a more mixed social composition than the London Borough of Southwark as a whole. The low electoral participation is often attributed to the unlikelihood of a change in political representation but may be due to an apathy generated in the poor social conditions of these boroughs.

The Advisory Services

One of our more difficult tasks was to try to establish how many of the solicitors listed in the *Law List* were in fact available to the general public for advice and information. There were 98 firms listed for the three Boroughs, after excluding solicitors who were obviously not in private practice—town clerks, those listed as working in the town halls, or with commercial firms. We then attempted to contact these 98. We approached them first with a letter and brief questionnaire designed to establish whether the firm was in private practice and gave legal advice free or under the statutory or voluntary schemes. We then sent a follow-up letter to those who did not reply and subsequently we telephoned those who still had not replied. A few of the questionnaires were filled in over the telephone, or at the interview.

Later we telephoned all who had told us that they provided legal advice to ask for an interview: not all agreed to this. At the interview firms were asked whether they would agree to record over a very short period of time those new clients who were seen free or under the voluntary or statutory scheme. We were in touch with these firms over a period of approximately ten months. After eliminating those solicitors working for the three local authorities it appeared that by that time 26 of the total of 98 firms (including one-man firms) were not practising in the Boroughs: 5 were not in private practice, 2 had moved their offices out of the area of the three Boroughs, 6 had amalgamated either with a firm within or outside the borough, 10 proved to be practising just outside the Borough boundaries, and 3 were listed at their private address. This left a total of 72 firms in private practice in the Boroughs. As the original names were taken from the 1967 *Law List*, any new firms which may have started to practise in the three Boroughs during 1968 were excluded from the survey. Of the remaining 72, 38 were in Islington, 24 in Southwark, and 10 in Tower Hamlets. Thus Islington had one firm per 7,000 of the population, Southwark one per 12,000, and Tower Hamlets one per 20,000. On average there were about three solicitors per firm in Islington and Southwark and about two per firm in Tower Hamlets. Thus the position in Tower Hamlets was relatively even worse in terms of individual solicitors than in terms of firms.

In Table 9 we list as at the time of our study the main local agencies other than solicitors providing advice[1] and indicate the number of hours they were open and also how many staff were available to advise callers.

In 1967–8 there was a total of nine citizens' advice bureaux in the three boroughs. But while Tower Hamlets had six, there were only two in Islington and one in Southwark. At that time there were also eight legal advice centres—four in Tower Hamlets, one in Southwark, and three in Islington. Each local authority provided some advice through its legal department and each had a rent officer who helped with housing difficulties. Advice was also offered by Members of Parliament, by the prospective Conservative candidate for Peckham, and by the Stepney Conservative Party, usually at stated times in local party offices, sometimes with councillors and, in one case, with a lawyer also present. In each borough the probation service also offered advice, though this was incidental to its main function.

The maps on pages 19–21 show the location of these agencies. In Tower Hamlets the solicitors and legal advice centres were concentrated mainly at the western end of the borough on the three main roads. Two citizens' advice bureaux, in Poplar and Bow Road, tried to fill the gap at the eastern end of the Borough but parts had no services, e.g. in the north-east and east round Old Ford area and Bow, and along the river, such as Shadwell and Isle of Dogs. Communications in the area mainly run from east to west (both the main roads and underground transport) although there is a bus service round the Isle of Dogs, and a few buses go north/south along the Burdett Road.

The services were also unevenly distributed in Islington.

---

[1] Agencies for whom the provision of advice is wholly incidental to their main function are excluded from the table. The role of such agencies is described in Chapter 3.

TABLE 9 LOCAL ADVISORY AGENCIES: HOURS OPEN PER WEEK AND NUMBER OF STAFF AVAILABLE

Agency	No. of staff available to public when open	No. of hours open per week*
ISLINGTON		
Citizens' Advice Bureaux		
Finsbury	1	30
Islington	2 for 2 days, 3 for 3 days	35
Total	3½ whole-time equivalents	
Legal Advice Centres		
Town Hall	1 lawyer	1
Islington	3 lawyers	2
Leysian Mission	1 lawyer	1–2 hrs per month
Total	4 lawyers + 1 lawyer once a month	
Local Authority		
Legal Department	Advice incidental	35
Rent Officer	4	35
Total	4	
Members of Parliament		
Islington East	1 lawyer	2
Islington North	1	2
Islington South West	2 including 1 lawyer	2
Shoreditch & Finsbury	2	3
Total	6 including 2 lawyers	
Probation Service		
350 Old Street	Advice incidental	22
3a Alexander Rd	Advice incidental	42½
67a Stoke Newington Rd	Advice incidental	14
SOUTHWARK		
Citizens' Advice Bureau		
Southwark	2	30
Total	2	

* For the specific purpose of giving information and advice.

Agency	No. of staff available to public when open	No. of hours open per week*
Legal Advice Centre		
Cambridge House	2 lawyers	19
Total	2 lawyers	
Local Authority		
Legal Department	Advice incidental	35
Rent Officer	3	$32\frac{1}{2}$
Total	3	
Members of Parliament		
Bermondsey	1	$2\frac{1}{2}$
Dulwich	1 lawyer	3 fortnightly
Peckham	1	2 fortnightly
Southwark	1	3 monthly†
Total	4 including 1 lawyer	
Conservative Candidate for		
Peckham	1 lawyer	2
	5 including 2 lawyers	31 hours per
Total	6 including 3 lawyers	month†
Probation Service		
Tower Bridge Office	Advice incidental	15
22 Kennington Lane	Advice incidental	$37\frac{1}{2}$
8a Camberwell Green	Advice incidental	$37\frac{1}{2}$
26 Camberwell Church St	Advice incidental	$37\frac{1}{2}$

TOWER HAMLETS

Citizens' Advice Bureaux		
Bethnal Green	1	32
Dame Colet House	1	10
Jewish Institute	1	18
Pilgrim House	2	20
Poplar House	2 (or 3)	$26\frac{1}{2}$
Toynbee Hall	2	33
Total	9 or 10	

* For the specific purpose of giving information and advice.
† Special appointments can be made at other times.

Agency	No. of staff available to public when open	No. of hours open per week*
Legal Advice Centres		
Bernhard Baron	1 lawyer	2
Dame Colet House	2 lawyers	2
Toynbee Hall	10 lawyers	2
University House	1 + 1 lawyer	22
Total	15 including 14 lawyers	
Local Authority		
Legal Department	Advice incidental	35
Rent Officer	4†	71
Total	4†	
Members of Parliament		
Bethnal Green	2	2 fortnightly
Poplar	2	2½ (3 times per month)
Stepney	1 lawyer	2
Total	6 including 1 lawyer	
Probation Service		
519 Commercial Rd	Advice incidental	12½
58 Bow Rd	Advice incidental	12½
377 Cambridge Heath Rd	Advice incidental	12½

* For the specific purpose of giving information and advice.
† Not all 4 officers available at any one time.

Most of the solicitors had their offices in the south-eastern corner of the Borough, and along the southern boundary. Others were dotted along Upper Street near the Town Hall near two of the advice centres. There were no agencies of any kind in the extreme north of the Borough and in the middle stretching east/west around Highbury, Caledonian Road, Holloway, and Arsenal underground stations. Communications were not as bad as in Tower Hamlets. The underground railway and the main roads run north to south, but the Borough is comparatively narrow from east to west.

In Southwark, as in Islington, solicitors' offices were con-

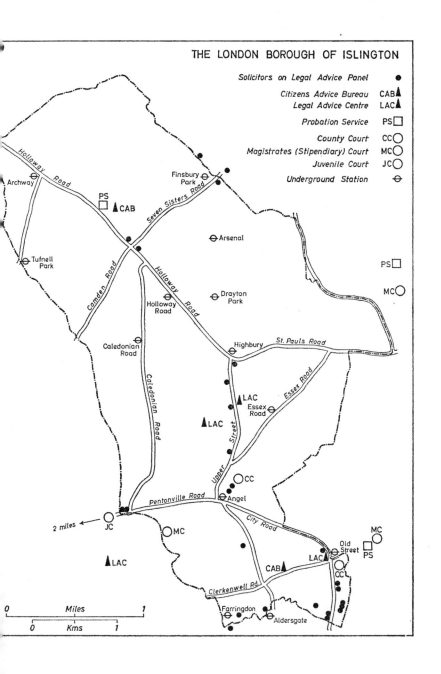

THE LONDON BOROUGH OF ISLINGTON

Solicitors on Legal Advice Panel   ●

Citizens Advice Bureau   CAB▲
Legal Advice Centre   LAC▲

Probation Service   PS□

County Court   CC○
Magistrates (Stipendiary) Court   MC○
Juvenile Court   JC○

Underground Station   ⊖

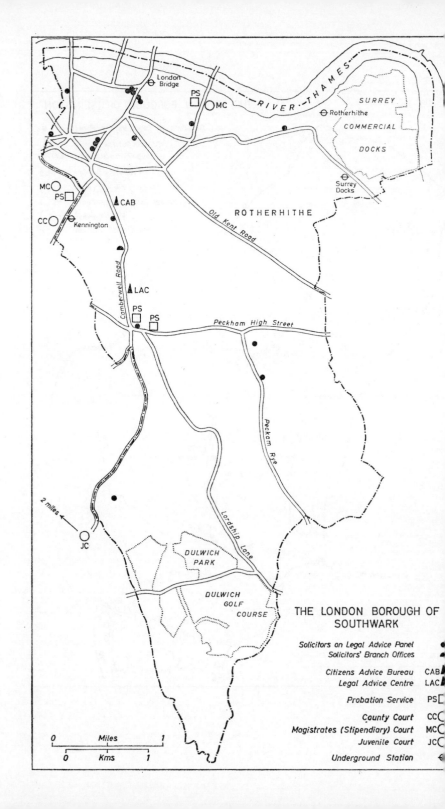

THE LONDON BOROUGH OF
SOUTHWARK

Solicitors on Legal Advice Panel
Solicitors' Branch Offices

Citizens Advice Bureau   CAB
Legal Advice Centre   LAC

Probation Service   PS

County Court   CC
Magistrates (Stipendiary) Court MC
Juvenile Court   JC

Underground Station

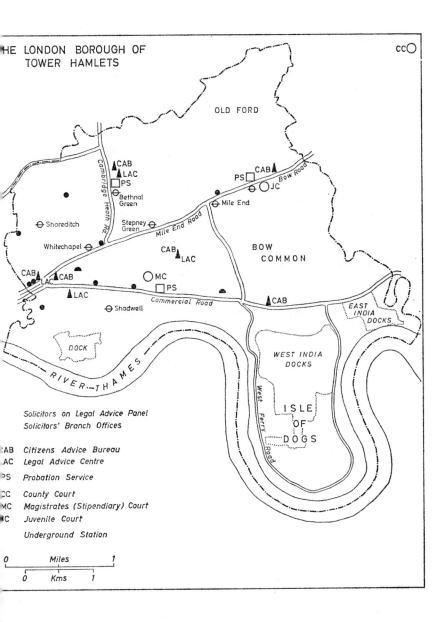

THE LONDON BOROUGH OF
TOWER HAMLETS

CC○

OLD FORD

CAB
▲LAC
▲PS
○ Bethnal Green

PS□ CAB▲
⊖ ○JC
Bow Road

⊖ Mile End

⊖ Shoreditch

Stepney Green ⊖
Whitechapel ⊖

Mile End Road

CAB
▲LAC

BOW
COMMON

CAB▲
▲LAC ▲CAB
▲LAC

○ MC
□ PS

Commercial Road

▲CAB

EAST
INDIA
DOCKS

⊖ Shadwell

DOCK

RIVER — THAMES

WEST INDIA
DOCKS

West Ferry Road

I S L E
O F
D O G S

Solicitors on Legal Advice Panel
Solicitors' Branch Offices

CAB   Citizens Advice Bureau
LAC   Legal Advice Centre

PS   Probation Service

CC   County Court
MC   Magistrates (Stipendiary) Court
JC   Juvenile Court

       Underground Station

0   Miles   1

0   Kms   1

centrated in one small corner of the Borough, in the north-west. The north-east (Bermondsey area) had very few agencies of any kind. Similarly there were none in Rotherhithe or in the southern end of the Borough around Dulwich. The one citizens' advice bureau was not very centrally located, although it was on one of the main roads to the north, near the Lambeth boundary. The main roads run north to south, and there are good bus services, but very limited underground transport facilities.

In all three Boroughs the most evenly distributed advice agencies were the offices where Members of Parliament or political parties provided advice. Some of these offices were however not on a main road, but in a side street—many of them hard to find for the first time on a dark and rainy winter evening.

Ease of access depends not only on geographical location but on the hours the agency is open. Of special importance is whether the agency is open in the evenings and on Saturday mornings to enable people to use it without taking time off work. In Islington all the legal advice centres and Members of Parliament held their sessions in the evening—generally at 6 p.m. or later. There were no other evening sessions and none were available on Saturday mornings. In Southwark only Cambridge House and the Members of Parliament were available in the evenings. The only agency available on a Saturday morning was one of the probation offices, while one of the Members of Parliament held a surgery every fortnight.

Tower Hamlets had a much wider range of services open in the evening. Not only did the political agencies and legal advice centres all provide evening services but two citizens' advice bureau (Dame Colet House and Toynbee Hall) were each open two evenings per week. In addition one of the rent officers was available up to 7.30 p.m. on two evenings per week. The citizens' advice bureau at Bethnal Green was open on Saturday mornings and the Bureau run by the Jewish Institute was open on Sunday mornings.

We describe the origin and function of these agencies in the next two chapters. In Chapter 2 we describe the work of the firms of solicitors particularly in relation to the legal advice scheme and also give some account of the agencies which provide advice on a national basis—not only the probation service which is nationally organized but the services provided by trade unions, newspapers, the courts, the police, and hospitals.

CHAPTER 2

Legal Advice Services

In this chapter we describe the main agencies which provide legal advice. First, we discuss the statutory and voluntary legal advice schemes, and the role of solicitors in private practice. Second, we describe the work of the full- and part-time legal advice centres which were operating in the three boroughs at the time of the survey. Third, we discuss the work of the legal departments of local authorities, which have a specific duty under the 1964, 1965, and 1968 Rent Acts to prevent the harassment of tenants in private accommodation, and therefore are a potential source of legal advice and help. The Rent Officer Service, a national service set up under the 1965 Rent Act, is a potential source of advice on legal rights under the Rent Acts whose work in the boroughs we describe.

Solicitors and the Legal Aid and Advice Scheme
The statutory provisions for legal aid and advice under the 1949 Act[1] are administered by the Law Society. Under the Act people with low incomes can obtain up to one and a half hours of advice on any matter of English law from a firm of solicitors in private practice which has a solicitor on the legal advice panel. At the time of our survey the scheme was confined to those with disposable income of less than £7.10s.0d. (£7·50) per week[2] and disposable capital[3] of under £125. A payment of 2s.6d. (12½p) has to be made, unless the applicant is receiving supplementary benefit. The solicitor giving the

---

[1] Legal Aid and Advice Act 1949.
[2] The limit on disposable income was increased to £9.50 in 1970 (when the fee receivable by the solicitor was also raised).
[3] Disposable capital means gross capital minus allowances for dependants and certain commitments and the first £3,000 of a house (raised to £5,000 after the survey was completed).

advice sends the pink application form to the legal aid committee to claim payment of the fee. This part of the scheme is financed by the Exchequer.[1]

In addition, there is the voluntary legal advice scheme run by the Law Society, which enables any person without any means test to receive thirty minutes of advice for £1·00. According to a leaflet published by the Law Society, any solicitor is permitted to decline to give advice under the voluntary scheme and need not give any reason.[2]

The advice under the statutory scheme may be given by any solicitor (or member of his staff) who has placed his name on the legal advice panel. The panel kept by the Law Society does not indicate whether a solicitor is willing to advise on all or only on some areas of the law. This is unlike the legal aid panels which indicate what types of work a solicitor is prepared to take and in which courts he will undertake litigation. In 1966 there were 13,360 solicitors on the legal advice panel in England and Wales, out of 21,672 with practising certificates. It is not known how many firms had members on the legal advice panel.

The civil legal aid scheme, set up under the 1949 Act, is controlled by the Law Society, which is responsible to the Lord Chancellor, who is advised by an Advisory Committee. At the time of our survey, the scheme was administered by thirteen area offices covering the whole of England and Wales, with some twenty-seven salaried local secretaries working for the local committees which consider applications for legal aid. All the area and local secretaries are solicitors, and are assisted by other solicitors acting as deputy and assistant secretaries. The area office staff do not normally offer an advisory service owing to the pressure of their administrative work. The Supplementary Benefits Commission (formerly National Assistance Board) carry out the financial assessments for applications for legal aid.

We sent all the solicitors who appeared to be in private practice and who, judging from their postal addresses, were apparently within the area of the three boroughs, a letter with a

[1] But see now Legal Advice and Assistance Act 1972.
[2] Law Society, *Voluntary Legal Advice Scheme* (undated leaflet).

three-page questionnaire[1] to ascertain whether they did, in fact, give advice free or at a nominal fee. Not all solicitors replied or were willing to give information and, as mentioned in Chapter 1, some firms had moved or amalgamated and some solicitors were found not to be in private practice.

There were 52 firms (23 in Islington, 20 in Southwark, and 9 in Tower Hamlets) who were in practice *and* on the legal advice panel *or* who told us that they gave advice free. During the autumn of 1968 we interviewed as many firms on the legal advice panel as were willing to see us. We also asked whether they would record information for us about their legal advice scheme clients where this was appropriate. Some firms said that they saw less than twenty people free or under the statutory scheme during the course of the year. These firms were not asked to record information for us. Some information was obtained from all but three firms on the legal advice panels, of which two were in Islington, and one in Tower Hamlets. A solicitor in 40 out of the 52 firms was interviewed, most during the autumn of 1968. One firm in Islington gave up practice between March and October 1968.

We give particulars below about those firms of solicitors which were practising in the three boroughs and either did legal advice work or were on the legal advice panel. Most of this information was obtained during the interviews, rather than by the questionnaire sent out earlier in the year.

We were able to establish when 35 of the 52 firms had first been established in the neighbourhood. Nine of the 35 firms had been established before 1900, including four before 1850 (3 of them in Southwark). Three firms were established between 1900 and 1919, 8 between 1920 and 1939, and the remaining 15 from 1940 onwards. Most of the offices were in a main street with public transport facilities or close to one.

We asked the firms whether they had branch—or main—offices elsewhere. Some 17 firms in the three boroughs (8 in Islington, 7 in Southwark, and 2 in Tower Hamlets) had no other office. No information was obtained for 10 firms. The remaining firms (25) had offices either in another borough or

---

[1] Copies of these are available for inspection in the British Library of Political and Economic Science.

outside London—in a number of cases more than one other office.

We also asked about the number of qualified solicitors in the firm. Eleven firms had one qualified solicitor and 16 firms had two qualified solicitors. There were 6 firms with three qualified solicitors and 5 with four qualified solicitors. One firm in Southwark had seven qualified solicitors. No information was obtained for 13 firms. Information was also obtained for all but 14 of the 52 firms contacted about the number of clerks (articled, managing, or legal executives). Ten firms said they had none and 15 had one or two clerks. A further 12 firms had between three and five clerks each, and 1 firm in Southwark had seven clerks. Questions were also asked about secretarial and other supporting staff. There were 11 firms which had one or two typists or receptionists, 10 firms with between three and five, 4 firms with six or seven, and 12 firms had over eight. No information was obtained for 15 firms.

We asked about the type of work undertaken. All firms did conveyancing and probate work. All firms, except one in Tower Hamlets, said they did divorce and matrimonial work, though a number said they would do this work only for existing clients. Eleven of the 52 firms said they did not do criminal work and 16 did not do commercial work. Only 3 firms regarded themselves as having specialities. Most firms did some rent tribunal work, but far fewer firms had done or would do redundancy or social security tribunal work. In some cases we were told that the firm had not done it because no one had ever asked them to do so. Nearly all the firms were prepared to undertake advocacy in courts or tribunals. In the case of 12 firms, it was estimated that one or more members of the firm would be doing advocacy for at least one day per week.

We asked about the firm's legal advice clients and the major sources from which they came. No information was obtained for 15 firms and a further three saw so few clients for statutory legal advice that it was valueless to ask about the source of recommendation. Citizens' advice bureaux were the source most frequently mentioned, while legal advice centres were mentioned by Tower Hamlets' firms, and the probation service by firms in Southwark. Courts, trade unions, and political parties also occasionally referred clients. Fifteen firms said that legal advice clients were seen by a partner (this tended to be true of the smaller firms), one firm said they would only be seen by an assistant solicitor, and three firms by either. One firm said that such clients were seen solely by a legal executive. Another 16 firms said legal advice clients would be seen by partners or assistant solicitors or legal executives or articled clerks, depending upon who was available at the time and the degree to which members of the firm specialized in different branches of the law.

Solicitors were asked how many clients had been given advice under the legal aid and advice scheme during the last fortnight. Many firms found this a difficult question to answer precisely because they said that numbers fluctuated and in the larger firms the partner interviewed did not always know how many might be seen by other members of the staff. Thus no information could be obtained for 30 firms. Eleven firms said they had see no one in the last fortnight, a further 9 firms said they had seen up to five people, 1 firm between five and ten people, and 1 firm between fifteen and twenty people. Some of the solicitors we interviewed told us that it was not the firm's practice to fill in the pink legal advice assessment form in order to claim the fee due from the Law Society: this was said to be the case in ten firms. In seventeen cases the forms were said to be sometimes filled in, while in eight cases it was said to be the usual practice to fill in the form. No information was obtained for 17 firms.

We asked for views about the legal aid and advice scheme. No views were obtained from 15 firms, while the rest were equally divided on whether the scheme was thought to be adequate or inadequate. Some of those who thought the scheme generally adequate did, however, make a few specific comments. Those who thought the scheme inadequate drew attention to aspects of the scheme thought to be particularly deficient. Most criticism was directed at the low income limits for clients,[1] the low remuneration for solicitors,[1] and the fact that letter-writing and preliminary investigations were not covered by the scheme.

[1] The income limits and fees payable to solicitors were raised after this survey was carried out.

Legal Advice Centres

In the three Boroughs there were eight legal advice centres (excluding one run by a political party), while the ninth, the Mary Ward centre, although in the borough of Camden, drew some clients from both Islington and Tower Hamlets (see Chapter 1, Table 1, and the maps, pp. 19–21). All but one of these nine centres were run from settlement houses.

The Mary Ward legal advice centre, responsible to the Council of the Mary Ward Settlement, was primarily financed by the Greater London Council. The remaining income came from clients who paid a registration fee of 3s.6d. (17½p), after an enquiry about their financial resources, for help with one case. In addition, the centre charged a further £2.4s.6d. (£2·22½) for providing representation, or in a more complicated case, e.g. involving the county court, social security tribunal, or quarter sessions, a fee of £3.5s.6d. (£3.27½). The centre was open five days a week from 10.30 a.m. to 12.30 p.m. and from 2.0 p.m. to 3.30 p.m.: on Wednesday evenings there was an extra evening session from 5.30 p.m. to 7.0 p.m. It was housed in the settlement buildings, where it had the use of a small waiting room and a very large room, which at other times was used for evening classes. In this room brief particulars about the client were taken and an interview was arranged with one of the rota of four voluntary interviewers. The client then waited in this room to see one of the lawyers. There were two full-time paid solicitors, and a rota of about twenty young barristers or solicitors who came when they could, particularly on Wednesday evenings. In addition to the lawyers, there were three part-time shorthand typists. The centre was managed by a full-time secretary who was an associate member of the Institute of Legal Executives.

The centre tried to ensure that the client received continuity of care from the lawyer who first saw him. But if a client called when the voluntary barrister dealing with the case was absent, one of the full-time solicitors or the office manager tried to help the client.

Mary Ward handled most types of work, but, in matrimonial problems where a divorce or separation was being sought, clients were advised to consult a solicitor and obtain legal aid.

The bulk of their work consisted in advising on landlord and tenant matters, and problems connected with employment. The centre not only advised on the law but wrote letters and arranged representation before the appropriate court or tribunal. In addition, many small accident claims were handled where the sums involved were too small for legal aid, or where preliminary work was required to see if there was the basis for a claim. Wills were drafted and advice was given on the administration of estates, but papers leading to a grant of probate were not prepared by the centre.

The legal advice centre at Cambridge House in Southwark, like Mary Ward, was housed in a building belonging to the settlement, founded in the 1880s. Legal advice has been given there since the 1890s. In 1939 one full-time salaried solicitor was employed. In 1944 there were three and in 1968 two full-time salaried solicitors. The centre, as in the case of Mary Ward, was primarily financed by the Greater London Council. Additional finance came from clients' contributions and some limited voluntary support. The means test for clients was not emphasized. Clients waited in a room shared with the family advice centre, where brief particulars about name, status, and the problem were taken by the receptionist. The lawyers advised in separate offices and shared the services of typists allocated exclusively to the centre.

Cambridge House, like Mary Ward, gave legal advice and helped to negotiate claims. It also assisted clients to apply for legal aid, but, since legal aid became available in the magistrates' and county courts, it no longer arranged representation. Many of the cases handled at the centre involved comparatively small sums which could, nevertheless, be of great importance to the client. Wills were drafted for people with low incomes unless their liquid capital resources were such that they could be expected to instruct a solicitor in private practice. All new clients were informed about the statutory legal aid and advice scheme. Since 1959 (when the legal advice section of the Legal Aid Act was implemented), it has been their policy to refer clients to solicitors under the legal advice and aid scheme where a matter could be dealt with under it, usually with a full statement of the case. The warden of the settlement informed social workers and other people referring clients to the legal advice centre about the statutory scheme. This policy has not, however, led to a significant reduction in the number of people coming for help to the centre.

The third centre which was operated on a full-time basis was that at University House in Bethnal Green. The service began as a poor man's lawyer service to give legal advice where none was available. It was extended in 1946 on a full-time basis to organize representation for magistrates' and county courts. The centre was run by one full-time paid lay worker, who acted as managing clerk, secretary, and legal social worker: volunteer lawyers served on a rota. It was the aim only to admit experienced barristers and solicitors to the rota, even though this could create problems when a busy barrister went on circuit. The lawyers came on Wednesday evenings only. The organizer interviewed all clients, conducted any correspondence, and referred those needing expert help to the Wednesday lawyers' session. Other lawyers were consulted by telephone and details of cases were occasionally sent to barristers on the rota who were out on circuit. Divorce cases were referred to private solicitors and representation was arranged in magistrates' courts for other matrimonial cases. The centre represented people in county and magistrates' courts where legal aid had been refused. Cases of harassment were referred to the Town Hall just around the corner, and other types of landlord and tenant problems were handled by the centre itself. Claims in both street and work accident cases were begun by the centre and some were settled. Clients came not only from Tower Hamlets but also from Hackney, Islington, and places to the north east such as Chingford and West Ham.

The centre was financed by a grant from the Greater London Council, from clients' fees, and from grants from the poor box at Old Street and Thames Magistrates' Courts. A rough means test was operated at University House: prospective clients were asked how much they earned and how much they had in savings. If a case was thought to be of particular importance, it was taken regardless of the client's income, if it would otherwise be dropped. Clients were charged 3s.6d.(17½p) for every new case. If representation was arranged the minimum charge was £3.5s.6d. (£3·27½), and the maximum £6.11s.od. (£6·55). The actual fee paid to the young barrister might be higher, but the balance was met by the centre. All charges were waived for clients who were very poor.

In late 1967 these three full-time centres were hoping to receive a further grant for three years from the Greater London Council. Letters of support for Mary Ward Legal Advice Centre were received from, amongst others, the President of the local Law Society, who said that it 'would be a social calamity if your Centre and others like it were not to continue fully to operate'. (A similar letter was received at Cambridge House from the South London Law Society.) Although there were 1,200 solicitors in Holborn, they were 'finding it impossible fully to serve the needs of the public for legal advice under the Legal Aid and Advice Act 1949 because overhead expenses which solicitors have to meet have so increased it is no longer economically possible to do the work'. Some of the greatest support for Cambridge House came from local solicitors, who also contributed financially towards it. Mary Ward Centre, Cambridge House, and University House eventually received a one-year grant from the Greater London Council, based on 1967 figures, for 1968.[1]

The oldest of the legal advice centres—Toynbee Hall—started as a tenants' protection association in 1898. The centre was open every Wednesday evening and was staffed entirely by voluntary lawyers and lay workers. It was financed by voluntary contributions received from clients—about £3 was collected each Wednesday (about 1s.od. (5p) per client)—and it had the financial backing of the settlement. In addition, costs were recovered from insurance companies when cases were settled. There was no means test for clients, though less work was done for clients who appeared able to afford the cost of a solicitor.

At the time of the survey, the centre was organized by a layman, one of the Toynbee residents, who signed all letters and opened all incoming letters. Three other lay people helped with the preliminary interviewing of new clients and there were usually three voluntary secretaries to type the

[1] All three were still running full-time legal services in 1972.

correspondence. Ten lawyers, barristers, and solicitors in local government and private practice provided the legal advice. Each lawyer retained his 'client', although the lay organizer took messages and gave information if the lawyer was not present. Most of the lawyers came every Wednesday. There was a turnover of about two lawyers each year, but at the time of our survey five had been advising at Toynbee for over three years—three of them for over five years.

The advice sessions were held in rooms used at other times for old people's welfare. The dining room for the old people was used as the waiting room for the advice centre. Leading off it were five small rooms where the lawyers saw their clients and the secretaries typed the letters written out by the lawyers. The centre had some cupboard space for files in one of the offices and the organizer kept the main records in his flat. The lawyers were discouraged from taking files away with them. Every Wednesday evening, well before opening time (6.30 p.m.), the big waiting room filled up with old and new clients. Old clients were seen first, while new clients gave a few details about their problems to the lay interviewers.

The policy at the Toynbee centre was to refer divorce and most other matrimonial problems to private solicitors, though some advice was usually given about the possibility of a divorce or steps which should (or should not) be taken. Criminal cases were also referred to private solicitors. Otherwise the centre itself handled landlord and tenant, debt, accident, assault, defences or statements of claim, but could not usually undertake to make telephone calls on behalf of the client, although the organizer did this occasionally. Indeed, the organizer sometimes visited clients who were too old, ill, or domestically tied to attend the centre in the evenings. Claims up to about £500 were begun and the smaller claims negotiated to a settlement. The centre organized representation in all courts, particularly magistrates' and county courts, and before the rent, social security, and industrial tribunals. Clients paid £2.4s.6d. (£2·22½) for representation, though there were limited funds to cover this for poorer clients. If the court were outside London, the client had to pay the travelling expenses.

The Bernhard Baron Settlement legal advisory service was started about thirty years ago, organized by the warden of the settlement. Every Thursday evening a session was held with one lawyer from a rota of about six and one layman (an accountant/J.P., and a long-standing member of the settlement), who also acted as interpreter for German- or Russian-speaking Jews. A client was normally interviewed initially by the receptionist, before being seen by the lawyer. No charge was made to clients, although if a client could afford a lawyer he was usually referred to one. Letters were written on behalf of clients and the attempt was made to negotiate a settlement in, for example, accident cases. When a case required court proceedings, the client was referred to a private solicitor. No lawyer was recommended individually, but the client was shown a list of the local solicitors on the legal aid and advice panels. Most of the problems were personal injuries claims, hire purchase, faulty goods, and matrimonial problems. The centre also took up housing applications and received some requests for financial aid.

The third legal advice service run by a settlement in Tower Hamlets was that at Dame Colet House. The sessions were started in the early 1960s by a group of Oxford graduate lawyers who used to work at the youth club. The settlement provided two rooms for the use of the lawyers. The lawyers paid individually for the letters and telephone calls made on behalf of clients. No charge was made to clients nor was there any means test. There was a rota of twelve lawyers, both solicitors and barristers, of whom two attended at each session. Clients' cases were handled by the lawyer on duty who was not necessarily the one who first saw the client. The lawyers regarded the service as primarily an advisory and letter-writing service. Letters were written for clients and settlements negotiated, but any cases which had to go to court or required a writ or summons were referred to a solicitor. Representation was not arranged. The problems were predominantly personal injury claims, landlord and tenant, matrimonial and hire purchase problems. Like Bernhard Baron, the centre dealt with a few problems of a less 'legal' type, like housing applications and transfers.

The newest legal advice sessions were started in March 1968, based on the new Society of Friends settlement house in Islington.[1] It was founded by a small group of lawyers in conjunction with the Toynbee Hall lawyers, but was, in fact, independent of both Toynbee Hall and the Friends organization. A small sum was received from Toynbee to set up the service, which, by the autumn of 1968, was self-financing from the contributions made by clients. Three practising barristers gave advice while a non-practising barrister organized the service: letters were signed by the honorary secretary. The Friends Neighbourhood house was situated in a residential square five minutes' walk away from the main street (Upper Street). The centre used a room normally allocated to a pre-school play group. With the rising number of clients using it, the centre moved to church hall premises in Upper Street in January 1969.

Letters were written for clients, but not many telephone calls were made as the service was run on a voluntary part-time basis. Clients were represented, particularly at tribunals and magistrates' courts, and at the county court for urgent landlord and tenant cases. Clients were referred to local solicitors if legal aid could be obtained and for other cases which had to go to court.

There were two other legal advice services in Islington. The Leysian Mission, situated at the south eastern end of the borough, was founded in 1886 primarily as a medical mission. A legal advice session was held monthly in the settlement's premises, which were built in 1905. The porter at the settlement made appointments for clients to see the adviser at other times if it was urgent. Advice was given by a practising barrister, who had been running these sessions since 1959, although legal advice had been given there since before 1939. The adviser drafted letters for clients to sign and drew up wills: no representation was arranged. There were no means tests for clients, but they were expected to make a contribution.

Islington Metropolitan Borough Council started a legal advice session in the late 1940s and from 1950 had close links

[1] Several more sessions have started in Islington since the time of the survey.

with the London School of Economics Law Department.[1] The new borough continued this service, which operated usually on Mondays and Tuesdays from 6.0 p.m. or 6.30 p.m., dropping to one session each week in the summer. At other times of the year an extra session was arranged when demand was heavy. A maximum of six appointments was made for each session, and the Town Clerk's Department drew up the yearly rota of advisers and made the appointments. The lawyers were solicitors or barristers of whom some were in private practice or from the London School of Economics. No charge was made to people using the service. Letters were written on behalf of persons seeking advice.

Local Authority Legal Departments and Rent Officers

Before 1964 local authorities could only give advice or support information services either in connection with landlord and tenant matters, or local authority or government services.[2] Since the 1964 Protection from Eviction Act, local authorities have also had the task of prosecuting landlords who harass or illegally evict tenants. In most cases this function was allocated to the legal department of the local authority, under the control of the town clerk.

The town clerks of all three boroughs were lawyers. The legal departments in the three boroughs were organized in different ways. In Islington the division was headed by a chief assistant solicitor and four assistant solicitors. There were three solicitors in Tower Hamlets in addition to the town and deputy town clerks. In Southwark legal staff within the property division under the town clerk's responsibility were given Rent Act responsibilities. There was an assistant town clerk (a solicitor) and two assistant solicitors as well as some unadmitted law clerks. The council had other legally qualified staff: the town clerk, deputy town clerk, and two assistant town clerks, and two more assistant solicitors. The property division maintained a rota from its unqualified staff so that enquirers, generally

---

[1] This session has since ceased.

[2] There is power under the 1948 Local Government Act, s. 134, to give *information* only on local government departments and services, while the 1933 Rent and Mortgage Interest Restrictions (Amendment) Act, s. 12, empowers local authorities to give information about landlord and tenant matters.

sent up by the enquiry centre or doorkeeper, could usually be seen immediately. In Islington and Tower Hamlets, there were public counters in the offices of the legal sections of the town clerks' departments to which members of the public could come. In Southwark members of the public were referred to the property division from the information centre in the town hall.

All three departments appeared to be active in undertaking their Rent Act duties. At Tower Hamlets, for example, public health inspectors had been asked to notify the legal section of the town clerk's department about any tenants with defective rent books or no rent books at all. After a visit from a tenant, letters were written to landlords and signed by the head of the department or town clerk: landlords sometimes came to see the staff so that problems were settled by agreement. Legal problems unconnected with eviction or harassment law were referred elsewhere, usually to citizens' advice bureaux or to legal advice centres or local solicitors.

The staff of the housing section of the Islington town clerk's department organized a free legal advice session three times a week at the town hall in Upper Street. At the public counter of the department, enquiries were sorted and referred on to the legal department (if there was a problem of harassment or eviction), or to the free advice session or other appropriate departments. No one in the department actually purported to give legal advice: a brief interview at the department might, however, be the first step towards receiving advice from the legal department or rent officer.

The Rent Officer Service was set up following the 1965 Rent Act. The duties of the officers were to fix rents for unfurnished decontrolled accommodation. The rent officer is a statutory officer employed by the Ministry of Housing and the service is paid for by a Ministry of Housing grant.[1] No rent officer can be dismissed except with the approval of the Ministry.[2] The administrative and clerical staff are members of the town clerk's department. In Tower Hamlets there was one chief rent officer and three other rent officers, while in Southwark there were three

[1] Rent Act 1965, s. 22(8).
[2] Ibid., s. 22 (3).

and in Islington four. Their offices are provided by the local authority, although paid for by the Ministry. In Southwark, the rent officer moved to premises away from the Town Hall to emphasize his independence of the local authority. In Tower Hamlets the main office was in the former Limehouse Town Hall, and there were also offices in Bow Road (in the north east end of the borough) and in E.1 (in the north western part of the borough).

The function of rent officers is to determine rents of unfurnished tenancies and the staff help applicants to fill up the relevant forms.[1] Problems about furnished tenancies were referred to the rent tribunal, and of harassment and eviction to the town hall. A problem concerning the tenant's status, e.g. whether he was a controlled or decontrolled tenant, would normally be referred to the citizens' advice bureau. In Tower Hamlets the Rent Officer might suggest an applicant should see a lawyer or visit a legal advice centre, if his case were coming up before the Rent Assessment Committee. The Tower Hamlets rent office staff might explain about rent rebates to elderly people and send off the forms to the borough treasurer. At that office most other problems were referred to the nearby citizens' advice bureau with whom there was a good working relationship.

In this chapter we have described the principal legal advice services available in the three boroughs at the time of the survey. In particular, we have described the firms of solicitors available in private practice, the scope of the full-time legal advice centres and volunteer legal advice sessions, and the legal departments and rent offices whose work may have a legal aspect to it. In the next chapter we describe the general information and advice agencies which play important advisory or referring roles.

---

[1] Though there are some dangers in this. See *Chapman* v. *Earl* [1968] All. E.R. 1214.

CHAPTER 3

General Advisory Services

In this chapter we describe some of the major general advisory services available to residents in the three Boroughs at the time of the survey. First, we describe the citizens' advice bureaux and then the role of Members of Parliament. We then discuss certain departments of the local authorities, including housing, public health, welfare,[1] children's[1] and family advice centres. Then we go on to describe the general advisory work of the probation service, and the potential advice role performed by the police and local courts. Towards the end of the chapter we discuss briefly the work of hospitals, trade unions, national newspapers, and local associations like tenants' groups, in either providing advice or acting as a referral agency.

Citizens' Advice Bureaux
Citizens' advice bureaux, or in some cases groups of bureaux, are locally independent but closely linked through regional representation to the National Citizens' Advice Bureaux Council. This is an associated group of the National Council of Social Service which, with the support of the parent body, provides the background information and supporting services on which the work and organization of bureaux are based. The council also maintains a register of bureaux which attain an acceptable standard of work and organization.

There were over eighty bureaux in Greater London in 1968. Some were independent, others were associated with local councils of social service or settlements, and still others were administered in groups. In most boroughs there was some form of co-ordinating machinery for the bureaux in the area and most bureaux had a local advisory committee. The Family

[1] Now reorganized as part of the Social Services Departments.

Welfare Association was responsible for nineteen citizens' advice bureaux in nine of the Inner London boroughs and the City of London, while the London Council of Social Service provided an advisory service for the other independent citizens' advice bureaux in three Inner London and seventeen Outer London boroughs. The London Council of Social Service provided the secretariat for the London Regional Citizens' Advice Bureau Advisory Committee, on which all London bureaux are represented on a borough basis.

The London Council of Social Service was financed by the Greater London Council, the Inner London Education Authority, and voluntary sources, while part of the Board of Trade grant made available since the report of the Molony Committee on Consumer Protection[1] was earmarked specifically for the citizens' advice bureau department of the L.C.S.S. The secretary of this department, who had an assistant and full-time secretary, acted in an advisory capacity to all the L.C.S.S. bureaux and was on all the citizens' advice bureaux advisory committees ex officio. Individual L.C.S.S. citizens' advice bureaux were responsible for raising their own finance, although the L.C.S.S. citizens' advice bureaux secretary might be called upon to advise on estimates or other matters. The L.C.S.S. did not expect 100 per cent local authority finance before opening a new bureau. Most L.C.S.S. bureaux were, in fact, about 85 per cent local authority grant aided. In Tower Hamlets, however, where the L.C.S.S. was responsible for five of the six citizens' advice bureaux, the local authority was directly responsible for about 60 per cent of the cost of the four L.C.S.S. citizens' advice bureaux, while the fifth (the Jewish Institute) was self-financing. Four of them were run from settlements and religious organizations, and the borough council met part of the cost of three settlements and in addition paid the salaries of two organizers. Jewish religious voluntary sources paid for the whole cost of the Jewish Institute citizens' advice bureau, while the Presbyterian Church paid for part of the salaries at Poplar House.

Under the 1961 constitution of the Family Welfare Association, the citizens' advice bureau service constituted one of its

[1] *Final Report of the Committee on Consumer Protection*, H.M.S.O., 1962 Cmnd. 1781.

five departments. The association paid the cost of office accommodation in Denison House, together with telephone, heating, lighting, postage, stationery, and services which were shared with other departments, notably accountancy. The salaries of the citizens' advice bureau officer, her two assistants and secretary were paid by the local authorities in which the Family Welfare Association bureaux were located. Their contributions were paid on a proportionate basis depending on the number of bureaux in the borough. The local authorities also contributed towards the salaries of relief staff and staff in training, again on a proportionate basis depending on the number of citizens' advice bureau workers in each borough. In view of the limited resources of the Family Welfare Association, any new bureau had to be 100 per cent grant aided by the local authority. The Family Welfare Association citizens' advice bureau officer negotiated annually with each local authority for the grant for eighteen of the nineteen Family Welfare Association bureaux for the following year. The exception—the one bureau in Tower Hamlets affiliated to the Family Welfare Association—raised its own grant from the local authority, which was supplemented from voluntary sources. In 1966 there was doubt whether the new Southwark Borough Council would continue to finance the only citizens' advice bureau in the borough. Although there had been an information centre at Camberwell since 1949, after 1965 the new borough of Southwark thought that, as the numbers using it were falling, there was less of a demand for a citizens' advice bureau as well. But, in fact, the use made of that bureau had steadily increased.[1] Islington had expressed interest in the establishment of a third citizens' advice bureau in the centre of the borough, but as a result of financial stringency the council had not yet agreed to meet the costs involved.[2] There was no means test for citizens' advice bureau clients, although most offices had collecting boxes for contributions and many displayed notices saying that it was a service which relied partly on voluntary support.

There were two important differences between bureaux run

[1] See Family Welfare Association, *Citizens' Advice Bureaux in Central London*, Report 1966–7, p. 33.
[2] A third bureau was opened in August 1970. Family Welfare Association, *Citizens' Advice Bureaux in Central London*, Report 1970–1, p. 20.

by the Family Welfare Association and those which were not. The Family Welfare Association retained close control over administration and staffing: all the bureau staff were employed by the association and the citizens' advice bureau officer allocated staff to each bureau. By contrast, the other bureaux were autonomous and loosely affiliated to the London Council of Social Service, which tried to maintain common standards and policies in each bureau in the London area. The second difference stemmed from the first: nearly all staff in the Family Welfare Association bureaux were full-time workers paid on standard salary scales. The Family Welfare Association had ten voluntary workers, each of whom have to agree to do a minimum of three days' (now two days') work each week. Most workers in other London bureaux, however, were voluntary workers and were not required to give any minimum period of attendance. Approximately two-thirds of all the organizers were paid an honorarium or salary, but the size of this depended on the grants and financial support available to the bureau: about one quarter of the total staff were paid. In 1965 discussions were held between the Family Welfare Association and the London Council of Social Service on the possibility of establishing a united headquarters for all bureaux in Inner and Greater London,[1] but no agreement was reached.

These discussions did, however, give rise to a joint training scheme run by the Family Welfare Association and the London Council of Social Service, while the National Citizens' Advice Bureaux Council had overall responsibility for training and training standards. The joint training scheme was held twice a year, and had been in operation for two years at the time of the survey. The course lasted for nine weeks, and lectures and discussions were held one day a week. Each day was devoted to one topic like landlord and tenant, employment or consumer problems, marriage and divorce, office administration and interviewing. Both organizations aimed to send workers who had done three months' or more work in a citizens' advice bureau. Although both organizations ran the joint training scheme, their attitudes to in-service or probationary training

[1] Ibid., 1966–7, p. 5. Discussions began again in 1971, and agreement was reached to amalgamate the two by mid. 1972.

differed. Family Welfare Association workers, some of whom had a social science diploma or a degree, did up to one year of in-service training, six months of which was on a probationary basis, during which the worker was placed in two citizens' advice bureaux. In addition, the Family Welfare Association organized visits of observation for its staff in training. L.C.S.S. bureau organizers were themselves responsible for training their new workers. They organized suitable visits of observation for workers or held one-day training or refresher courses, usually in conjunction with other nearby citizens' advice bureaux.

There were four Family Welfare Association bureaux in the three boroughs covered by this survey—two in Islington, the only bureau in Southwark, and one of the six citizens' advice bureaux in Tower Hamlets. The other five bureaux in Tower Hamlets were under the jurisdiction of the London Council of Social Service. All four Family Welfare Association bureaux were open full-time, usually 10.0 a.m. to 5.0 p.m.: the citizens' advice bureau at St Margaret's House in Bethnal Green was also open on Saturday mornings. In addition to the full-time paid workers, there were part-time workers at Islington and Bethnal Green, also paid; a third worker had not yet been appointed in Southwark. The other five bureaux in Tower Hamlets presented a more varied picture as regards staff and hours of opening. Two were part-time bureaux—one at Dame Colet House and the other at the Jewish Institute. At the latter the organizer and secretary ran other Jewish voluntary agencies from the same office, and thus could answer queries and give some help to callers outside office hours. Dame Colet citizens' advice bureau had a retired civil servant as organizer and a second worker was present at evening sessions. The remaining three citizens' advice bureaux (Pilgrim House, Poplar House, and Toynbee Hall) were full time. Poplar House opened five days a week, Pilgrim House citizens' advice bureau four and a half days per week, while Toynbee Hall had similar opening hours but extended two afternoon sessions into the evening. These three bureaux were all organized by a full-time paid organizer, assisted by a number of voluntary workers. At Toynbee Hall and Pilgrim House there were always two workers on duty, while at Poplar House there were usually two, but the organizer aimed to have a third worker whenever possible.

Some of the bureaux have honorary advisers. At the Islington citizens' advice bureau there were both legal and tax advisers. Poplar House had three young solicitors who acted as legal advisers and ran advice sessions weekly for about eight or nine clients. Pilgrim House had access to a solicitor who acted as legal adviser but was not frequently consulted. There was no longer a legal adviser at Southwark. At the Finsbury citizens' advice bureau there were no regular advice sessions, but the organizer had a legal adviser whom she consulted on the telephone. At the Jewish Institute there was no formal legal adviser, though the organizer contacted a lawyer/friend when necessary. At the Dame Colet, St Margaret's House, and Toynbee Hall citizens' advice bureaux there was no official legal adviser. All of them referred clients, or consulted the legal advice centres at Dame Colet, University House, and Toynbee Hall respectively.

The bureaux in Islington were situated at the extreme southern and northern ends of the borough. The one in Finsbury was in shop premises in a busy street by a bus stop, on the edge of the city boundaries. It had a large waiting room with tables displaying a collection of leaflets on a very wide range of subjects, some of which were also displayed in the window. There was a small room where clients were interviewed in private. The northern Islington bureau was situated in a side street off the Archway end of Holloway Road. The citizens' advice bureau, since the summer of 1968, had three small interviewing rooms in a large Baptist Mission building. Clients waited in the draughty and unheated entrance hall. The Southwark citizens' advice bureau, like the one in Islington, was in a side street off a busy main road (the Walworth Road). The door opened straight into a large waiting room, at one end of which one of the workers interviewed clients. There was a small room used by the organizer or for any particularly private interviews.

All but one of the citizens' advice bureaux in Tower Hamlets had premises in settlement buildings, or buildings belonging to voluntary or religious organizations. The citizens' advice bureau at Toynbee was situated at the extreme western end of the borough, near Aldgate East underground station. Its premises were the newest and were custom built, lying off a covered way leading to the older buildings in the Toynbee Hall complex. The waiting room was shared by the family advice centre and by clients coming for marriage guidance appointments. The organizer had a large office and the bureau had the exclusive use of two other small rooms. All interviewing was done in private. Dame Colet citizens' advice bureau was housed in the new settlement buildings, and was situated about seven minutes' walk away from the main Mile End and Commercial Roads, amongst some of the new housing estates belonging to the Greater London Council and Tower Hamlets. Clients waited in the entrance hall of the settlement, and were interviewed in private in the organizer's room, which was also used by the legal advice centre on Mondays. Pilgrim House citizens' advice bureau was the most north-easterly of the Tower Hamlets citizens' advice bureaux. The settlement which used to house Pilgrim House ceased to exist since the Second World War and the citizens' advice bureau had an office in Poplar Town Hall at the eastern end of Bow Road. The citizens' advice bureau had the exclusive use of a large room on the first floor which was partly partitioned at the sides by filing cabinets to give some feeling of privacy. Clients waited outside in the passage on two benches opposite the lavatories.

Poplar House citizens' advice bureau covered the southern and eastern ends of the borough, including the Isle of Dogs. It had offices in the East India Dock Road in the basement of a Presbyterian settlement building.[1] There was a small waiting area and all interviewing was done in four interviewing rooms. The two rooms on the front could be extremely noisy as the lorries thundered past to and from the docks. The citizens' advice bureau at St Margaret's House in Bethnal Green had a basement site with waiting room and space outside to park prams.

The sixth citizens' advice bureau in Tower Hamlets was situated at the western end of the borough, not more than five minutes' walk from Toynbee Hall. This bureau at the Jewish Institute had been in the building containing the synagogue and other Jewish voluntary organizations since their other

[1] This citizens' advice bureau has now moved to a different site.

offices were bombed during the war. In fact, there had been an advisory service run by the United Synagogue since 1905 to help Jewish immigrants from Central Europe: it was affiliated to the citizens' advice bureaux Council in 1939. The organizer and secretary used one large room on the first floor and there was another room for any particularly private interviews. The organizer was full time and paid by the United Synagogue. He also did a considerable amount of youth work and prison welfare work.

The purpose of a citizens' advice bureau, as explained in a National Citizens' Advice Bureaux Council publication, is 'to make available to the individual accurate information and skilled advice on many of the personal problems that arise in daily life; to explain legislation; to help the citizen to benefit from and to use wisely the services provided for him by the State, and in general to provide counsel to men and women in the many difficulties which beset them in an increasingly complex world'.[1] Citizens' advice bureaux are prepared to assist any person coming to their offices. Where the enquiry involves a difference of opinion between the client and another individual or organization, the general policy of the citizens' advice bureau service is to act as an impartial intermediary— to get both sides of the problem, but also where appropriate to put the client's point of view to the landlord or tenant, employer, trader, or government department by correspondence or by telephone.

In practice bureaux differed in their own interpretation of what constituted 'advice' or 'counsel'. They differed also in the number of telephone calls made or letters written on behalf of clients. The number of calls and letters were partly affected by the number of visits made to the bureau and the secretarial facilities available.

It was the policy of the citizens' advice bureaux that all enquirers with legal problems should be referred to solicitors in private practice under the legal aid and advice scheme. The National Citizens' Advice Bureaux Council tried to ensure that clients made their own choice of solicitor from the *Law List*, in conformity with the policy of the Law Society. Clients

[1] National Citizens' Advice Bureaux Council, *Aims and Methods* (undated), p. 1.

were referred to solicitors under the legal advice and voluntary schemes. But one bureau in the Boroughs no longer informed clients about the £1 voluntary advice scheme, having found that solicitors in that area either charged more or refused to give advice for £1. In these circumstances it was held to be damaging to the reputation of the citizens' advice bureau service in the client's eyes to mention the £1 scheme. Clients referred to legal advice sessions attached to citizens' advice bureaux underwent a means test, which was liberally administered. Clients were asked to sign a document stating their means. Such sessions, in the eyes of headquarters, were seen as filling a gap in the present legal aid and advice scheme. The work which they did was limited in scale. Honorary legal advisers drew up wills for old age pensioners, clarified points on appeals before tribunals, and any other small or obscure points which need not be referred to solicitors in private practice. They were used also as a means of ensuring that a client of limited means who needed legal advice actually obtained it. In addition, the honorary legal advisers were consulted by bureau staff themselves on problems with a legal aspect where the lawyers' knowledge was needed; for example, in connection with legal procedure. Honorary legal advisers were not permitted to arrange or undertake representations either in courts or tribunals.

Members of Parliament and Political Parties[1]

Members of Parliament and political parties play an important role in the provision of advice. The three boroughs were represented by eleven Members of Parliament in the House of Commons. All were Labour and in the autumn of 1967 four of them were Ministers, two of them Cabinet Ministers. All ran constituency surgeries, five weekly, five fortnightly. One, the Rt Hon. R. V. Gunter, ran a monthly session, but, as his constituency (Southwark) was just over the river from the

[1] This information was collected in late summer and autumn of 1967. In the 1968 borough elections many Labour councillors in Islington and Southwark lost their seats. Southwark's 54 councillors and 10 aldermen were reduced to 33 councillors and 10 aldermen after May 1968. Islington, which had been 100 per cent Labour, became 52 Conservative to 15 Labour, plus three Independents (including aldermen). After the 1971 borough elections all three reverted to Labour control.

Houses of Parliament, more people came to see him by personal appointment at the House. The surgeries were held in Labour Party offices or rooms where other party meetings and activities were held. Some of the Members of Parliament conducted their surgeries on their own; the wife of the Member of Parliament (Mr W. S. Hilton) for Bethnal Green attended the interviews to act as her husband's secretary. Mr G. Reynolds (North Islington) usually had with him a local party committee member. Other Members of Parliament, for example Mr R. W. Brown (Shoreditch and Finsbury) and Mr I. Mikardo (Poplar) had local councillors present at the surgery, while in Bethnal Green there was always either a borough or Greater London Council councillor available to see people in another room. In the Dulwich and Peckham constituencies both borough and Greater London councillors attended fortnightly, alternating with the Member of Parliament. In S.W. Islington local councillors held a weekly surgery on a different night from the Member of Parliament, while in Southwark councillors held surgeries at the Town Hall. The Members of Parliament for Bermondsey, Southwark, East Islington, and Stepney did not have councillors sitting with them. Two Members of Parliament were practising lawyers. Sir Eric Fletcher (East Islington) was a solicitor, and Mr S. C. Silkin (Dulwich) a Q.C.; while a third, Mrs F. A. Corbett (Peckham), was a qualified barrister who had never practised.

Mr A. Evans (S.W. Islington) often had a lawyer present, and advice was given on legal, parliamentary, and local government matters. Mr R. W. Brown (Shoreditch and Finsbury) referred constituents to solicitors in appropriate cases. Mr I. Mikardo (Poplar) used to have a solicitor/councillor present at his surgery, but at the time of the survey consulted him by telephone or letter, fairly infrequently. Other non-lawyer Members of Parliament referred clients to nearby legal advice centres: one Member of Parliament also referred clients to citizens' advice bureaux. These Members of Parliament also occasionally consulted lawyer/Member of Parliament colleagues in the House of Commons, although some of them had acquired sufficient experience to help with certain types of problem; for example, notices to quit.

In the autumn of 1967 there was one Conservative candidate covering Islington and one in Tower Hamlets, while there were three prospective candidates in Southwark, and an association with a secretary in Bermondsey. Only two of these candidates were interviewed, the one for Bethnal Green (working as a solicitor in South London) was reluctant to be interviewed, while the Islington local Conservative Party offices did not provide the necessary information. Our description of services provided in the three boroughs by the Conservative Party may, therefore, be incomplete. Mr Ivan Lawrence, candidate for Peckham, a practising barrister, held a weekly surgery on Thursday evenings. Mr J. Gordon (candidate for Southwark) was a solicitor, practising in the borough. He did not hold a formal surgery in the constituency at the time of the survey. In Tower Hamlets, the Stepney Conservative Association ran a legal advice session from their offices in the Commercial Road. This service was started after the 1966 election when the then candidate (a practising barrister) became aware of the number of legal problems raised by local people. Advice was given by a lawyer and the service was organized by a lay woman, who wrote letters and made telephone calls on behalf of clients. Clients were referred to solicitors on the legal aid panels if their case was likely to go to court.

The Liberal Party in the autumn of 1967 had two prospective candidates (both in Islington). There were two constituency associations in both Tower Hamlets and Southwark, and three in Islington. No formal surgeries were being held at that time, although the candidates or party officials would advise callers and take up problems on their behalf. The North Islington Liberal Party was at the time of our survey considering trying to get a solicitor to hold advice sessions in their party rooms, while the candidate for East Islington hoped to hold a formal surgery if premises and finances could be found.

Local Authority Departments: Information, Housing, Children,[1] *Welfare,*[1] *Public Health*
Local authority services constitute another potentially important source of information at the local level. Two

[1] Now reorganized as part of the social services department.

boroughs ran a specific information service. In Southwark the information centre was started in 1949 by the Metropolitan Borough of Camberwell.[1] The Tower Hamlets information service was set up by the borough in December 1965 after the London government re-organization, originally attached to the borough librarian, but since October 1967 under the control of the borough public relations officer. Tower Hamlets information service aimed to give information on any question. But the main role of both these information services was to help people find the local government department which could deal with their query. Some advice was given, but not legal advice, as this was not permissible for a local authority information service except in connection with the Rent Act, and then by the legal department. The Southwark information centre was in the Southwark Town Hall (formerly Camberwell Town Hall), which housed the Southwark town clerk's department. Enquirers at the entrance hall were generally referred to the information centre, located just inside the front door, run by two women who were experienced in the work, but had no formal training or qualifications. At the beginning of 1968 the council started a second centre in Bermondsey based on the district reference library, using existing staff but with the help of the press and publicity officer. Information was available, as for the library, from 9.30 a.m. to 8.0 p.m. and on Saturdays from 9.30 a.m. to 3.0 p.m.

The Tower Hamlets information service had a ground floor office in the Bethnal Green library. There was a waiting area with tables, chairs, and displays of leaflets and maps, and two desks for the two members of staff who gave advice and information.

Other local authority services may give advice or information in addition to their ordinary statutory functions. One department, however, by virtue of its statutory duties, gave considerable assistance of a legal nature to certain people. Public health inspectors can require certain defects in private housing to be put right; for example, when a landlord has failed to repair a defective roof or leaking drains. Some public health inspectors interpreted their duties more widely than others

[1] Under general powers given in the Local Government Act 1948.

and were prepared to stretch a point on behalf of a person with bad housing conditions. In addition, of course, the inspectors came across or were consulted about other problems, particularly landlord and tenant cases. Tower Hamlets public health inspectors notified the town clerk's department of any tenant without a rent book or with a defective one. The health department had a total establishment of about twenty-nine inspectors, including both district and specialist inspectors, and in addition there was always a number of pupil inspectors.

Maternity and child welfare clinics and health visitors were also asked for advice or information, and acted as referring agent for some types of legal problems. The staff in the clinics were trained nurses, some with training as health visitors. In Islington there were eight maternity and child welfare clinics and a number of branch centres (mainly for infant welfare), open half a day or more each week.

Children's departments also gave some incidental advice to clients and callers on legal problems. Since 1965 all three local authorities had set up family advice centres. In Islington one was run in conjunction with a voluntary agency. The one in Southwark was financed exclusively by the local authority but run by Cambridge House. The two part-time workers were responsible to the warden of the settlement and their office was on the ground floor of the settlement, where they shared a waiting room with the legal advice centre. There were three family advice centres in Tower Hamlets, all staffed by child care officers responsible to the senior child care officer in their area who, in turn, was responsible to the assistant children's officer. Two of these centres (at Toynbee Hall and on the Isle of Dogs) were staffed by part-time child care officers and the third, which moved from Wapping to the former Shadwell Town Hall, was staffed by two child care officers. The senior worker left the Shadwell centre in the early part of 1968. The Shadwell centre was less case-work oriented than the other two in Tower Hamlets and the one in Southwark: its policy was to help the community organize and obtain such facilities as better play space for children, and to help individuals to obtain improved housing and other social services. One of the two officers occasionally accompanied clients to social security

C

appeal tribunals. The Shadwell centre referred people for legal advice either to one of the nearby legal advice centres or to local solicitors.[1] In Southwark there was much cross-referral between the family advice centre and the legal advice centre.

Housing and welfare departments also gave some incidental information and advice. Housing departments had public counters at their main offices which usually dealt with lettings and rents. If a caller showed his notice to quit at the counter, he was not always referred to a citizens' advice bureau or advice centre, though practice varied from one authority to another. In Islington such a caller might be referred to the legal advice service organized at the time from the Town Clerk's department but in Tower Hamlets he was less likely to be referred on. The staff on the public counter in the housing section of the town clerk's department in Islington, as has already been mentioned, made appointments for the legal advice centre in the Town Hall. In the autumn of 1967 the Tower Hamlets main office moved from a central position in the borough to offices in a side street at the extreme western end of the borough. In Islington the housing department was in the Town Hall in Upper Street, while in Southwark it was in the Bermondsey area. All offices were open during normal office hours, five days per week.

The welfare departments were, in 1968, all separate departments in these three boroughs. In Tower Hamlets the public counter and offices of the department were split between the section dealing with homeless families and that dealing with welfare services for the old and disabled. Their offices were in the same building as the health department, which was a converted warehouse. In Southwark, although not split into sections for homeless or disabled people, the welfare department had four area offices, all with public counters to which members of the public could come with requests for help.

The Probation Service
The Probation Service is a national service, financed 50 per cent

---

[1] After this survey was completed, legal advice sessions with volunteer lawyers have started at this family advice centre.

by the Home Office and 50 per cent by local authorities, and administered by area probation committees (composed largely of J.P.s), normally based on county boundaries. In the case of Inner London there is one probation committee with, among others, representatives of the stipendiary magistrates from the courts in Inner London. Since the reorganization of the London boroughs in 1965, juvenile court boundaries have been the same as the new London borough boundaries, but this was not true of the petty sessional and magistrates' court areas. Thus probation officers may be consulted by clients from outside the main borough in which they operate.

At the time of the survey, two of the three offices serving Islington and one of the offices serving Southwark were not in these boroughs. Tower Hamlets was the only Inner London Borough where the juvenile court, magistrates' court, petty sessional and probation area boundaries were all coterminous. The number of staff based on an office varied considerably; for example, there were twenty-three at the Islington/Hackney office, of which only three or four officers dealt with Islington, while there were six at another Islington office. There was no standard pattern for the hours at which offices were open to the general public.

Anyone could come in and ask to see a probation officer, although the receptionist might screen and refer elsewhere; for example, if the enquirer obviously wanted the housing department, the receptionist would direct the enquirer to it. A client would either be seen by a duty officer or be referred by a duty officer to the probation officer responsible for the geographical area in which the client lived. A number of probation offices are either in the magistrates' courts buildings or very close by. This was true of two offices covering Islington and Hackney, one in Southwark and two in Tower Hamlets, one of which was close to the domestic and juvenile court and the other fairly near the stipendiary magistrate's court.

The provision of advice is incidental to the statutory duties of supervision and after-care. We were told that landlord and tenant problems were usually referred to a citizens' advice bureau or town hall, although some initial advice might be given. Visitors were, however, given help with matrimonial problems, both from the legal and personal point of view. In a cruelty or neglect case, the client might be advised to see a solicitor, while in a desertion or maintenance case the client might be helped to make her application in court.

All the probation offices had lists of solicitors who undertook legal aid and advice work, extracted from the *Law List*. Clients were shown this list, or possibly told which was their nearest solicitor. Some senior probation officers said that they still referred clients to legal advice centres, though much less frequently since the statutory legal advice scheme had been introduced.

The Courts

At the courts, our visits and interviews led us to believe that some unofficial 'legal' advice was provided, both by the officials, the clerks and warrant officers, and by the stipendiary magistrates. The Thames and North London Magistrates' Court buildings have been on their present site in their existing form for some fifty to sixty years. It is said to have been part of the tradition in working class areas for people to come and see the magistrate to ask for help and advice. One chief clerk told us that 'hordes of people' used to wait outside the courts in the 1920s, but there were now much fewer calls for help of this kind. The London Stipendiary Magistrates' Courts were open six days a week.

Those who wanted to make an application to the magistrate were seen initially by the warrant officer (a member of the police force working within the court). Some warrant officers would themselves advise a deserted wife on which type of application she should make, or advise persons up on a criminal charge to go to a solicitor or legal advice centre. Some visitors— particularly those with matrimonial cases—were referred to the probation officer and in the preceding section we have discussed the advising role of the probation officers. A person who wants to take out a private summons, for example, in a neighbour dispute, can make an application to the stipendiary before the normal court proceedings begin. The magistrate may grant the summons asked for or give some general advice about how to handle the matter. He might suggest a different course of action, as in a dispute between tenants; for instance, he might ask the police to call and to warn one tenant against assaulting the other. In addition, a magistrate may help people in court. (The Magistrates' Courts Act[1] actually places the magistrate under a duty to help unrepresented defendants in domestic proceedings.) In some magistrates' courts the chief clerks were on occasions consulted by probation officers when advising a client on a matrimonial problem. Part of the role of the chief clerks may involve indirectly advising people both in court— e.g. by asking questions to see if there is a possible defence to a charge. Clerks also act as collecting officers to supervise the payment of fines and maintenance orders, and incidental advice might be given to a woman on what to do about her maintenance order when her husband goes abroad. Some enquirers at the courts ask for a solicitor and then the staff may be able to help by showing the *Law List*. Some courts kept no lists of solicitors so that the enquirer would be told to 'walk up the High Street' to find one; some warrant officers, on the other hand, gave the name of the nearest firm of solicitors or legal advice centre.

Petty Sessional courts in London deal mainly with licensing (both liquor and betting), rates, and minor traffic offences. Although the courts, at the time of the survey, had full-time staff (the J.P.s are lay), they sat in buildings not used exclusively for magistrates' proceedings, so that the full-time offices were some distance away from the buildings (e.g. a mission hall or council premises) where the hearings were held. Requests for advice at these offices were mainly related to the payment of fines or issuing of licences. These courts did not have the same application procedure as the stipendiary magistrates' courts, nor were the J.P.s themselves asked for help and advice in the same way.

Rent tribunal offices, also another national 'court' service, gave a certain amount of advice to callers. They also helped people to make out their applications and see the case through the rent tribunal hearings. The administrative offices of the rent tribunals covering Islington and Tower Hamlets were moved at the end of 1967 to the same building in the northern

[1] The Magistrates Courts Act 1952, s. 61.

part of Islington. The staff of the East London Tribunal went out from that office to the boroughs they covered and were available in Tower Hamlets one day each week. The callers at the office came mainly from Islington and neighbouring boroughs. The office was open from 9.30 to 4.30 and until 7.30 on Thursdays. The policy was to help both tenants and landlords, and the counter staff assisted people to fill in application forms. Callers with legal problems were generally referred to a citizens' advice bureau or solicitor: the tribunal staff did not advise on how to issue a valid notice to quit. Any cases of unlawful eviction, harassment, or lack of a rent book were referred to the town hall. Most applicants were unrepresented at the hearings.

There were five county courts for the three boroughs, some of which were noticeably busier than others. Part of the reason may have been that the less busy seemed to be less conveniently located. The staff at the courts helped to fill in forms in a simple case of money owing to the court, but on anything more complicated they referred the caller either to a citizens' advice bureau or legal advice centre, and explained the facilities available under the Legal Aid and Advice Act. At one county court in Tower Hamlets we were told that few people came for advice. Registrars of the courts said that their policy was not to allow staff to give advice in the sense of giving an opinion on the success or future of their case or on what action should be taken, although form filling in a possession action was permitted.

The Police
The police, like the courts, operate nationally, but are normally locally administered. In London, however, the Metropolitan Police comes directly under the Home Secretary, while there is a separate force for the City. In each of the three boroughs there is one police divisional area (with five stations in Islington, eight in Southwark, and seven in Tower Hamlets). Some police stations are open twenty-four hours per day and are manned in three shifts. A superintendent of a busy station in Islington said: 'You name the problem: we get it.' The police were careful to avoid giving advice in the sense of legal advice

which might be given by a solicitor. But in some parts of the three boroughs the police stations were the only national or local agency available. In some cases the police act, especially if it is an emergency (for example, a family made homeless); in other cases they refer the person to another agency.

The police generally referred matrimonial problems to the probation officer, while problems over children were normally referred to the children's department. Landlord and tenant problems were also referred to the appropriate agency—for example, harassment to the town hall (although a police constable might be sent to escort the caller back to his house) or to the rent tribunal. Minor assaults (i.e. those not serious enough for the police to prosecute) were referred to the court where the complainant would go before the magistrate to ask for a summons. In accident cases the police would advise an injured person to report it to his insurance company and to see a solicitor. The police also referred people to citizens' advice bureaux, legal advice centres, and the Ministry of Social Security. The police told us that there were many people in these three areas who were not used to going to solicitors. We were told at one station that a small number of problems were brought to them each year, for example about dismissal without notice from jobs or faulty goods and services.

Hospitals

Hospitals, like the police, do not act as an advice-giving agency but as a referring agency when their help or advice is sought. Advice may, however, be proferred to accident victims on the initiative of the hospital authorities. For the survey, enquiries were made at some of the hospitals. One hospital in Islington sent a formal note to all accident victims advising them of their rights and suggesting that the patient should see a solicitor, while another hospital in the same borough told patients to see the medical social worker if they had any problems. This appeared to be the more general practice: the patient might therefore have to take the initiative of contacting the social work department before he was told about possible rights and claims, and the existence of the legal aid and advice scheme. Medical social workers gave information not only to patients injured in road or work accidents, but also to those who were bothered by such problems as hire purchase arrears, matrimonial, or landlord and tenant problems. Most hospitals advised patients to avoid ambulance chasers (either laymen or lawyers willing to take up a personal injury action on a commission fee basis). A few hospitals reported their continued existence, but again this was generally not discovered unless the patient mentioned it. Some hospital social work departments were willing to show patients a list of solicitors if asked to do so, while a few might go further and make an appointment for the patient, possibly even for the solicitor to visit the hospital. One or two hospitals said quite firmly that they would recommend a firm of solicitors well known to them and appointments would be made for the patient. If, in fact, that patient was a member of a trade union he would be encouraged to use their legal aid and advice facilities. Other problems, e.g. hire purchase, divorce, landlord and tenant, might be referred either to a citizens' advice bureau or to a solicitor.

Ministry of Social Security

Social security officers, like the hospitals, do not purport to give legal advice, but they may well be asked for advice on legal problems. Most offices have leaflets and posters on display informing people of changes in the law. Social security officers dealing with the supplementary benefit side have wider responsibilities and are willing to refer people to the rent officer, rent tribunal, or local authority on landlord and tenant problems. It is not the policy of the Ministry of Social Security to inform people claiming industrial injury benefit that they might also have a claim at common law, although if a person raised this question it might be suggested that he should see a solicitor or his trade union official.

Trade Unions

Certain trade unions provide a specific advice service to their members. Such schemes are usually limited to problems in connection with employment, such as accidents at work or loss of employment and redundancy. A member can consult his local branch secretary (usually honorary or part-time) or district secretary (usually a full-time official). Such officials rarely have any formal legal training, but often have considerable experience and knowledge of industrial accidents and problems about employment and redundancy. For example, in the Amalgamated Engineering Union with about $1\frac{1}{4}$ million members, district secretaries were prepared themselves to take up a problem over redundancy, while they would consult the legal department at their central office in London over more difficult matters and for help with accident cases. The legal department of the A.E.U. was run by two people, very experienced in industrial law problems, though not legally qualified. All accidents and requests for help were sifted, partly to see whether there was a case and also to make sure that the member was not in arrears with his membership dues (which precludes use of the trade union legal aid scheme). Then the bulk of the work was sent out to solicitors, who advised the member and possibly took up the case. The Electrical Trades Union legal aid scheme was available only for accidents at work and employment problems. That union referred other legal enquiries to citizens' advice bureaux or to private solicitors. The Civil Service Union had similar rules permitting legal aid only for accidents and employment problems.

Other unions such as the Transport & General Workers' Union advised on and processed much of the work themselves, either through the central legal department or regional offices (which have no legal staff). A Transport & General Workers' Union member did not have to make a payment for this service. The union had arrangements with solicitors in some towns, whom their members could also consult for their private legal problems, though the member had to pay privately for this service. The union also assisted its members by arrangements with specialist solicitors in respect of road traffic offences which occurred in the course of their employment, with the main exception of parking.

Some unions, such as the General & Municipal Workers' Union, run an advice bureau, so that members could consult an official at national office about a wide range of problems, not only connected with work. The Society of Graphical and Allied Trades offered legal advice administered on a branch level (at the time of the survey, up to 37s. worth) to any member on any matter except those arising out of the ownership of a private vehicle. The National Union of Furniture and Trade Operatives provided a secondary and limited legal advice service, which was available also to a member's family. The union decided in each case whether to pay for a solicitor to undertake the work. In none of these three unions was advice given by a legally qualified person.

Help was available only to a very limited extent to a member with private matters on which he might need legal assistance— for example, a divorce, house purchase, or motoring offences other than those occurring in the course of the employment. Many unions were prepared to recommend a member either to their own or to another solicitor, while other trade unions provided a limited advisory service.

Newspapers

Three national papers,[1] the *News of the World*, the *People*, and the *Sunday Mirror*, provided advisory services. The John Hilton Bureau, situated in Cambridge, financed by the *News of the World*, handled enquiries received by the paper. A large staff of experts was available to answer problems within their own specialities. The *Daily Mirror* and *Sunday Mirror* also ran an advice bureau, which was divided into departments dealing with, for example, social security benefits, hire purchase and consumer complaints, and employment problems. The more difficult legal problems were referred to the lawyer in the bureau, who was also willing to advise on wills and inheritance laws. The *People*'s bureau also handled problems and referred some cases to counsel for an opinion every week. The reader was advised on the basis of that opinion.

No other newspapers ran bureaux on the scale of the John Hilton or *Sunday Mirror* bureaux. Other papers were, however, prepared to answer readers' queries and might consult the legal department on legal problems. This was the practice in both the *Daily Mail* and the *Daily Sketch*: more general queries were handled by other staff members.

---

[1] Since the time of the survey the *Daily Express* has started 'Action Line'.

Miscellaneous

Finally, there may be miscellaneous groups of individuals and organizations in different areas from which people might get help and advice with legal problems. In Islington there was the Tenants' and Residents' Association (not to be confused with the Islington Tenants' and Ratepayers' Association). From 1958 the association held a surgery every Tuesday evening at 8.0 p.m. Membership of the association was a condition for obtaining advice and help: membership cost 12s.0d. (60p) a year or 1s.0d. (5p) per month (less for old age pensioners). Members usually made a contribution at the surgery. The association advertised its surgery occasionally in the local press, and also distributed leaflets. Landlord and tenant problems predominated. Letters were written on behalf of its members. A practising lawyer was usually present at the Tuesday evening sessions, while members were referred to solicitor contacts of the association rather than to local solicitors.

There were some immigrant organizations in the three boroughs, notably the Greek-Cypriot Brotherhood, whose headquarters was in the borough of Camden. The chairman was a Greek-Cypriot accountant. They received quite a number of requests, notably from Islington and Camden, for help of all kinds, e.g. for interpreters and for legal advice. People were referred to barristers and solicitors known to the brotherhood, who were usually Greek-Cypriot. A person with a landlord and tenant case might be referred to such a lawyer or to the appropriate town hall, if the person's English was adequate. No doubt other organizations for immigrants tried to help those coming to them for advice.

Local councillors were also another potential source of advice at local level. Some local Labour councillors,[1] as mentioned earlier, sat with members of parliament at their surgeries or held their own on other nights; for example, Southwark councillors held surgeries in the Town Hall. Some councillors in the three boroughs, until the 1968 elections, appeared to have no formal arrangements for surgeries. Those

---

[1] This information was correct up until the May 1968 borough elections. It does not cover the work in Islington and Southwark of the Conservative councillors between 1968 and 1971.

councillors who were interviewed said that the bulk of the requests for help were in connection with housing; they sent any legal problems to a lawyer.

Other agencies, for example, the marriage guidance and family planning associations, occasionally received requests for help and gave advice or suggestions for referrals incidental to their main functions. Similarly local priests, both Anglican and Roman Catholic, and other religious leaders in the community gave information and advice. No doubt there were many others who were consulted by people in search of advice with whom we failed to make contact.

Summary

The services provided by all these organizations differed not only from one type of agency to another but also within the same group of agencies. Citizens' advice bureaux were prepared to write letters or make telephone calls on a person's behalf, but did not normally arrange representation in court or go with a client to a tribunal hearing. Some citizens' advice bureaux contacted lawyers personally either to give advice or to take a case to court, while others gave the client a list of solicitors and suggested which to visit. Some of them frequently wrote letters or made telephone calls: it was not necessarily the busiest citizens' advice bureaux which did the least telephoning and letter writing.

Legal advice centres also varied in the services they gave. Some never arranged representation or wrote briefs or drafted pleadings or statements of claim. Others saw these as among the most important aspects of their work. Four of the advice centres arranged representation, while five hardly ever did so. But all of them wrote letters and some made telephone calls on their clients' behalf, and negotiated small claims.

Probation officers advised callers on the social and legal aspects of matrimonial, children, and affiliation problems. They wrote letters on these subjects and tried to arrange the matter amicably, or in some instances actually spoke for the client in the magistrates' court. They were not prepared to do so much for other types of problem. Instead they tended to refer clients to other agencies.

Members of Parliament and political parties also gave varied services. The lawyer Members of Parliament and some candidates were qualified to give legal advice. All Members of Parliament wrote letters on behalf of clients, but would not go very far into a case involving personal injuries, although some legal advice centres and some citizens' advice bureaux did do this. Occasionally Members of Parliament consulted lawyer colleagues and arranged for legal representation at a tribunal, but this was rare.

Local authority legal departments and rent officers carried out their statutory functions so that the legal department might write to a landlord who had been harassing a tenant and as a last resort prosecute that landlord in the magistrates' court. Rent officers also wrote to landlords, arranged meetings, and a hearing in connection with their duties. Neither organization would normally do more for other problems than give a little advice and refer the caller to another agency.

In the next three chapters we set out the findings from our survey about the use made of the main agencies described in Chapters 2 and 3.

PART TWO

The Survey of Agencies

CHAPTER 4

The Use of Advisory Services

We describe in Appendix I the ways in which the data was collected and explain why we adopted this method of research. In this chapter and the two succeeding chapters we analyse the information recorded for us. Here we describe the use made of the agencies. In Chapter 5 we show some of the characteristics of the users, and in Chapter 6 we analyse in greater detail the information collected for us by the citizens' advice bureaux, legal advice centres, and solicitors.

Coverage

As mentioned in Appendix I, our statistical data excludes visits made on departmental problems, i.e. those problems coming to a department because it is its duty to deal with them. This exclusion relates in particular to local authority departments when handling their day to day work. We have also excluded, unless otherwise stated, visits made to agencies whose offices were not situated within the borough concerned. (This exclusion affects probation offices and a legal advice centre.) Visits to probation officers are, therefore, under-represented as three offices (two which partly served Islington, one which partly served Southwark) were outside the borough boundaries and one legal advice centre is also excluded. Unless otherwise stated, we include visits made to agencies by persons living outside the boroughs. The figures show the work load over a twelve-week period as estimated from our data covering varying periods, as described in Appendix I.

In the classification of agencies, we have grouped together certain local authority services: legal departments, housing departments, and the rent officer service are in our first group, which we refer to loosely as 'legal and housing services', while children's departments, family advice centres, information, maternity and child welfare, and welfare departments were placed in the second group, which we refer to loosely as 'social services'. It must be remembered however, that not all departments of all local authorities could record information for us (see Appendix I, p. 233). These two groups of local authority services do not cover every office in the borough. Similarly,

TABLE 10 NUMBER AND PERCENTAGE OF VISITS BY AGENCY
(Calculated from estimated number of visits for a 12 week period)

Agency	Number of estimated visits for 12-week period		Percentage of estimated visits for 12-week period
Local authority legal and housing services	1,692	(141)	11
Local authority social services	2,634	(268)	17
Members of Parliament and political parties	372	(36)	2
Legal advice centres	2,330	(392)	15
Citizens' advice bureaux	7,488	(676)	48
Probation service	984	(82)	6
Total:	15,500	(1,595)	100%

Note: Parenthetical figures represent the number of recorded visits on which the calculation was made. Only the offices of agencies situated in the three boroughs are included. Visits on departmental problems are excluded.

only three of the eleven Members of Parliament recorded for us, and only one of the parliamentary candidates and one political legal advice service. All the legal advice centres operating within the three boroughs recorded information for us, with the exception of the part-time centres in Islington, the Leysian Mission (which runs one session per month), and the poor man's lawyer service at Islington Town Hall. The third centre in that borough—Islington Legal Advice Centre—did not open until April 1968.

Part 1: The Use of Advisory Services
In Table 10 we show the total visits recorded for the six groups of agencies estimated for a twelve-week period. About half of

TABLE 11 NUMBER AND PERCENTAGE OF VISITS BY AGENCY AND BY
BOROUGH, AND THE NUMBER OF VISITS PER ONE THOUSAND OF POPULATION*
(Calculated from estimated number of visits for a 12-week period)

Borough and agency	Number of estimated visits per 12-week period		Number of estimated visits per 1,000 of population
Borough of Islington (population: 235,340)†			
Legal advice centres	0	(0)	0
Citizens' advice bureaux	1,716	(143)	7
Probation service	132	(11)	0·6
Local authority legal and housing services	1,368	(114)	6
Local authority social services	792	(66)	3
Members of Parliament and political parties	156	(13)	0·7
Total:	4,164	(347)	17
Borough of Southwark (population: 295,900)†			
Legal advice centres	648	(54)	2
Citizens' advice bureaux	1,464	(122)	5
Probation service	648	(54)	2
Local authority legal and housing services	180	(15)	0·6
Local authority social services	1,230	(113)	4
Members of Parliament and political parties	108	(9)	0·4
Total:	4,278	(367)	14
Borough of Tower Hamlets (population: 196,830)†			
Legal advice centres	1,682	(338)	9
Citizens' advice bureaux	4,308	(411)	22
Probation service	204	(17)	1
Local authority legal and housing services	144	(12)	0·7
Local authority social services	612	(89)	3
Members of Parliament and political parties	108	(14)	0·5
Total:	7,058	(881)	36

* This table includes visits by persons resident outside each borough.
  † 1966 Census material supplied by the Registrar-General.
  Note: Parenthetical figures represent the number of recorded visits on which the
calculation was made. Only the offices of agencies situated in the three boroughs
are included. Visits on departmental problems are excluded.

the visits recorded were made to citizens' advice bureaux and over a quarter to our two groups of local authority services.

In Table 11 we show the estimated number of visits over a twelve-week period per 1,000 of population in the three boroughs.

There were thirty-six estimated visits per 1,000 of population for the twelve-week period in Tower Hamlets, and less than half this rate of visits in Islington and Southwark (seventeen and fourteen per 1,000 of population respectively). There was not a great difference in the number of visits made to the local authority social services and to Members of Parliament in the three boroughs. The main difference was in the rate of visits to legal advice centres and citizens' advice bureaux. Nine estimated visits per 1,000 of population were made to legal advice centres in Tower Hamlets, two in Southwark, and none were recorded for Islington.[1] The difference between boroughs in the rate of estimated visits to citizens' advice bureaux was even more marked: twenty-two per 1,000 in Tower Hamlets, five per 1,000 in Southwark and seven per 1,000 in Islington. As pointed out in Chapter 1, Tower Hamlets had more facilities: it had six of the nine citizens' advice bureaux, and four of the nine legal advice centres.

In Table 12 we show the number of estimated visits over a twelve-week period for different types of problems. The category 'miscellaneous' includes requests for advice about how to change one's name, social welfare enquiries, immigration, road and noise nuisance, and educational problems.

Over a quarter of all visits were made on landlord and tenant and other housing problems including house purchase and homelessness. Matrimonial problems were the next largest category of problems for which people sought advice, and related to these were problems about custody of children, affiliation, and family relationships. Employment problems and personal injuries constituted the third and fourth most common types of problems about which people sought advice.

In Table 13 we show the percentage of different types of problems about which visits were made to the different

[1] See Appendix I, where we explain that the two legal advice centres in Islington operating in the autumn of 1967 did not record for us.

TABLE 12 NUMBER AND PERCENTAGE OF VISITS BY TYPE OF PROBLEM
(Calculated from estimated number of visits for a 12-week period)

Type of problem	Number of estimated visits for 12-week period		Percentage of estimated visits
Landlord and tenant	631	(336)	23
Housing and house purchase	582	(59)	4
Homeless: seeking accommodation	192	(17)	1
Compulsory purchase orders	51	(5)	0·3
Debt	912	(109)	6
Faulty goods and services	462	(50)	3
Wills, winding up estates	294	(35)	2
Personal injuries	1,073	(136)	7
Employment, redundancy	1,211	(118)	8
Matrimonial	1,928	(192)	12
Affiliation	81	(10)	0·5
Custody of children, adoption	255	(24)	2
Family relationships	293	(33)	2
Personal and financial difficulties	555	(53)	4
Social security	840	(93)	5
Criminal (including motoring offences)	387	(42)	2
Insurance (motor, house, etc.)	201	(23)	1
Neighbour	213	(24)	1
Information: civic and national	162	(15)	1
Income tax, rate rebates	451	(42)	3
Social welfare enquiries	234	(24)	2
Educational	132	(11)	1
Miscellaneous	1,241	(129)	8
Not ascertained	119	(15)	0·7
Total:	15,500	(1,595)	100%

Note: Parenthetical figures represent the number of recorded visits on which the calculation was made. Only the offices of agencies situated in the three boroughs are included. Visits on departmental problems are excluded.

agencies. The agencies have been grouped together as in Table 10.

As nearly half of all estimated visits were made to citizens' advice bureaux, it is not surprising that they dealt with the greatest percentage of every type of problem over the twelve-

TABLE 13 PERCENTAGE OF VISITS BY TYPE OF PROBLEM AND AGENC
(Calculated from estimated number of visits for 12-week period)

Type of problem	Local authority legal and housing services	Local authority social services	Members of Parliament and political parties	Legal advice centres	Citizen's advice bureaux	Probation service		Total
Landlord and tenant	33	11	3	13	41	0	100	(33
Debt	3	26	3	25	43	1	100	(10
Faulty goods and services	3	0	0	14	83	0	100	(5
Wills, winding up estates	4	0	0·7	28	67	0	100	(3
Personal injuries	3	2	1	46	49	0	100	(13
Employment	1	12	1	15	68	3	100	(11
Matrimonial, affiliation, children, family relationships	0	20	0·9	14	37	28	100	(25
Social security	3	21	0	0·7	66	9	100	(9
Criminal	3	2	0	30	47	19	100	(4
Income tax, rate rebates	19	8	3	6	65	0	100	(4
Housing, house purchase, homeless, compulsory purchase orders	7	28	18	5	41	0	100	(8
Personal and financial difficulties	0	29	0	0·5	55	15	100	(5
Miscellaneous	10	29	1	11	47	1	100	(22
Not ascertained	7	40	7	33	13	0	100	(1
Total:	11	17	2	15	48	6	100	(1,59

Note: Parenthetical figures represent the number of recorded visits on which th
calculation was made. Only the offices of agencies situated in the three borough
are included. Visits on departmental problems are excluded.

week period. But for some matters a disproportionate shar
of the work went to other agencies. Local authority lega
departments and rent officers received a third of all estimate
visits about landlord and tenant problems, while citizens
advice bureaux received 41 per cent. Citizens' advice bureau
received 41 per cent of estimated visits about problems con
cerning housing, house purchase, and homelessness, while th
local authority social services received 28 per cent of thes
visits. Members of Parliament received 18 per cent of th
estimated visits about housing problems, in contrast to 2 pe
cent of all visits on all problems, excluding departmenta
problems. No visits were made to the probation service o
housing matters, while the remaining 12 per cent were made t
local authority legal and rent officer services, and to lega
advice centres.

On debt problems, local authority children's, welfare

information departments, and family advice centres, together with legal advice centres had more estimated visits than citizens' advice bureaux. Citizens' advice bureaux and legal advice centres together dealt with nearly all visits about wills and winding up estates, personal injuries, and employment. No doubt some of these visits may have been made by the same person who was referred by the citizens' advice bureau to a legal advice centre.

Nearly half the visits about criminal problems were made to citizens' advice bureaux, nearly a third to legal advice centres, and most of the remainder to the probation service. On both social security problems and income tax and rate rebates, most visits were made to citizens' advice bureaux. Both the probation service and local authority social services received some visits about social security problems. Visits on income tax and rate rebates were also made to local authority legal and housing services. The majority of visits about personal and financial difficulties were made to citizens' advice bureaux, and most of the remainder to the probation service or to the local authority social services.

In Table 14 we show how the client had come to visit the agency. The category 'other' includes self-referrals, those who said they saw the sign, and referrals by a miscellaneous group of people including Members of Parliament, local councillors, and general practitioners.

The greatest proportion of clients visiting the probation service, citizens' advice bureaux, and the local authority social services had visited those agencies before. The largest proportion of clients visiting legal advice centres had been recommended to do so by citizens' advice bureaux. In the case of visits to local authority legal departments and rent officers the largest percentage gave 'other' as their source of recommendation. Nearly one quarter of clients visiting the local authority social services gave 'other' as their source of recommendation, while nearly a fifth of the clients visiting citizens' advice bureaux were recommended to do so by persons in the 'other' category.

Friends, neighbours, and relatives were an important source of recommendation for some agencies recording for us: this

TABLE 14 PERCENTAGE OF VISITS BY SOURCE OF RECOMMENDATION AND AGENCY

(Calculated from estimated number of visits for 12-week period)

Source of recommendation	Local authority legal and housing services	Local authority social services	Members of Parliament and political parties	Legal advice centres	Citizens' advice bureaux	Probation service	Total
Client has been before	22	36	3	27	41	46	35
Friend, neighbour, or relative	14	25	26	24	26	6	23
Local authority	11	4	0	7	3	2	5
Probation officer	0	0·2	0	4	0·6	7	1
Magistrate, court official	0·7	0	0	0·6	0·8	11	1
Ministry of Labour, labour exchange, youth employment	0·7	0·5	7	0·5	0·3	1	0·6
Police	3	3	0	0·7	2	3	2
Citizens' advice bureau	5	3	0	30	3	2	7
Other (self-referral, saw sign, notice)	36	21	13	6	19	6	18
Not ascertained	9	8	52	1	4	13	7
Total:	100	100	100	100	100	100	100
	(141)	(268)	(36)	(392)	(676)	(82)	(1,595)

Note: Parenthetical figures represent the number of recorded visits on which the calculation was made. Only the offices of agencies situated in the three boroughs are included. Visits on departmental problems are excluded.

was the case in about a quarter of all visits to Members of Parliament, legal advice centres, citizens' advice bureaux, and the local authority social services. 'Local authority' was the source of recommendation in over a tenth of visits to local authority legal departments and the rent officer service. The probation service, court officials, and police were not important sources of recommendation to the agencies recording for us, with one exception: over a tenth of estimated visits to the probation service were recommended by court officials.

All agencies were asked to record what services they provided for people calling at their offices. In Table 15 we show whether visits led to telephone calls being made, or letters written, or whether other services were provided. We asked agencies to record what they did as a result of the visit recorded, not what had been done on previous occasions, or what they proposed to do on a subsequent visit. The category 'Forms filled in' includes legal aid forms, pension and supplementary pension books. The category 'Drafted defence, pleadings' covers any formal legal document required for possible court proceedings.

The category 'representation arranged' signifies arrangements made for a client to be represented formally in a court or tribunal proceedings.

Over half of the estimated visits to the probation service, citizens' advice bureaux, and to the two groups of local authority services led to advice or information only. In the case of about a quarter of estimated visits to Members of Parliament and over a third of visits to legal advice centres, the service provided was advice or information only. Just under two-thirds of the estimated visits to Members of Parliament led to letters being written on the client's behalf: this was the case in one third of visits to legal advice centres. In the other agencies, letters were written for much fewer visitors.

Telephone calls were made more frequently than letters written at citizens' advice bureaux: over a fifth of estimated visits resulted in that service. The same was true in the case of local authority social services. Forms were occasionally filled in for visitors to citizens' advice bureaux, legal advice centres, and local authority social services. Only legal advice centres and citizens' advice bureaux occasionally drafted letters or wills, defences, and pleadings. Only legal advice centres arranged

TABLE 15 PERCENTAGE OF VISITS RESULTING IN SERVICES BY AGENCY (Calculated from estimated number of visits for 12-week period)

Services provided	Local authority legal and housing services	Local authority social services	Members of Parliament and political parties	Legal advice centres	Citizens' advice bureaux	Probation service	Total
Advice or information	70	64	24	38	56	61	56
One or more letters	13	4	63	33	9	12	14
One or more telephone calls	1	21	3	2	22	13	16
Both letters and telephone calls	4	3	10	7	5	7	5
Forms filled in	1	4	0	6	6	2	5
Client came to report	0	0·5	0	0·5	0·2	0	0·2
Drafted letter, will	0	0	0	2	2	0	1
Drafted defence, pleadings	0	0	0	0·9	0·2	0	0·2
Representation arranged	0	0	0	4	0	0	0·7
Not ascertained	11	4	0	6	0	4	3
Total:	100 (141)	100 (268)	100 (36)	100 (392)	100 (676)	100 (82)	100 (1,595)

Note: Parenthetical figures represent the number of recorded visits on which the calculation was made. Only the offices of agencies situated in the three boroughs are included. Visits on departmental problems are excluded.

TABLE 16 PERCENTAGE OF VISITS LEADING TO REFERRAL BY AGENCY
(Calculated from estimated number of visits for 12-week period)

Referral	Local Authority Legal and Housing services	Local Authority Social services	Members of Parliament and political parties	Legal advice centres	Citizens' advice bureaux	Probation service
None	35	43	93	79	51	38
To: Solicitor in private practice	9	1	4	10	15	16
Citizens' Advice Bureau honorary legal adviser	0	0	0	0	0·8	0
Legal advice centre	9	3	0	0	9	4
Trade union lawyer	0	0	0	0	0	0
Political party legal advice	0	0	0	0·1	0·1	0
Court official	0·7	0·5	0	1	0·6	13
Probation officer	0	3	0	0	2	2
Town hall legal dept.	6	3	0	0·1	1	0
Member of Parliament	0	1	0	0	0·2	0
Local councillor	0	0	0	0·1	0·8	0
Citizens' advice bureau	4	2	0	0	0·3	0
Police	1	1	0	0	0·3	0
Children's Department	0	3	0	0·5	0·2	1
Ministry of Social Security Voluntary agency (including N.S.P.C.C. and W.R.V.S.)	0	3	0	2	2	4
Ministry of Labour Housing department	7	2	3	0·5	1	0
Public health department	7	3	0	0	0·4	0
Welfare department	0·7	2	0	0·5	0·5	0
Other	17	20	0	1	8	4
Not ascertained	3	5	0	8	3	4
Total:	100 (141)	100 (268)	100 (36)	100 (392)	100 (676)	100 (82)

Note: Parenthetical figures represent the number of recorded visits on which the calculation was made. Only the offices of agencies situated in the three boroughs are included. Visits on departmental problems are excluded.

representations for their clients: this was done in the case of 4 per cent of estimated visits to them.

In Table 16 we show the extent to which visitors were referred to other agencies. The category 'other' includes general practitioner, legal aid committee of the Law Society, and employer, while the category 'not ascertained' covers all those cases where the agency did not record whether any referral was made or to whom the person was referred.

Agencies differed considerably in the extent to which they referred their clients elsewhere. This seldom occurred as a result of visits to Members of Parliament: as we have seen, they tended to contact others by letter. But two thirds of visits to the probation service and to local authority legal and housing services led to a referral compared with about half the visits to local authority social services and citizens' advice bureaux.

Visits made to the probation service and citizens' advice bureaux not infrequently led to a referral to a solicitor in private practice. Other agencies were less likely to refer callers to solicitors. Referrals to legal advice centres resulted from nearly a tenth of visits to citizens' advice bureaux, and local authority legal and housing services.

We asked most agencies to record for us whether a visit was the first on the particular problem or whether previous visits had been made. This information was not available for some local authority departments (maternity and child welfare) and rent officers. We found that 67 per cent of estimated visits to citizens' advice bureaux were first visits on that particular problem: the corresponding figure for legal advice centres was 52 per cent and for the probation service 46 per cent. Visits within the last three months on the same problem had occurred in 20 per cent of cases. Contact over a greater period of time (over three months) was more common in the case of the citizens' advice bureaux. About 35 per cent of estimated visits to legal advice centres had been preceded by visits made within the last three months, and 10 per cent over three months ago. In the case of the probation service, 22 per cent of estimated visits had been preceded by a visit made within three months, and 8 per cent by a visit over three months ago.

We should have liked to assess every recorded visit according to the importance to the client and its legal complexity. As explained in Appendix I, we were only able to do this for visits made to citizens' advice bureaux and the probation service (see Table 17). The research worker herself assessed the problem in the citizens' advice bureaux, while the probation officers did this for themselves. The figures are based on the visits recorded for all nine citizens' advice bureaux.

We did not classify according to legal complexity problems which were not of great importance to the client, or which could not be remedied by an advisory service or where some simple information, advice, or help was required. Thus, visits were regarded as of minor importance where all that was wanted was to have a pension book signed or to know how to claim an income tax refund, or when a lonely lady came to claim that her tenants were persecuting her. We were concerned that our classification should include all cases where there was a legal problem or the possibility of a legal solution to a problem. This involved a wider definition of legal problems than the work which lawyers are normally expected to undertake. For example, a lawyer might have been able to give considerable help on the legal aspects of a supplementary benefit claim, although extremely few lawyers have any experience in this area and are, thus, ill-equipped to offer any advice, except on how a fair hearing at a tribunal should be conducted.

We used this classification for problems arising from visits to citizens' advice bureaux because one of the authors (Rosalind Brooke) was herself making the classifications on the days she was present. As she was only able to be present for two out of the five (or six) working days (or their equivalent in the case of bureaux open only part time), she was only able to assess just under a quarter (23 per cent) of cases coming to bureaux during the recording period. The results are shown in Table 17.

All debt, personal injuries, and criminal problems were considered to be either minor or major legal problems. Others which were very likely to be assessed as legal problems were those about landlord and tenant matters, matrimonial, family and custody of children, and housing, homelessness or compulsory purchase order problems. Few about income tax or

TABLE 17   PERCENTAGE OF LEGAL PROBLEMS HANDLED BY CITIZENS'
ADVICE BUREAUX

Type of problem	Not a Legal Problem	Minor Legal Problem	Major Legal Problem	Total
Landlord and tenant	19	46	36	100 (31)
Debt	0	57	43	100 (4)
Faulty goods and services	44	31	25	100 (9)
Wills and winding up estates	40	60	0	100 (5)
Personal injuries	0	25	75	100 (9)
Employment, redundancy	42	58	0	100 (15)
Matrimonial, affiliation, children, family relationships	3	21	76	100 (21)
Social security	64	18	18	100 (12)
Criminal	0	0	100	100 (3)
Insurance	100	0	0	100 (3)
Neighbour	33	67	0	100 (3)
Information	100	0	0	100 (5)
Income tax, rate rebates	71	29	0	100 (7)
Housing, house purchase, homeless, compulsory purchase orders	29	43	29	100 (7)
Personal and financial difficulties	100	0	0	100 (3)
Miscellaneous	76	24	0	100 (13)

Note: Parenthetical figures represent the number of recorded visits on which the calculation was made.

rate rebates were considered to be legal problems. Neighbour problems were classified as minor legal if they were legal at all. Over half of the estimated visits about faulty goods and services were considered to be legal in some degree.

The probation officers themselves assessed visits made to them by stating whether or not the client would have been wise to see a solicitor. We give the results of this assessment in Table 18. The category 'Unclassified' in this table includes all those visits where the officer concerned made no assessment, or where the officer stated he or she did not know whether the client would be wise to see a solicitor. The range of problems in this table is considerably shorter than in preceding tables,

TABLE 18 PERCENTAGE OF VISITS TO PROBATION SERVICE BY NEED TO
CONSULT A SOLICITOR AND TYPE OF PROBLEM

| | Seriousness of problem | | | | |
Type of problem	Wise to see a solicitor	Not wise to see a solicitor	Not applicable for client to see a solicitor	Unclassified	Total
Matrimonial	39	44	10	7	100 (100)
Affiliation	39	31	15	15	100 (13)
Social security	0	55	11	33	100 (9)
Criminal	11	67	22	0	100 (9)
Custody of children, adoption	53	26	5	16	100 (19)
Personal and financial difficulties	0	74	16	11	100 (19)
Family relationships	33	56	11	0	100 (9)
Other	47	29	12	12	100 (17)
Not ascertained	0	0	0	0	0
Total:	34	45	11	10	100 (195)

Note: Parenthetical figures represent the number of recorded visits on which the calculation was made. All probation offices are included, but visits about departmental problems are excluded.

as over half the visits recorded for us by the probation service were about matrimonial problems, and nearly a quarter were about family relationships, custody of children, or affiliation matters. The category 'Other' includes landlord and tenant matters, debt and employment problems. Percentage figures in this table are for visits over a one-week period.

In over half the visits recorded about custody of children and adoption, and in nearly two-fifths of matrimonial and affiliation cases it was considered that the caller would be wise to see a solicitor. In no cases on social security or in connection with personal and financial difficulties was it thought wise for a client to see a solicitor. In few of the visits about criminal problems was it considered wise for the client to see a solicitor. In nearly half of the recorded cases about 'other' problems clients were considered to be wise to see a solicitor.

Solicitors
As mentioned in Chapter 2, we interviewed as many solicitors as possible during the autumn of 1968. During the course of

these interviews we asked each solicitor whether he would be willing to record for us details of all new clients coming to him during the course of one week. Some solicitors were unwilling to do this, partly because they were unsure what use would be made of this information (one solicitor was worried about the extent of knowledge we would gain of his practice), partly because of the time and numbers of staff involved, and partly because of fears that this would be a breach of confidence with clients. A few solicitors said there was no point in recording details for us because the number of clients in whom we were interested (i.e. those receiving free advice or advice under the statutory scheme) was so small. Two solicitors were unfavourably inclined because there had been criticisms of lawyers and their work in a book written by one of the directors of the survey.

In the end only twenty-two out of a total of fifty-one promised to record details of new clients. Some of these firms agreed to record all new clients, whether fee-paying or not. Others were only willing to record details of new clients receiving advice either under the statutory scheme or free: they were unwilling to record all clients for one or more of the reasons given above. By the end of January 1969, however, we had only received schedules from ten firms, while another six had written to say either that they would do it in the future or had been unable to do the recording for us. The recording had not been done either because there were no new clients, or because the practice in the borough was being given up, or because the solicitor concerned had been in court for a considerable number of weeks and had thus given no advice under the statutory scheme. No replies were received from the other six firms when reminder letters were sent out.

In the following brief discussion of the questionnaires received it must be borne in mind that they relate to ten firms only, and secondly that all ordinary fee-paying clients have been excluded in order to make the data comparable. In addition, clients for whom no detail on payment was recorded have also been excluded. So the data relates to clients who were seen under the statutory or voluntary legal advice schemes or who were seen free or for a nominal fee, e.g. 10s. (50p) or less. We received eighty-nine schedules from the ten firms, but the data is based on forty-five, as the rest were excluded for the reasons we have stated. The results of this survey were very disappointing but we nevertheless thought it useful briefly to summarize the findings to show the use which can be made of a study of this kind in the hope that at some stage a better response rate may be obtained in a later survey.

Slightly more of the clients were men than women. About a third came from outside the three boroughs: Southwark firms had the highest proportion of clients from outside the borough. Nearly a quarter of the clients were immigrants from the West Indies, Cyprus, or Eire. The majority of new clients came as a result of a referral from a citizens' advice bureau, the court, the local authority, police, or probation department. Over a third of the visits were on matrimonial problems: landlord and tenant problems, personal injuries and criminal cases were the most common other types of problem on which help was sought. In the majority of cases a specific service was given other than advice—letters, telephone calls, the drafting of a document, or representation in court. In only about a tenth of the cases did the solicitor think that a lawyer's help had not been required. Nearly half the clients were not seen by a partner in the firm but by an articled clerk, legal executive, assistant solicitor, or secretary. In three-quarters of these cases the service was provided free and in only about a third was the service provided under the legal aid and advice scheme. Over a third of the visits took less than twenty minutes.

Data for Agencies which did not record information
Some local organizations were willing to discuss their work with us but were unable to allow us to record it, though their counterparts in other boroughs or even in the same borough were able to do so. The rent officer for Tower Hamlets was unwilling to record information for us and unable to give us any estimate of the number of callers at his three offices. However, he was able to tell us that between the setting up of the rent officer service in the borough in 1965 and January 1966 there had been 1,050 applications to the rent officer. The public relations officer in Tower Hamlets was also unable to agree to keep records for us of the work undertaken in the Information

Centre; but it appeared that most of the requests for information handled at this centre fell outside the scope of this survey. Between March 1966 and March 1967 the centre had handled about 7,000 enquiries, of which about 4,000 had been made by letter or telephone, and about 3,000 by a personal visit. Publicity in the form of posters and advertisements in local newspapers probably accounted for the increase from three enquiries per day when the centre opened to thirty per day in November 1967. Between 3 per cent and 5 per cent of these enquiries were referred to citizens' advice bureaux, legal advice centres, or solicitors; in addition some landlord and tenant enquiries were referred to the town hall. It was estimated that in total about 5 per cent of their enquiries were 'legal', the most frequent being landlord and tenant problems, but also included were problems of hire purchase, employment, and personal injuries.

Two other departments of the Tower Hamlets Borough Council were visited and the research worker was allowed by the council to spend a day sitting at the public counter. She spent one Monday early in November in the main (lettings) office of the Housing Department. There were approximately thirty-eight callers between 8.45 a.m. and 4.30 p.m. (the office shuts at 5.00 p.m.). Thirty-three of these enquiries were exclusively about the housing waiting list, applications and transfers, offers of flats, repairs and maintenance of these. Two visitors made general requests for information while the remaining visitor wanted to find the electricity board. The remaining two had a legal aspect; both of these were about the possibility of being rehoused by the council: one West Indian had an eviction order (he had previously had his rent reduced by the Rent Tribunal). The other enquirer's flat was in a clearance area and he was complaining of rats. In view of the very high proportion of enquiries relating exclusively to routine housing department work we did not consider it worth asking the department to record further information for us.

One of the team spent a Wednesday in the same week in the general office of the environmental section of the Tower Hamlets Public Health department. The department allowed the research worker to sit beside the clerical worker/receptionist

D

to whom callers made their request for help. There were twenty-six personal callers to the office, and in addition there were telephone and letter requests for help made straight to the public health inspectors in another room. They were all requests for help and information coming within a public health inspector's statutory duties. The vast majority were about housing conditions and rehousing on medical grounds, while two were about bad food and slaughtering, one from builders about drains on test, and one was about rats in the street and house. Statistics collected weekly by the office showed that the preceding week there had been 141 requests for help (65 personally, 45 by telephone, and 31 by letter). The biggest proportion of these were about housing conditions; there were eighteen miscellaneous problems and thirteen about rats and bugs. Because all of these problems related to the work of the department, and because there were so many members of the department who would be asked for advice and help, we decided not to ask the department to record information for us.

All eleven Members of Parliament were interviewed, but only a few recorded information for us which is included earlier in this chapter. The Member of Parliament for Bermondsey (Mr R. Mellish) had thirty people come to his constituency surgery one evening in November when the research worker was present. The Members of Parliament for Dulwich and Peckham estimated that they generally had between ten and twelve people each at their fortnightly surgeries. The Member of Parliament for East Islington (Sir Eric Fletcher) thought he had about fifteen people at his weekly surgery, while the Member of Parliament for Shoreditch and Finsbury (Mr R. Brown) estimated he had about forty. In Tower Hamlets the Member of Parliament for the Isle of Dogs (Mr I. Mikardo) had twenty to thirty people or more at his surgery. That constituency had an office at the eastern end of the East India Dock Road with a full-time agent who was also a councillor for a nearby London borough. The agent estimated that for every person seen by the Member of Parliament he would see and help another three people.

The Liberal Party constituency organizations at the time of

he research enquiries in October/November 1967 were running
10 formal surgeries and officials and candidates could not give
:stimates of the numbers coming to them individually with
)roblems, although the candidate for North Islington thought
1e received one problem in about six weeks.

Neither the police nor the courts would record systematic
nformation for us. Interviews with them were, however, useful
n giving some impression of how they handled enquiries for
nformation, and what they were about. The station officer
tt Islington police station considered that 60 per cent of his
ime was spent in giving advice, while the station sergeant in
)outhwark thought on average about twelve people might
:ome in for advice and help on each shift, making a total of
hirty-six in twenty-four hours, seven days per week.

Magistrates and county courts do not keep records of all
hose coming to the court offices with requests for information
tnd advice. General enquiries at the stipendiary magistrates
:ourts most probably bear some relation to the level of applica-
ions made to the magistrate himself. The Warrant Officer at
:lerkenwell Court considered that for every applicant put up
o the magistrate there might be twice as many referred elsewhere or helped in some other way. At that court during
)ne week in March 1968 there were five applications on Mon-
lay, three on Tuesday. In the preceding week at Thames
:ourt in Tower Hamlets, there were nine applications on
Monday and seven on Tuesday. At Tower Bridge Court in
)outhwark the Chief Clerk estimated the maximum number of
tpplications would be twenty, the average being between
hree and six per day, while the Warrant Officer thought there
night be between five to ten people per day wanting to make
tn application. At North London Court in a week in February
here had been twenty applications on Monday and eleven the
ollowing Tuesday. At Old Street Court (covering parts of
slington and Hackney) there were twenty-seven applications
n the first three days of a week in March (twelve on Monday,
iine on Tuesday, and six on Wednesday).

At Lambeth County Court some statistics were available on
he number of callers in connection with another survey.
Γhe Chief Clerk thought they might get as many as seventy

callers on a busy day and during three days early in December 1967 they had had seventy-one callers on a Friday (a further seventeen telephone calls), sixty-three on a Monday (plus sixteen telephone calls) and fifty-two on Tuesday (plus twenty-nine telephone calls). These calls would include those made by solicitors and their staff on behalf of clients. One of the office clerks at the court estimated that approximately ten to twenty people each week were in need of legal advice. Their problems might be matrimonial, or breach of promise to marry, while others would be about hire purchase agreements. The Registrar at Bow County Court thought they got few requests for advice. This may reflect the ambiguity inherent in impressionistic interviews, not backed up by visits of observation. There is a difference because a person may make a request which could lead to advice (which it is county court policy not to allow staff to provide, as court staff cannot appear to be assisting either party), or information (i.e. how to fill in a form or file a defence), or referral elsewhere (e.g. to a magistrates' court for a separation order).

At the time of the survey the Rent Tribunal offices in Islington were keeping records for the Ministry of Housing. In one week in February 1968 there were twenty-six personal callers on Monday, seven on Tuesday, six on Wednesday, and thirteen on Thursday. The Clerk thought Islington residents constituted the majority of visitors, although the figures would include a few from Camden and Barnet; requests for help from Tower Hamlets and the eastern boroughs were more likely to be made by letter or when office staff went to those boroughs.

Neither the hospital staff nor the trade union officials whom we interviewed could give any information on the number of people they advised or referred elsewhere. Trade union officials were, however, able to give information on cases taken to tribunals or courts, or settled privately out of court. The A.E.U. in London alone handled each year 250 appeals on social security benefits, and between 200 and 300 redundancy appeal cases, of which three were taken to the Divisional Court. The Transport & General Workers' Union in 1966 settled out of court 4,800 personal injury claims in its thirteen regional offices recovering a total of £1 million. The London ffice, which dealt with the more serious cases, settled another ,500 cases, recovering £1 million. The same union sent between 600 and 700 cases to lawyers and took about 160 ases to court.

The newspapers could give some information on the size of their correspondence, for example the *Daily* and *Sunday Mirror* in 1967 received nearly 82,000 letters on social security, hire purchase, employment, matrimonial, and other problems and wrote nearly 80,000 letters. The *People*'s Advice Bureau handled between 3,000 and 4,000 queries per week and sent about 100 cases per week to counsel for an opinion. The *News f the World* John Hilton Bureau dealt each year with 150,000 letters, over 30 per cent of which were on social security and 7–8 per cent were about matrimonial problems. The other newspapers did not purport to deal with problems or to encourage people to write to them. This is reflected in their figures. The *Daily Sketch* legal department dealt with about 50 legal problems each year, while the paper as a whole received many more queries which did not have a legal aspect. The *Daily Mail* sent between ten and twelve letters per week to its legal department for advice.

A local, specialized organization like the Greek-Cypriot Brotherhood (which covers more than Islington and Tower Hamlets) had between fifteen and twenty people per week coming with problems needing help and advice. The Islington Tenants' Association had between six and ten people at its weekly surgery. We did not contact two tenants' associations in Tower Hamlets so we have no knowledge of their numbers or practice.

Summary

We have set out in this chapter the systematic data which we obtained about visits to many of the local agencies in the three boroughs. For some individuals, particularly the Members of Parliament, we were only able to obtain an estimate of the number of people they saw and helped. We were not able to obtain systematic information about the use by residents of the three boroughs of national organizations like trade unions, the police, or newspaper advisory services.

CHAPTER 5

The Users of Advisory Services

In this chapter we describe some of the characteristics of those who visited the agencies which recorded information about their work. The information collected for us was limited, for reasons explained in Appendix I. Thus, the characteristics we use are restricted to social class and occupational status, marital status and sex.

We estimated the proportion of visits made by men of each social class resident in the three boroughs, compared with the proportion of each social class in the borough. As described in Appendix I, postal districts were used to decide whether or not a person was resident in one of the three boroughs. This allocation to a borough could only be approximate because postal districts cross borough boundaries.

The census statistics do not include four of the classifications which we have had to use (student, unemployed or sick, retired and in prison). Some agencies were unable to spare the time to elicit actual occupation for those who said they were out of work, or sick or were retired, and in some instances it might have upset the client to be asked for more details. In those few agencies where briefing procedures were not comprehensive, the agency workers did not always appreciate that a normal occupation should be obtained, even for those not currently at work.

The four extra groups (student, unemployed or sick, retired, in prison) accounted for just under 11 per cent of visits from men resident in the three boroughs. The census statistics show 3 per cent of the male population unclassified by social class, while the category 'not ascertained' in our statistics covered 12 per cent of visits. The large proportion whom we were unable to classify limits the reliability of the comparison with total population. If, however, those whom we failed to classify were not biased towards any particular social class, it appears from Table 19 that social classes I and II used the services much less and social class III slightly less than average. The heavy users came from social class V.

TABLE 19 PERCENTAGE OF VISITS BY SOCIAL CLASS OF CLIENT COMPARED WITH SOCIAL CLASS OF RESIDENTS OF BOROUGHS: (MALES ONLY)

Social class	Visits*		Residents of three boroughs†
Class I	1	(6)	2
Class II	5	(27)	8
Class III non-manual	6⎫37	(32)⎫(215)	49
Class III manual	31⎭	(183)⎭	
Class IV	17	(95)	22
Class V	18	(100)	16
Unclassified	23	(130)	3
Total:	100	(573)	100

* Calculated from estimated number of visits for a 12-week period. Parenthetical figures represent the number of recorded visits on which the calculation was made. Male clients of all agencies are included who were resident in a postal district wholly or partly within the borough boundaries. Visits on department problems are excluded.
† 1966 Census of Population.

We looked to see how far the use made of the different agencies with offices in the three boroughs varied by social class. Visits by both men and women were examined: married women were attributed to the social class of their husbands. For about a third of the visits no information was obtained. This is higher than in Table 19 because of the difficulty of asking about the occupations of husbands of divorced and separated women. All visits about departmental problems were excluded. It seemed that social classes I and II made very little use of legal advice centres. These were particularly used by skilled manual workers. Apart from this, there was no great difference in the social class usage of different agencies.

In Table 20 we show the problems on which people of different social classes sought advice from the agencies. There were extremely few visits from persons in social class I. Members of social class II sought advice on landlord and tenant problems more frequently than persons in other social classes. On the other hand, the higher social classes were much less likely to seek advice from these agencies on social security, income tax, or problems involving goods or to ask for help with their personal and social problems. The clearest pattern emerged in the case of advice on personal injuries—the lower the social class, the higher proportion of visits on this type of problem.

TABLE 20 PERCENTAGE OF VISITS BY SOCIAL CLASS OF CLIENT AND TYPE OF PROBLEM

(Calculated from estimated number of visits for 12-week period)

Type of problem	Class I	Class II	Class III non-manual	Class III manual	Class IV	Class V	Unclas-sified	Total
Landlord and tenant	11	26	21	22	22	22	27	24
Debt	11	4	1	10	5	8	4	6
Faulty goods and services	0	2	4	4	3	3	3	3
Wills, winding up estates	0	0	2	3	3	1	1	2
Personal injuries	0	3	6	9	9	12	3	7
Employment	0	13	15	8	12	11	3	8
Matrimonial, affiliation, children, family relationships	17	3	5	5	2	4	5	4
Social security	0	2	5	5	5	6	4	5
Criminal	0	2	2	3	2	4	2	3
Income tax, rate rebates	0	2	2	2	4	4	3	3
Housing, house purchase, homeless, compulsory purchase orders	0	1	1	1	1	1	2	1
Personal and financial difficulties	0	0	2	3	4	3	5	4
Miscellaneous	60	27	35	28	40	32	41	30
Total:	100	100	100	100	100	100	100	100
	(10)	(61)	(117)	(427)	(221)	(234)	(525)	(1,595)

Note: Parenthetical figures represent the number of recorded visits on which the calculation was made. Only the offices of agencies situated in the three boroughs are included. Visits on departmental problems are excluded.

We looked to see if there were any significant differences in the way by which people had come to visit a citizens' advice bureau (referred by friends, seeing the office, etc.). No clear pattern emerged.

In Table 21 we show how far the services provided to clients varied according to social class. In general the higher the client's social status, the less likely he was to receive extensive services. Advice and information only was given as a result of over two-thirds of estimated visits by non-manual workers and as a result of less than half of the visits by semi-skilled and unskilled manual workers. Letters, telephone calls, and other specific services were most commonly undertaken for the lower social classes.

TABLE 21 PERCENTAGE OF VISITS RESULTING IN SERVICES BY AGENCY, BY SOCIAL CLASS OF CLIENT

(Calculated from estimated number of visits for 12-week period)

Services provided	Class I	Class II	Class III non-manual	Class III manual	Class IV	Class V	Unclas-sified	Total
Advice or information	77	68	68	62	48	48	54	56
One or more letters	23	3	8	11	18	20	15	14
One or more 'phone calls	0	16	12	14	17	18	16	16
Both letters and 'phone calls	0	10	4	4	6	5	4	5
Forms filled in	0	0	4	6	4	5	4	5
Client came to report	0	0	0	0	1	1	—	—
Drafted letter, will	0	2	2	1	3	1	1	1
Drafted defence, pleadings	0	0	0	—	0	1	0	—
Representation arranged	0	0	1	1	0	—	—	1
Not ascertained	0	2	2	1	3	1	7	3
Total:	100	100	100	100	100	100	100	100
	(10)	(61)	(117)	(427)	(221)	(235)	(524)	(1,595)

Note: Parenthetical figures represent the number of recorded visits on which the calculation was made. Only the offices of agencies situated in the three boroughs are included. Visits on departmental problems are excluded.

In Table 22 we show the extent to which referrals varied with a person's social class. The category 'voluntary agency' includes the N.S.P.C.C. and the W.R.V.S., while 'other' includes general practitioner, employer, and legal aid committee.

Slightly more visits in the higher social classes than in the lower led to referrals. But there were marked differences in the agency to which different social classes were referred. The higher the social class the more likely was referral to a solicitor in private practice. Manual workers and clerical workers were much more likely than the higher social classes to be referred to legal advice centres, the town hall legal department, probation officers, and the Ministry of Social Security.

In the remainder of this chapter we discuss such differences as there were in the use of the agencies according to sex and marital status. Relatively more estimated visits were made by men to legal advice centres (58 per cent), while relatively more visits were made by women to local authority social services. Women also made more visits to the probation service (57 per cent of estimated visits). There was no variation in the proportion of visits made to local authority legal and housing services, Members of Parliament and political parties, and citizens' advice bureaux.

TABLE 22   PERCENTAGE OF VISITS LEADING TO REFERRAL, BY SOCIAL CLASS OF CLIENT
(Calculated from estimated number of visits for 12-week period)

Referral	Class I	Class II	Class III non-manual	Class III manual	Class IV	Class V	Unclassified	Total
None	51	48	43	51	52	53	56	52
To: Solicitor in private practice	26	15	15	13	10	6	6	11
Citizens' advice bureau honorary legal adviser	0	0	1	—	1	1	—	—
Legal advice centre	0	2	8	7	7	8	5	6
Trade union lawyer	0	0	0	0	0	0	0	0
Political party legal advice	0	0	0	—	—	0	0	—
Court official	0	2	1	2	1	1	2	2
Probation officer	0	0	1	2	2	2	1	1
Town hall legal department	0	0	3	1	2	1	3	2
Member of Parliament	0	0	0	—	0	0	1	—
Local councillor	0	0	0	1	1	0	—	—
Citizens' advice bureau	0	0	1	1	1	1	1	1
Police	0	0	2	0	1	0	1	1
Children's department	0	0	1	—	1	1	1	1
Ministry of Social Security	0	0	1	1	2	4	1	2
Voluntary agency (including N.S.P.C.C. and W.R.V.S.)	0	2	1	1	1	1	1	1
Ministry of Labour	0	2	2	1	1	3	1	1
Housing department	0	0	1	1	3	1	3	2
Public health department	0	4	0	2	2	1	2	2
Welfare department	0	0	1	0	1	3	1	1
Other	23	15	10	8	6	7	9	8
Not ascertained	0	2	4	4	3	5	27	4
Total:	100	100	100	100	100	100	100	100
	(10)	(61)	(117)	(427)	(221)	(235)	(524)	(1,595)

Note: Parenthetical figures represent the number of recorded visits on which the calculation was made. Only the offices of agencies situated in the three boroughs are included. Visits on departmental problems are excluded.

Single people, who made 20 per cent of all estimated visits, made only 5 per cent of estimated visits to Members of Parliament and political parties. Married people, however, who made

54 per cent of all estimated visits, made 79 per cent of estimated visits to Members of Parliament. This is perhaps not surprising, since most visits were made concerning local authority housing matters. Married people made also proportionately more visits to local authority legal and housing services (62 per cent of estimated visits), to legal advice centres (57 per cent), and the local authority social services (58 per cent).

There was some variation in the incidence of problems between the sexes. Men made far more estimated visits about problems connected with personal injuries, employment, and personal and financial difficulties (over 61 per cent for each category); and 83 per cent of estimated visits about criminal problems. Men and women made nearly the same percentage of estimated visits (i.e. between 50 per cent and 55 per cent each) about landlord and tenant matters, debt, income tax and rate rebates, housing, and faulty goods and services. Women made the largest proportion of estimated visits about matrimonial, children, and family problems (65 per cent), wills and winding up estates (66 per cent), and social security (60 per cent).

We analysed the visits about different types of problems according to the client's marital status. Single people, who made one fifth of all estimated visits, made over one third of estimated visits about criminal problems, and over one quarter of estimated visits about faulty goods and services, wills, personal injuries, employment, and income tax. They made about one fifth of estimated visits on other types of problems, except for matrimonial and affiliation problems, where they made only 7 per cent of estimated visits. Married people, who made over half (54 per cent) of all estimated visits, made proportionately more (between 57 per cent and 60 per cent) of estimated visits about landlord and tenant problems, faulty goods and services, personal injuries, housing and house purchase matters. Married people, however, made less than one third (30 per cent) of estimated visits about social security matters, and 44 per cent of estimated visits about income tax and rate rebates. People who were separated, although they made 8 per cent of all estimated visits, made over 23 per cent of estimated visits about matrimonial and related problems and personal and financial difficulties (21 per cent). Widowed people with 11 per cent of all estimated visits made 20 per cent of visits about wills and winding up estates, and 32 per cent of visits on social security matters.

CHAPTER 6

Variations among Operational Units

In this chapter we set out some information about individual advice bureaux and legal advice centres to see whether there was any variation between individual agencies. We were not however able to evaluate the reasons for the differences which we found from the information collected for the study.

1. Citizens' Advice Bureaux

Our figures for each citizens' advice bureau are again based upon the workload over a twelve-week period as estimated from our data for visits during one or two weeks, as described in Appendix I. In Table 23 we show the percentage of visits about different types of problems. In this and subsequent tables, individual bureaux are indicated by letters of the alphabet (for reasons of confidentiality). The categories 'miscellaneous' and 'not ascertained' include those visits where the bureau did not record the subject of the enquiry and visits on problems such as change of name, immigration, and emigration.

There were wide variations in the proportion of visits made on different types of problem. While Bureau F, which received 20 per cent of all visits, handled 46 per cent of personal injuries cases, Bureau C, with the same percentage of estimated visits, handled 34 per cent of problems about faulty goods. Bureaux A and B, with 23 per cent of visits, handled 39 per cent of visits about landlord and tenant matters. Bureau I handled 38 per cent of visits about social security matters: this was because many elderly immigrants living in the neighbourhood took their pension and supplementary pension books to be signed, as they could not read English. Bureau E received 40 per cent of the visits about criminal problems, although the

TABLE 23   PERCENTAGE OF VISITS BY TYPE OF PROBLEM AND CITIZENS' ADVICE BUREAU

(Calculated from estimated number of visits for 12-week period)

Type of problem	A	B	C	D	E	F	G	H	I	Total	
Landlord and tenant	11	28	22	5	10	12	10	4	0·4	100	(128)
Debt	3	19	9	19	15	25	3	8	0	100	(35)
Faulty goods and services	9	13	34	0	13	28	0	3	0	100	(33)
Wills, winding up estates	6	36	18	6	12	12	6	0	3	100	(17)
Personal injuries	7	7	12	5	12	46	9	8	0	100	(47)
Employment	3	15	22	9	18	21	10	2	2	100	(71)
Matrimonial and affiliation	2	20	20	11	16	19	8	3	2	100	(68)
Social security	7	7	15	4	9	17	4	0	38	100	(64)
Criminal	0	13	13	7	40	13	7	3	3	100	(16)
Neighbour	0	0	15	8	39	23	8	0	8	100	(14)
Information	22	22	15	0	30	0	0	4	7	100	(15)
Income tax, rate rebates	4	25	25	4	12	20	8	0	2	100	(25)
Housing, house purchase, homeless, compulsory purchase orders	3	7	25	7	25	25	0	1	7	100	(32)
Children, family relationships	0	7	19	7	32	19	7	4	7	100	(18)
Personal and financial difficulties	8	0	8	8	24	51	0	0	2	100	(28)
Miscellaneous, and not ascertained	7	17	24	12	9	5	14	4	9	100	(65)
Total:	6	17	20	7	15	20	7	3	5	100	(676)

Note: Parenthetical figures indicate the number of recorded visits on which the calculation was made.

bureau received only 15 per cent of all visits. That bureau also received the largest proportion of visits about children and family relationships. This may be because Bureau E operates from the same building as a local authority family advice centre. Of all visits about wills one bureau (B) received 36 per cent, while a bureau in another borough handled 18 per cent.

This may be because Bureau B is in a borough with few legal advice centres.

Matrimonial problems were more evenly distributed among the bureaux. Visits about debt problems were also fairly evenly spread, although Bureau F handled proportionately more and Bureau C handled proportionately less. Problems about employment and redundancy were also evenly spread amongst the bureaux in relation to the total visits which they received.

In Table 24 we show the extent to which bureaux referred clients to other organizations or individuals. The category 'other' includes general practitioners, employers, some local authority services, and the police.

TABLE 24 PERCENTAGE OF VISITS LEADING TO REFERRAL BY CITIZENS' ADVICE BUREAU
(Calculated from estimated number of visits for 12-week period)

Referral	Citizens' advice bureau								
	A	B	C	D	E	F	G	H	I
None	56	50	29	47	42	70	54	66	80
To: Solicitor in private practice	8	21	22	9	5	15	20	13	4
Citizens' advice bureau honorary legal adviser	0	0	0·8	0	4	0	0	0	0
Legal advice centre	21	12	9	18	14	2	0	5	0
Probation officer	0	2	2	4	2	2	2	0	0
Voluntary agency (including N.S.P.C.C. and W.R.V.S.)	5	0	2	2	1	0	9	0	9
Other	15	15	33	30	21	7	25	0	7
Not ascertained	0	0	2	0	11	4	0	16	0
Total:	100	100	100	100	100	100	100	100	100
	(39)	(104)	(122)	(45)	(95)	(123)	(44)	(38)	(66)

Note: Parenthetical figures indicate the number of recorded visits on which the calculation was made.

There were large variations in the extent to which bureaux referred clients to other agencies: 20 per cent of the visits to Bureau I led to referrals and 71 per cent to Bureau C. Bureaux B, C, and G referred just over 20 per cent of their visitors to a solicitor in private practice, while Bureaux A, D, E, and I referred less than 10 per cent of their callers to solicitors. Only two bureaux made referrals to their honorary legal adviser: Bureau E referred 4 per cent and Bureau C 0·8 per cent.

Bureau A (which referred few people to solicitors) referred 21 per cent of their visitors to legal advice centres. Bureau D, which also made a low proportion of referrals to solicitors, referred 18 per cent of clients to legal advice centres. Bureau E, which had close links with one particular legal advice centre, referred 14 per cent of visitors to this or another centre. Bureaux G and I referred none. Three bureaux (A, H, and I) made no referrals to probation officers, while the others referred 4 per cent of their visitors to them. Bureaux C and D referred clients in 30 per cent or more of their visitors to other organizations and individuals.

Bureaux F and I, which were least likely to refer people elsewhere, were most likely to do something for the client themselves in addition to giving advice or information. This was true for 70 per cent of visitors at Bureau I and 57 per cent of visitors at Bureau F. The other bureaux ranged from 38 per cent (Bureau B) to 45 per cent (Bureau H). In all but three bureaux letters were written as a result of 8 per cent to 12 per cent of visits. The exceptions were Bureaux B and D, where letters were written as a result of only 5 per cent of estimated visits, and Bureau H as a result of 21 per cent of estimated visits. (Bureau H is a part-time bureau and recorded the smallest number of visits.) Bureaux workers were far more likely to make telephone calls than write letters: at Bureaux A, F, and G telephone calls were made as a result of over 30 per cent of visits, while at four bureaux (B, C, E, and H) calls were made as a result of between 15 per cent and 21 per cent of estimated visits; at Bureaux D and I calls were made as a result of about 10 per cent of visits. At all bureaux, with the exception of A and H, where no form-filling was done, 5 per cent and under of estimated visits involved the completion of forms (including legal and pension books): Bureau I filled in forms as a result of 48 per cent of estimated visits.

In Table 25 we show the proportion of visits made to different bureaux by the social class of the visitors. Some variations in the proportion of visits made by different classes can be explained by misunderstandings about the classification system (e.g. the extensive use of the category 'housewife' by bureau I, and 'retired' by bureau D) and by the fact that some bureaux did not obtain as much information about occupation as other bureaux. Nevertheless, we found considerable differences between the bureaux. While bureau A was disproportionately used by the higher social classes, the reverse was the case with bureaux F and G.

TABLE 25 PERCENTAGE OF VISITS BY SOCIAL CLASS OF CLIENT AND CITIZENS' ADVICE BUREAU
(Calculated from estimated number of visits for a 12-week period)

| Social class | Citizens' advice bureau | | | | | | | | | |
	A	B	C	D	E	F	G	H	I	Total
Class I	3	1	2	0	0	0	0	0	0	1
Class II	10	6	4	4	6	3	0	8	5	5
Class III non manual	8	13	15	9	18	3	5	8	5	10
Class III manual	46	26	27	18	25	25	25	29	47	28
Class IV	10	15	18	29	18	18	14	11	15	17
Class V	13	14	16	4	17	24	16	5	5	15
Unclassified	14	26	19	35	16	28	41	40	27	24
Total:	100	100	100	100	100	100	100	100	100	100
	(39)	(104)	(122)	(45)	(95)	(123)	(44)	(38)	(66)	(676)

Note: Parenthetical figures indicate the number of recorded visits on which the calculation was made.

More visits were recorded by women (340) than men (333) but the percentage of *estimated* visits by men was higher (51 per cent). This can be explained by the fact that a high proportion (74 per cent and 61 per cent) of visits were paid by women to bureaux H and I, which were part-time, and thus the weight allocated was lower than that for the other seven bureaux.

Two bureaux were visited by men more often than by women: at bureau A 72 per cent of estimated visits were made by men, and at bureau E 61 per cent. Bureaux G, H, and I were more used by women, who made between 61 per cent and 74 per cent of estimated visits. The remaining four bureaux (B, C, D, and F) were visited nearly equally by men and women (48 per cent to 54 per cent of estimated visits were made by men). The greater use made by men of bureaux A and E can possibly be explained by the fact that both lie on the edge of the city and the main business and commercial area of the City of London.

We classified callers by borough of residence. As explained in Appendix I, we were not able to ask for the precise address and had to classify by postal districts, some of which cross borough boundaries. The allocation of place of residence to borough is therefore only approximate.

We found that some bureaux have a wider catchment area than others which mainly serve people resident in the immediate neighbourhood. Two bureaux (A and E) had the smallest proportion of visits (over half of their visits) made to them by residents of the boroughs in which they were situated. Both bureaux were situated on the edge of the city but just within the borough boundaries. Four bureaux (all in Tower Hamlets) received over three-quarters of all their estimated visits from residents of that borough.

Information was collected about the country of birth of their clients (see Table 26). 'Middle East and Asia' includes people born in Aden, Burma, Iran, and Malaysia. The categories 'Not ascertained' and 'Not classified' cover people for whom no information was recorded, but includes five recorded visits by people whose country of birth was Australia, New Zealand, Canada, and the U.S.A.

At all bureaux, with the exception of Bureau I, over 60 per cent of clients were born in the United Kingdom. Only 33 per cent of the visitors to Bureau I were born in the United Kingdom: 61 per cent of its visitors were born in Europe or Israel. Much of the work of this bureau, as mentioned earlier, consisted of signing pension books for elderly Jewish immigrants. The next largest category (11 per cent) of all bureaux' clients

vere persons born in the West Indies. Bureaux B, C, and G
eceived however between 14 per cent and 18 per cent of their
stimated visits from people born in the West Indies, while
ureau I recorded no visits from West Indians. Just under
; per cent of all estimated visits to citizens' advice bureaux

TABLE 26 PERCENTAGE OF VISITS BY COUNTRY OF BIRTH OF CLIENT AND
CITIZENS' ADVICE BUREAU
(Calculated from estimated number of visits for a 12-week period)

Country of birth	Citizens' advice bureau									
	A	B	C	D	E	F	G	H	I	Total
United Kingdom and Northern Ireland	74	61	67	76	68	78	82	79	33	69
Pakistan	5	0	0	2	5	0·8	0	5	2	2
India	0	0	0	0	5	0	0	0	0	0·8
West Indies	5	18	14	7	5	12	14	5	0	11
Africa	3	6	2	2	2	5	0	0	0	3
Eire	8	8	12	4	3	0·8	2	3	0	5
Cyprus, Malta, Gibraltar	3	0	2	0	3	0·8	0	0	0	1
Europe and Israel	0	2	2	0	4	0	2	5	61	5
Middle East and Asia	0	1	0	0	2	0·8	0	0	3	0·8
Not ascertained and not classified	3	5	3	9	1	2	0	3	2	3
Total:	100 (39)	100 (104)	100 (122)	100 (45)	100 (95)	100 (123)	100 (44)	100 (38)	100 (66)	100 (676)

Note: Parenthetical figures represent the number of recorded visits on which the
calculation was made.

vere made by people born in India or Pakistan, and over
; per cent of all visits by people born in Africa. People born in
Eire made 5 per cent of all estimated visits to bureaux, while
bureaux A, B, and C received between 8 per cent and 12 per
cent of their estimated visits from clients born in Eire. The most
cosmopolitan bureau was E, to which visits were made by
people born in every group listed.

*. Legal Advice Centres
Our data for legal advice centres includes information recorded
by all six centres, including the centre which is situated in the

borough of Camden, but excluding those in Islington. Thre
of these centres open daily and three are part-time evenin
centres, as indicated in Chapter 1.

In Table 27 we show the differences in the type of probler
dealt with by each centre. The list of problems has bee
shortened since most visits were made about the seven types (
problem listed. The category 'other' includes visits abou
faulty goods and services, custody of children, income ta>
rate rebates and housing problems.

TABLE 27   PERCENTAGE OF VISITS BY TYPE OF PROBLEM AND LEGAL ADVIC
CENTRE
(Calculated from the estimated number of visits for a 12-week period)

Type of problem	Legal advice centre						
	O	P	Q	R	S	T	
Landlord and tenant	31	14	19	6	6	16	
Debt	7	10	10	17	20	8	
Wills, winding up estates	4	6	3	2	6	5	
Personal injuries	22	20	18	26	9	22	
Employment	11	12	6	6	3	8	
Matrimonial and affiliation	11	8	18	4	30	6	
Criminal	2	5	8	4	0	5	
Other	12	25	18	26	26	30	
Not ascertained	0	0	0	9	0	0·6	
Total:	100	100	100	100	100	100	100
	(54)	(107)	(78)	(47)	(34)	(179)	(499)

Note: Parenthetical figures indicate the number of recorded visits on which th
calculation was made.

At Centre O nearly a third of the visits were about landlor
and tenant problems, while under a fifth were on these problem
at the other centres. At Centre R over a quarter of visit
concerned personal injuries, while at Centres O, P, and T
just over a fifth of visits were about personal injuries. Th
proportion of visits about employment problems varie
between 12 per cent of visits at Centre P, and 3 per cent o
visits at Centre S. The latter received the highest proportio

f visits about matrimonial and affiliation problems (30 per
ent of problems). All centres had between 2 per cent and
per cent of visits about wills and winding up estates. Debt
roblems were 20 per cent of visits to Centre S, 17 per cent
o Centre R, and 10 per cent or less to the other four
entres.

Most centres made either no referrals at all, or only to a very
imited number of individuals or organizations. At four of the
ix legal advice centres, over 75 per cent of estimated visits
ed to no referrals. Centre R referred 45 per cent of visitors and
Centre S referred 63 per cent of visitors. Both these centres,
however, had the highest proportion of visits where no informa-
ion had been recorded as to whether a referral had, or had
not, been made (24 per cent and 18 per cent respectively of
stimated visits). These two centres (R and S) referred more
of their clients to solicitors than the others (21 per cent and
5 per cent of estimated visits). At centres O, P, and T between
o per cent and 13 per cent of visitors were referred to solicitors.
The full-time centres (O, P, and Q) referred a smaller propor-
ion of clients to solicitors than two of the part-time centres
R and S). Four centres (P, Q, S, and T) referred a small
roportion of clients to a court official (3 per cent or under of
stimated visitors). Centres O, P, R, and T made few referrals
o other organizations or individuals (5 per cent or under of
stimated visitors), while centre Q referred 9 per cent of
stimated visitors, and centre S referred 18 per cent of estimated
visitors.

In Table 28 we show the sources of recommendation of
clients visiting legal advice centres. The category 'other'
ncludes self-referral, saw the notice, general practitioner, and
employer.

In nearly half of estimated visits to centre Q the client had
been before, while in over half of visits to centre O the source of
recommendation had been a friend, neighbour, or relative.
Centre O is situated in a settlement building which has been
in that borough for eighty years and is well known in the
neighbourhood. The source of recommendation for half of
estimated visits to centre T was a citizens' advice bureau. That
centre operates in a settlement where there is also a full-time

citizens' advice bureau, although neighbouring bureaux also refer to it. For half the visits to centre P, the source of recommendation was 'other'. The two remaining centres (R and S) had no predominant source of recommendation, although for about 60 per cent of cases either a citizens' advice bureau had recommended the visit, or the client had visited the centre

TABLE 28 PERCENTAGE OF VISITS BY SOURCE OF RECOMMENDATION AND LEGAL ADVICE CENTRE
(Calculated from estimated number of visits for a 12-week period)

Source of recommendation	Legal advice centre						
	O	P	Q	R	S	T	Total
Client has been before	4	8	45	26	32	24	20
Friend, neighbour, or relative	54	0·9	10	11	24	14	16
Local authority	13	3	8	4	0	0·6	6
Probation service	4	2	6	0	0	2	3
Magistrate, Magistrates' and county court official	0	0·9	1	0	0	0·6	0·7
Ministry of Labour, labour exchange, youth employment	2	0	0	0	0	0	0·3
Police	0	0·9	0	2	6	2	0·8
Citizens' advice bureau	15	34	26	34	29	50	31
Other	9	50	3	21	9	5	22
Not ascertained	0	2	1	2	0	3	2
Total:	100	100	100	100	100	100	100
	(54)	(107)	(78)	(47)	(34)	(179)	(499)

Note: Parenthetical figures indicate the number of recorded visits on which the calculation was made.

before. All centres, except centres O and T, received about one third or one quarter (26 per cent to 34 per cent) of their estimated visits as a result of a recommendation by a citizens' advice bureau. Centre T had 50 per cent of visits and Centre O had 15 per cent from this source. Centres O and Q had the highest proportion of visits made at the recommendation of the local authority or the probation service (17 per cent and 14 per cent of estimated visits respectively). Other centres received

9 per cent or less of their estimated visits as a result of recommendations from these two sources.

Some 33 per cent of estimated visits resulted only in advice or information. At centres O and T the proportions of such visits were 48 per cent and 40 per cent respectively, while at the other extreme at centres P and Q 23 per cent and 31 per cent of estimated visits involved only advice or information. Letter-writing varied from one centre to another. At centre P, 62 per cent of estimated visits led to letter-writing. At centre S, letters were written after only 2 per cent of estimated visits, but this centre had the highest proportion (18 per cent) of visits for which no information was recorded. Three centres (P, Q, and T) made telephone calls as a result of 4 per cent or less of estimated visits; the other three centres made no telephone calls. Form filling was done more extensively in centre O. Two centres, P and Q, drafted letters and wills (for 3 per cent and 4 per cent respectively of estimated visits). Three centres (O, P, and T) drafted formal legal documents for clients (for 2 per cent and under of estimated visits). These centres (P, T, and Q) arranged representations (in 8 per cent or less of visits) while it was not the policy at the other three centres to do so.

Most of the visits to three centres (Q, R, and T) were made by people living within the borough (in between 47 per cent and 64 per cent of estimated visits). Information on residence was unfortunately not recorded by centre S. Both centres O and P received the majority of estimated visits (58 per cent and 70 per cent) from people living in other parts of the London area (i.e. at an address in a London postal district). Centre P in fact received 23 per cent of estimated visits from people living in Islington, although it is situated in the borough of Camden. Centres Q and T also received visits from people living in other parts of London (33 per cent and 17 per cent of estimated visits respectively). Few visits were made to these centres by people living outside London (4 per cent or less to centres P and T, and none were recorded at the other four). Centre R did not record information for a high proportion (43 per cent) of its clients.

In these six chapters we have set out to describe the agencies available at the time of the survey and the role which they played in referring people for legal help or in providing legal assistance themselves. In Part III we describe our findings based on the survey of the sample population in the three boroughs.

PART THREE

The Survey of Population

CHAPTER 7

Concepts and Definitions

The main purpose of the population survey was to make an assessment of the character and, if possible, of the extent of any unmet need for legal services in the three boroughs over a period of time. We also took the opportunity to try to find out the extent of people's knowledge of the available legal and advisory services and to probe attitudes and opinion about lawyers and the legal system.

The Need for Legal Services
Our primary problem was to evolve a working definition of need for legal services. The concept of 'need' in any context evolves a judgement of some kind, which, in the case of legal services, is essentially a professional one, but different lawyers would take different views on the scope of legal problems. Is a lease presented for signature a 'legal problem' on which the would-be tenant needs the help of a legally qualified person? Is the rent card issued by local authorities to council tenants with conditions printed on the back a 'legal problem'? Are repairs which various categories of landlord have failed to carry out 'legal problems'?

We decided to concentrate on a range of problems that were legal in the sense that the law provides a solution or framework of rules for solving them. Some were matters which would be considered 'legal' by any definition, such as the purchase of a house or having an accident giving rise to personal injuries. Others were problems in which lawyers have traditionally played little part—such as disputes over entitlements to social security benefits. We realized that in such areas we would be bound to find a high level of unmet need in the sense that few respondents would have been to see a lawyer. We decided to cover a wide spectrum of problems stretching from those which are normally perceived as 'legal' by both lawyers and laymen to those which are seen as 'legal' by lawyers but not by laymen, and to those like social security problems which are not normally seen as 'legal' by lawyers but could in our view be appropriately included.

The concept of unmet need for legal services cannot be a static one. Lawyers are aware that they are serving too limited a class of clients on too narrow a range of problems. As new ways of providing legal services are evolved, so new needs will come to be recognized and new legal remedies will come to be developed by extensions or developments in the law. But at any time there will always be some problems which are clearly perceived by lawyers or laymen as more 'legal' than others. Our aim here is to define the extent of unmet need for the main categories of problems which could at the time of the survey be regarded as 'legal'.

In view of differing perceptions of what is legal, it would not have served our purpose to have asked people baldly whether they had had legal problems. Many would have failed to mention problems that we regarded as legal because they did not think of them in this way. Moreover, we did not want respondents to think in terms of law as they perceived it. Not only would this have led to differing interpretation but it might also have tempted them to claim more contact with lawyers than they had in fact had. Equally we wanted to find out about the use of advisers other than lawyers and by mentioning legal problems we might have limited information to advice from lawyers. Our basic method was therefore simply to ask respondents whether they had had particular problems— a landlord who had not done repairs, an accident, instalment payments which they could not keep up, a purchase of defective goods, etc. Our questionnaire covered seventeen such situations.

In addition to the difficulty of selecting and defining these situations or problems, we also had to decide on a definition of need for advice for those faced with them. One possible definition of need for advice on a legal problem is where a prudent person of moderate means would take advice from a lawyer or some other competent person. But what constitutes prudence? Obviously there are different degrees of prudence and the need for help would vary with a whole range of factors. One would be knowledge of the law, another the means of the individual, another the relative importance of the problem to different individuals.

When assessing a person's need for advice, were we to take any account of whether people thought they knew the law or not? For example, when someone receives a notice to quit from his landlord, an unquestionable need for legal advice can only be identified *after* the event—when, for instance, the notice to quit has had the effect of making the tenant who was protected under the Rent Acts leave his home. If he had obtained advice, he would have been told that the Rent Acts gave him full protection, that he could therefore stay on and ignore the notice to quit. But what if the tenant who receives the notice to quit is familiar with the provisions of the Rent Acts and thus 'knows' that the notice has no legal validity unless it is backed up by an order of the county court? Does he need advice? On one view he does—simply because he may be under a misapprehension. The tenant who relies on what he believes to be the right interpretation of the relevant legislation runs a risk. On the other hand, if the tenant knowing nothing simply sits tight and refuses to move out and the landlord abandons the attempt to evict him, he can be said *after the event* to have had no need for advice, as he managed without it and came to no harm apart from the worry created by the situation.

We decided that it was wrong to be wholly guided by what actually happened to the citizen—whether he did or did not come to harm. If this criterion had been used many, who in our view needed advice, would have been excluded. Instead, we decided that there was a need for advice whenever its absence created a genuine danger that the citizen might suffer substantial loss or disadvantage. We decided, moreover, to count the probability of worry and nervous tension as part of loss or damage. A tenant who is threatened with imminent expulsion may suffer considerable anxiety. If this tenant is entitled to the full protection of the law the injury is aggravated; but even if he is unprotected, he is still at a disadvantage, as he ought to be able to arrange his affairs with the knowledge of whether or not he has the right to stay. Without advice he may assume that he is entitled to stay on and thus have less time to find alternative accommodation. If he is a furnished tenant he may fail to apply for the limited security of tenure he could have obtained from the rent tribunal, application for which must be made before the notice to quit expires.

In such a case there can be little doubt that the loss or disadvantage from not taking legal advice is important. But there are other circumstances where an arbitrary line has to be drawn when deciding what is and what is not significant loss or disadvantage. Moreover, ideally the line needs to be varied according to individual circumstances. For example, a relatively affluent person who buys defective goods worth £5 may regard the amount as too small to be worth the effort of ascertaining whether there is a remedy at law. On the other hand, the loss of £5 would be important for someone with a very low income. Depending on their financial and other circumstances, some people may feel that a potential loss of £15 is sufficiently important to make it desirable to follow up an unsatisfactory consumer transaction; for others the equivalent figure may be £50.

We decided, therefore, that there was a need for advice if there was a risk of substantial loss or disadvantage which could be important for the individual concerned, and, when deciding whether there had been a need for advice at an earlier stage, to take no account of the final outcome. Our definition therefore depends on what is regarded as 'substantial' and on what is regarded as 'important'. Thus need had to be specially defined for each type of legal problem. The definitions we finally adopted are given in the next chapter.

It is difficult if not impossible in a questionnaire administered to a large sample to go into the special personal circumstances of each respondent in relation to each problem. Such an intensive investigation of each case was at all events beyond the means at our disposal. We therefore had to content ourselves with a definition which could be applied on a somewhat rough and ready basis to a very large number of individuals. We accepted that this would be likely to lead to some error but there was no alternative and a degree of 'error' is in any event inevitable in an inquiry where the subject matter is as difficult to pin down precisely as the scope and nature of a legal problem. We tried to minimize the problem by erring always on the side of the conservative view when determining whether or not there was a need for advice. Thus our estimate of unmet need is an underestimate rather than an overestimate, as in many situations we have not counted as need for advice circumstances which could quite reasonably be defined as indicating need. In view of this difficulty of delineating need we have also shown the number of persons who were faced with problems which were not of the importance to fall within our narrow definition of need.

The Design of the Questionnaire

Conscious of all these difficulties, we experimented with the use of a relatively open-ended questionnaire administered by persons with legal knowledge specially recruited for the purpose. While these exploratory depth interviews gave us useful leads on the information which needed to be collected, we soon abandoned this approach. The open-ended form of question in which we invited respondents to tell us about problems produced a mass of interesting information. But we could not be sure that the same questions were put by each interviewer faced with similar circumstances and that the same type of information was recorded. Also we found that persons with legal training tended to have individual approaches and attributed importance to different aspects of similar problems. Nor were all of them particularly good in establishing rapport in the interview situation. The style of questioning acceptable to a client who has chosen to consult a lawyer is not always acceptable to a client who has not and may never have done so. In view of this experience we changed our interviewer recruitment policy before the pilot. We ultimately selected our interviewers on the basis of experience of interviewing and not on the basis of knowledge of the law.

Meanwhile, the questionnaire went through a total of twenty-three drafts! In the light of our pre-pilot experience we abandoned the more open-ended approach of the early drafts and confined both interviewers and respondents with more narrow and precise questions. But there appeared to be a limit to which this process could be taken without losing the co-operation of the respondent or creating antagonism. For those respondents who had had major legal problems, the subject matter of the questionnaire was potentially distressing. They were asked to recall incidents which had often aroused strong emotions at the time and had left emotional scars. Naturally they wanted to tell their stories in their own way, and relate to the interviewer not only the facts we wanted collected but often much more—including what they had felt about the whole situation and their opinion of other persons involved in the case. We found it useful to draft questions which made this possible. We instructed interviewers to allow respondents to develop their own stories about each incident or situation, as long as the specific information we wanted emerged and was checked by further questioning before proceeding to the next series of questions.

In earlier drafts of the questionnaire we had asked respondents a series of hypothetical questions. If they were faced with a variety of situations would they try to get advice—if so, from whom and for what reason? We found that respondents found it hard to answer such questions. Often they appeared to have never envisaged being placed in the situation, and thus had no ready response. This made them uneasy in the interview situation. Also we were not satisfied that the answers given bore any real relationship to what the respondents would in fact have done if they had actually been faced with those problems. We therefore abandoned questions of this kind, partly to make the interview proceed more smoothly and partly because we distrusted the predictive value of the responses we obtained.

The questionnaire[1] which finally emerged consisted of a number of distinct parts. After ascertaining the composition of the household and enquiring about their present housing, respondents were asked whether they had been in any one or more of seventeen specific situations. Those who had been in any of these situations were then asked about the action and

[1] Copies of this questionnaire are lodged at the British Library of Political and Economic Science.

advice, if any, they had taken. After these 'situation' questions there followed questions to ascertain the respondent's knowledge of legal and advisory services. The next section was designed to find out more about the respondent (education, job, etc.). Then followed questions on income and assets. Finally there were questions to identify the respondent's attitude to the legal system.

The most difficult part of the questionnaire to design was the main section dealing with specific situations. Once legal need was broken down into a large number of component parts, it was clear that the number of persons who would *currently* be in one of the situations would be small and we would obtain far too few respondents with positive responses for meaningful analysis. This emerged clearly in our pilot work. In order to obtain a sufficient quantity of 'needs' of each type for meaningful analysis, we decided to ask respondents to recall needs over the relatively long period of seven years. This took respondents back to 1960, when the statutory legal advice scheme was introduced. Some needs for legal services are of a sufficiently traumatic character for it to be unlikely that a respondent would forget completely that such a need had ever arisen. But in the case of matters which had seemed relatively unimportant to the respondent, it was likely that an incident which had occurred several years earlier would have been forgotten and the volume of need would to that extent be under-stated. It was likely, however, that some respondents would attribute incidents which had actually occurred in the 1950s to the 1960s. There were, moreover, certain types of need such as criminal and matrimonial problems involving highly personal matters which some respondents might conceal from our interviewers. And, as with the more traumatic needs, it was likely that the years in which the need had arisen would be incorrectly reported.

If we had asked respondents to tell us of all the problems they had had in the seven-year period the questionnaire would have had to be enormously expanded to leave space for second, third, fourth, or even further instances of each situation. Having tried this approach, we decided that it posed insuperable obstacles with a sample of our size and a question-

E

naire which was already difficult to handle. Moreover we would not have been able to assume that all incidents occurring in the seven-year period had been recalled and that incidents occurring before 1960 had not been reported as falling within that period. For these reasons we ultimately decided to limit our respondents to the most recent incident of each sort even when they had had multiple cases. It was extremely disappointing to us not to be able in this study to quantify the total volume of need over the seven-year period or annually. In order to do this it would be necessary to interview a much larger number of respondents with a much shorter period of recollection.

As a further means of increasing the number of respondents giving positive responses, we asked wives about their husbands' experience and husbands about their wives' experiences. While there were some questions which husbands were normally most qualified to answer (e.g. accidents at work, wrongful dismissal) and others which wives were probably most qualified to answer (e.g. purchases of faulty goods) there were still other questions which the party most equipped to answer might sometimes be the wife and sometimes the husband, such as housing problems. We were aware that there were dangers in asking either party to the marriage about matters which had not concerned them directly, but we believed it would be rare for matters of such relatively major importance as those covered by the survey not to be extensively discussed between husband and wife. Moreover, sometimes both were present at the interview.

This procedure inevitably led to some loss of data and a risk of unreliable data, particularly in the case of questions about income and capital. We decided to deploy our limited resources on the maximum number of interviews rather than to instruct interviewers to ascertain income from the other party by making further visits to the same household. Thus, not only were there some respondents who were unable to state the income of their husband or wife, but some respondents who may have had an incorrect impression of their husband's or wife's earnings.

The Classification by Financial Resources

A straight classification of respondents by income group would have been an extremely crude instrument for measuring ability to pay for legal services. Capacity to pay legal or other bills depends not simply on income but on the number of persons who have to be supported out of that income. Moreover, housing costs vary widely according to the type of tenure, when the housing was first acquired, and many other variables which have little connection with current financial resources. One way of overcoming these difficulties is to compare the disposable income available to each family after housing costs have been deducted with the basic supplementary benefit scale rate for that family.

The scale provides for standard allowances for a wife and for dependent children according to age. Thus each family can be graded according to whether it is above or below the basic supplementary benefit level for that family. This was the method used for classifying families in an earlier study in which one of the present authors participated.[1] It has also been used by the Department of Health and Social Security.[2]

The method used here is a variant of this approach. As the focus of this study is on legal services, it seemed appropriate to use eligibility for either free legal aid or legal aid subject to contribution as the method for classifying financial resources. To ascertain which respondents might have been entitled to legal aid in either form is to answer a question which has an importance in its own right in a study of this kind. Just as the basic supplementary benefit represents the official current standard of poverty so the free legal aid limit represents the current official standard of indigency for the purpose of purchasing legal services. There is moreover the advantage of having a higher resources level up to which contributory legal aid can be provided. Beyond this level of resources, the assumption is apparently made that people can manage on their own in the market for legal services unless legal costs are exceptionally high. More-

---

[1] Brian Abel-Smith and Peter Townsend, *The Poor and the Poorest*, Occasional papers on Social Administration No. 17, Bell, 1965.
[2] See, for example, Department of Health and Social Security, *Two Parent Families*, Statistical Report Series No. 14, H.M.S.O., 1971.

over account is taken of capital resources as well as income resources as legal costs may be defrayed out of savings.

Our questions on financial resources and our coding procedure were developed with extensive help from what was then the Ministry of Social Security. Our aim was to collect the main information needed to do a legal aid assessment without over burdening our questionnaire with a mass of detail which might have only been relevant to very few, if any, respondents. Thus we cannot say that we have taken into account every circumstance which would have been used in a full assessment. For example, eligibility for legal aid depends on expected income over a year. We based the assessment on usual income without enquiring into any changes which were likely to occur during the next year. Moreover, we had to rely on oral statements made in the course of an interview and were not able to verify any of the statements made to us and, as mentioned earlier, not all respondents were necessarily equipped with correct information about their husband's or wife's resources. For all these reasons we can only claim that our classification gives an approximate indication of eligibility for free or contributory legal aid.[1]

In the analysis of the survey material we usually separate capital and income assessments. When, however, we consider current eligibility for legal aid, we combine these criteria to produce what we describe as our strict or combined legal aid assessment.

The Sample

The sample was drawn by random selection from the electoral register. The field work was undertaken from twelve to eighteen months after the information for the register had been obtained. A total of 2,666 names was used in the main survey. Owing to the lapse of time between the preparation of the register and the survey, there were 408 ineffective addresses. We interviewed 1,651 respondents out of the remaining 2,258—73 per cent.

Further details on the response rate are given in Appendix II, where comparisons are also made to check the representative-

[1] A copy of the classification form is lodged in the British Library of Political and Economic Science.

ness of our sample against the sample census of population. Our sample had a slightly lower proportion of males and single persons, and a much lower proportion of Commonwealth immigrants than were enumerated in the census. Using the Registrar General's classification by social class, higher social class males were slightly over-represented and the lower social class males under-represented. A high rate of geographical mobility may well be associated with a variety of legal problems. For example, we may have missed those with the most severe housing difficulties. This bias in our sample should be borne in mind in interpreting the findings reported in the following chapters.

We classified wives by the social class of their husbands. Only 2 per cent of our sample were in social class I (professional and managerial), 8 per cent were in social class II (intermediate), and 11 per cent were in social class III (non-manual). Seventy-one per cent of our respondents were manual workers: 37 per cent were skilled (social class III), 20 per cent semi-skilled (class IV), and 14 per cent were unskilled (class V). We assessed 60 per cent of the sample as entitled to legal aid (in 11 per cent of cases there was no information about income and/or capital). (For details see Appendix II, Table 3.) As many as 86 per cent of our respondents had left school at 15 or earlier and 8 per cent had left school at the age of 16; only 2 per cent had any full time education beyond the age of 18. Ninety per cent had no educational qualifications at all.

CHAPTER 8

The Need for Advice

As explained in Chapter 7, we decided to approach the problem of ascertaining need for legal services and how far that need was met by asking whether respondents had been in any of seventeen specific and common situations which we thought involved in varying degrees 'legal problems' during the last seven years. In this chapter we explain the situations and the definitions of need which we finally adopted. Our criterion, as explained in Chapter 7, was whether the loss or disadvantage which the client might potentially suffer was 'significant' and 'important'. In general, we decided that for our present purpose small losses or disadvantages would not be counted as giving rise to a need for advice; for example, minor defects in consumer goods or minor repairs to housing. Moreover, we excluded cases where, though the loss may be significant, one would not expect someone to resort to law even if well advised. We therefore, for instance, ignored debts owed to the respondent by friends or members of his family.

Taking a Lease
All respondents were asked whether they paid rent or whether they owned the dwellings in which they were interviewed. Only 139 respondents (8 per cent) said they had bought or were buying their homes; 1,370 (83 per cent) were tenants or married to the tenant. Of these only 16 had leases of more than 21 years. About half of the tenants (629) were council tenants. There were 39 respondents (2 per cent) who were lodgers (defined as someone who normally has one or more meals provided by the household to whom he pays rent), and 102 (6 per cent) were in other categories, mainly parents or children

of the rent payer and his or her spouse. One respondent refused to answer this question.

All the 1,370 tenants (or spouses of tenants) were asked what kind of papers they had about their tenancy. Those who said that they had a rent book or, in the case of council tenants, rent cards (1,139), or a letter from the landlord (23), or a lease signed before 1960 (39), or those with miscellaneous unspecified documents (26) or those with no document of any kind (63) were asked no further questions on their housing status. Those, however, who said that they had signed a formal written agreement since 1960 (there were 54 such cases) were asked whether they had taken it to anyone to advise them on it before they signed. (Interviewers were instructed to regard as a formal written agreement 'any typewritten or printed document in formal style, signed by the tenant, whether or not it was also signed by the landlord'.) It is well known that formal leases frequently, indeed normally, contain clauses which are decidedly unfavourable from the tenant's point of view. It is, therefore, wise, if not always productive of results, to get legal advice before signing such an agreement.

Whether it is productive will depend on a variety of factors— including a realistic but informed judgement on whether there is any real prospect of getting the unfavourable provisions in the document removed or amended, or on whether the tenant is in a position to find other accommodation, if the landlord refuses to alter the draft. It was impossible to investigate these questions satisfactorily in a standardized questionnaire. We decided that where a tenant had a house from the local council it would not for our purposes be advantageous to try to obtain advice. Very few, if any, prospective council tenants would think of consulting an independent adviser on the wording of the standard document used by the council, as it would seem unlikely that the council would be willing to amend it if the prospective tenant objected to terms in it. We decided therefore that for our purposes we would assume there was no point in taking independent advice as to whether to accept the terms offered. There were therefore 54 tenants of private landlords who had signed a formal agreement who were counted as having had *a need for advice*.

Repairs Undone

We asked respondents whether they had at any time from 1960 onwards been the tenant of a landlord who had failed to do repairs for which he was responsible. There were 310 respondents, just under one fifth of the total, who said that they had. Of these, 172 were unfurnished private non-council tenants, 118 were unfurnished council tenants, 17 were furnished non-council tenants, and 2 said they were furnished council tenants. There was one respondent who could not tell us what type of tenancy the family had. In virtually every case (291 out of 310) the tenant had taken the obvious initial step of telling the landlord or his agent about the need for repairs. In fifteen cases he had not yet done so but intended to, in one case the matter had been put right before the landlord had been told, and in three cases the respondent did not know whether the landlord had been told.

Respondents were asked whether the repairs had eventually been done and, if so, by whom. In 211 cases of the 310 (68 per cent) they had not been done by the time of interview, including 18 in which the premises were due for demolition. In 22 cases the tenant had done them himself; in only 64 cases (20 per cent) had the landlord done them, including 8 cases where they had been done badly and 13 in which they had taken 'unreasonably long'; in four cases the landlord and tenant had done them together. In nine cases there was no reply to the question.

We coded the repairs needed according to our estimate of their seriousness. It was impossible to do this precisely, but in order to make the classification as consistent as possible, the coding was done by one person in the office from information obtained from the interviewer. Thus major faults included: roof fell in; dry rot in bedroom; roof leaked for over a year; damp in bathroom, toilet didn't work; damp and dangerous wall in front hall. Minor faults included: paintwork cracking; house needed redecoration; windows in living room broken; sash cords not working; immersion heater tank leaking; ceiling cracked. In some cases the condition of the premises was so bad as to make it more appropriate to describe it as 'generally dilapidated'.

The breakdown into the different categories was as follows:

	Total
General dilapidated condition	41
Serious faults	126
Minor faults	134
Don't know and no answer	9
Total:	310

We decided that respondents were *in need of advice* if the condition was one of general dilapidation or if serious repairs had been left undone or were done badly or unreasonably slowly, provided in each case the tenant had told the landlord of the need. There were 123 cases which met these tests.

Attempted Eviction

A threat of eviction can be one of the most serious problems a family can face. We asked all respondents whether since 1960 they had had a landlord who had tried to evict them. There were 60 respondents (4 per cent) who said that they had, of whom 43 were unfurnished tenants, 15 were furnished tenants, and 2 were council tenants.

We took the view that all these 60 tenants had had *a need for advice*. Anyone threatened with eviction needs to know whether the landlord has the right to evict him and, if so, when this right can be enforced. Even the tenant who thinks he enjoys the protection of the Rent Acts is well advised to take expert advice as a check on his opinion.

We attempted to discover what methods were used by landlords to get their tenants to leave and in particular whether there were any cases of extreme 'Rachmanite' harassment of the type identified by the Milner Holland Committee. Most respondents said that the landlord merely requested them to leave. Formal notice to quit seemed relatively rare. Only 13 out of the total of 60 respondents said they had had written notice. We found only three cases of possible harassment. One tenant said that the landlord 'tried to make our lives unpleasant' by dragging dustbins through the passageways and by turning up the radio very loud. Two other respondents said that the landlord 'made life difficult', but did not specify the precise nature of such difficulties. Of these three respondents, none had taken advice.

Attempt to Evict

We did not think that there would be many people resident in these three boroughs who would have been landlords and might have wanted to evict a tenant, but we did nevertheless ask about this possible need for advice. In the event there were eighteen respondents who said they had had such a problem since 1960—in eight of these cases the tenancy was furnished, in ten it was unfurnished. In all such cases there was, in our view, a *need for advice*.

Buying a House

One situation in which the ordinary citizen almost certainly requires expert advice and help is when buying a house. For most of those involved, this is the largest single financial transaction they will undertake in their lives and the complexities are such that few can be expected to handle the work on their own. We therefore considered that all who bought houses had a *need for advice*. There were 74 (4 per cent of the total respondents) who said that they had bought a house since 1960.

Defective Goods

Anyone who buys goods which prove to be defective may need advice. There are a variety of remedies which may be open to a purchaser including an action for damages, in certain limited circumstances the right to return the goods, and frequently some qualified right to have the goods mended or repaired under a manufacturer's guarantee. It would have been impossible for us to discover which, if any, of the possible remedies might in fact have been open to the respondent without a careful examination of the transaction in question, which could not have been undertaken in a survey of this kind. We therefore had to content ourselves with a more superficial line of questioning designed to reveal the nature of the goods bought, whether they were new or secondhand, and the broad nature of the fault. We also asked how soon after getting the goods the fault was noticed and how soon after noticing it the respondent had complained.

Respondents were asked whether they had since 1960 bought either for cash or on hire purchase any goods worth more than £5 which were badly made, worked badly or did not work at all, or whether they thought they had been cheated. The question resulted in 270 positive responses (16 per cent of the 1,651 respondents). In 154 cases the item in question was electrical or gas equipment, in 85 furniture, in 17 a car or motor cycle, and in 12 goods of some other category. There were two cases where the respondent failed to specify the nature of the goods. The value of the goods in question was given as:

	Cases
Over £5 and under £10	18
Over £10 and under £25	39
Over £25 and under £50	62
Over £50 and under £100	111
Over £100 and under £500	32
Over £500	6
Don't know	2
Total:	270

Thus in 149 (55 per cent) of the 270 cases the item in question had cost more than £50. The relatively high proportion of major cases may have been due to the memory factor—one is more likely to remember a large than a small transaction that goes wrong. In 249 cases (92 per cent) the goods had been new and in 229 cases (85 per cent) they had been bought from an ordinary shop. There were only 13 cases which involved door-to-door salesmen and 7 which involved mail order firms. The remainder came from a variety of sources including private friends, the Ideal Home Exhibition, and purchases of fixtures and fittings from a previous occupier of unfurnished premises.

We did not think it right to assume that the advice was needed in all these 270 cases. The first step taken by a person who purchases defective goods will be to complain either to the retailer or to the manufacturer. One would hardly expect a consumer to consult an independent adviser until he has tried to get the defect cured or the goods exchanged and has failed to get satisfaction. We decided that advice was needed only in cases where complaints had been made which had failed to get results—either in the sense that the vendor ('the sales people or the manufacturer') had declined to do anything or had done it badly. This eliminated 39 cases when the respondent had made no complaint. In the remaining cases complaint had been made —in 122 cases immediately the fault was discovered, in 27 cases within one week, in 35 within one month, in 28 cases within six months, and in 18 cases after more than six months. In one case there was no information. In 109 (47 per cent) of the cases where complaint was made the 'sales people' had put it right. In 43 cases they had said they would, but had failed to do so. In 29 cases they had refused to put it right, and in 9 cases they had corrected badly. There were 41 cases which did not fit into any of these categories.

In some cases the complaint would have failed because the retailer or manufacturer had a valid defence which would have been clear to the consumer and explains why no advice was taken. For example, in some cases the purchaser might himself have been responsible for the fault, or it might have been due to ordinary wear and tear, or the complaint might have been made too late. We decided therefore to adopt a conservative approach and to disregard all cases where the fault was discovered more than a month after purchase, as such a fault may not be a defect in the goods themselves but rather the fault of the consumer. This left us with 184 cases where the fault had been discovered within one month of purchase. We also decided to disregard all cases where the fault reported did not appear to us to be serious and we classified 75 faults as falling within this category. Serious faults included: £385 car, many mechanical faults; £100 car, faulty brakes; £80 radiogram, radio made 'funny' noise and record player did not work; £24 tape recorder, didn't work; £43 rocking chair, rocker broke; £6 toaster, didn't work. Minor faults included: £30 wardrobe, wood split; £37 radiogram, valves went wrong; £40 kitchen suite, warped, cracked; £40 record player, on/off switch didn't work; £35 suede coat, lost colour after first cleaning.

When the cases were narrowed down in this way, we were left with only 27 cases which fulfilled all the conditions of a *need for advice* (a serious fault, noticed within one month of purchase, and where complaint to the vendor had brought unsatisfactory results).

Instalment Arrears

Merely to fall into arrears with instalment payments may not in itself constitute an immediate *need for advice*. Everything will depend on the action taken by the creditor. If the creditor does nothing, the debtor may eventually start paying again and ultimately complete his payments. But advice may become important at an early stage. For example, the failure to pay the instalments when they become due often automatically terminates the agreement and can also place on the debtor the obligation not just to permit the item to be repossessed but also to pay the full price or a certain proportion of the original price 'as compensation'. The courts will, however, protect a consumer from having to make such a payment if they consider it a 'penalty'—an extravagant sum held *in terrorem* over the hirer's head rather than a genuine pre-estimate of damages. The debtor therefore needs advice on whether the sum said to be due has to be paid and whether he could avoid paying on the ground that it is a penalty. Moreover, the legal position will often depend on whether the agreement was determined by the purchaser or by default. Paradoxically, the purchaser may in some circumstances be in a better position if he breaks the agreement than if he brings it to an end within the terms of the agreement. He will therefore need advice on what he should do if he finds himself for any reason unable to keep up the payments. He may also need to know that the creditor in a hire purchase agreement for goods worth under £2,000 is not allowed to repossess the goods on the debtor's default without a court order if more than one third of the price has been paid. If less than one third of the instalments have been paid there can be no repossession without a proper demand notice. If default makes the balance of instalments due the court can order that they be paid in instalments adjusted to the debtor's income. A person unable to keep up his instalments will therefore normally benefit from advice.

A total of 71 respondents reported that they had since 1960 been unable to keep up instalment payments where the total amount due was more than £5. In 56 cases the item was new, in 15 it was secondhand. In 19 cases the item was electrical or gas, in 23 it was furniture, in 18 it was a car or motorcycle, and in the other 11 cases the item fell into a variety of other categories. The amount involved was:

	Cases
Over £5 but under £25	11
Over £25 but under £50	14
Over £50 but under £100	17
Over £100 but under £500	23
Over £500	6
Total:	71

We thought it right to confine the *need for advice* to cases where the creditor had taken some positive action to get payment. In 36 cases the creditor appeared to have done no more than write to the debtor, pointing out the arrears. In some of these, the debtor seemed to have won extra time—by explaining that he was unemployed or ill or on strike. In others the creditor appeared to have given time without any such explanation. We decided that for the purposes of our study we would not include these within the category in *need of advice*, as the creditor had not gone beyond writing warning letters. We therefore confined cases where advice was needed to those where the creditor had taken further action—such as instructing solicitors or seizing the goods. In fourteen cases one or more solicitor's letters had been received; in two cases the creditor had taken the goods back; in one case he had taken the goods back and had also demanded payment of money still due; in ten cases court proceedings had been actually started, and in one they had been threatened.

There were twenty-eight cases where by this definition here was a *need for advice*.

Debtor Would Not Pay

Respondents were asked whether in the previous seven years they had ever been in the situation of being owed a sum over £5 which 'they wouldn't pay'. We included in this category debts in the form of court orders for husbands to pay maintenance to their wives or children. There was a total of 124 who said that they had been in the situation of being owed money by someone who would not pay—77 of whom had been owed money by friends or relatives, 33 who had business debts, 5 who had matrimonial obligations, and 9 other private debts. The number of matrimonial obligations seems at first sight surprisingly small. But the number was not far below the proportion in the national statistics. (Magistrates in 1967 granted 30,873 applications for maintenance,[1] being approximately 1 per 1,600 of the *total* population. On this basis our sample of 1,651 would have had about ten cases for a seven-year period of recall.)

A person who is owed money which the debtor refuses to pay may require advice on how to recover the debt. The only cases we thought it right to exclude were those where the money was owed by friends or relatives. It seemed to us unlikely that, save for the case of the deserted wife, even the well-informed creditor would normally wish to take legal proceedings against friends or family members. We decided that the 47 cases in the other three categories of debt did give rise to a *need for advice*, as in all these cases the debtor had refused to pay, presumably after various pressures had been exerted to secure payment.

Taken to Court for Debt

Respondents were asked whether since 1960 anyone had tried or threatened to take them to court for debt. A person in this situation might benefit from advice—even if he accepted that he owed the money claimed, as there might still be some valid defence against the claim or the possibility of counter-claiming. There were, in fact, 33 cases where the respondent said he had been taken to court for debt. For the purposes of this study however we decided conservatively to count as in *need of advice*

---

[1] The total represents affiliation orders and maintenance for married women and their children. Source: *Civil Judicial Statistics*, Cmnd. 4416, 1970, Table L, p. 19.

only those who thought they had not owed the money claimed. There were no less than 21 such cases (64 per cent of the 33): 14 cases of debts for goods or services, two of unrepaid loans, one matrimonial obligation, and four other debts.

Death in the Family

A death in the family may create a need for legal help, either to realize which member is a beneficiary, or simply to handle the mechanics of winding up the estate, paying the debts of the deceased, and distributing the assets. We decided that we would not be able to obtain enough information from respondents to be able to form a valid opinion on whether a particular death in the family had created a *need for advice*. Partly it was felt that many respondents simply would not have known enough of the circumstances to have had a clear idea of the situation. Also where there is a will the property is probably distributed in accordance with the testator's instructions—frequently without any need for professional advice. Where there is no will, the law provides rules for the distribution of the estate. (Thus if there is a surviving spouse, for example, he or she takes the personal effects, plus the first £8,750* and a life interest in half the remainder, if any. In the great majority of cases there is no remainder and so the surviving spouse takes everything.) The Personal Applications Department of the Probate Registry provides a valuable service for those who are unable to manage on their own and reference to this department would often avoid the need for other professional assistance.

We did not therefore have a category of *need for advice* but limited ourselves to finding out simply whether respondents or their families had taken any advice after a family death since 1960. In cases where there had been no will, we also tried to obtain some impression of the proportion of cases in which the assets had been distributed otherwise than in accordance with the legal rules of intestacy. So far as we know no attempt of this kind has previously been made in Britain.

There were 944 respondents who said there had been no death in the family since 1960 and 707 who said there had been

---

* Increased to £15,000 in 1972.

such a death. 'The family' for the purposes of this question was defined to include spouse (116 cases); parent (184 cases); child (16 cases); brother or sister (122 cases); aunt, uncle, nephew, or niece (68 cases); grandparent (53 cases); parent, son, or daughter-in-law (83 cases); brother or sister-in-law (44 cases); and aunt, uncle, nephew, or niece in law (14 cases). There were seven cases where the identity of the family member was not given. Since the extent of the respondent's precise knowledge of the particular circumstances of such deaths could vary greatly, we restricted our questions to matters upon which we thought we could reasonably expect correct information to be provided.

The first question we asked was whether the person who had died had left savings or belongings worth £50 or more. (The interviewer was told to prompt by reminding the respondent of savings, cash, furniture, a car, jewellery, the value of the house.) Where there was a positive answer to this question, the respondent was asked, 'On what principle were the goods shared out?' Interviewers were told that the object of this question was not to discover which relative got what, but rather the *basis* of distribution, e.g. 'Elsie got everything because she nursed the old man through his last months.'

In no less than 339 of the 707 cases (48 per cent) the respondent said that the value of the deceased's property had not amounted to £50. In 159 cases (22 per cent) the respondent did not know either how much had been left or how it had been distributed, and in one case there was no information. Excluding these two types of response, we were left with 208 cases in which the deceased's property had been reported as worth more than £50. In 68 (33 per cent) of these the respondent said that the deceased's property had been divided according to a will; in 115 cases (55 per cent) it seemed that the property had very probably been shared according to the rules of intestacy or it was not clear how it had been shared. In 25 cases (12 per cent) it appeared that it had not been shared in accordance with the rules of intestacy.

These last two categories are inevitably imprecise. We asked interviewers to obtain as much information as possible to enable us to decide whether the rules of intestacy had been applied. But it was only in obvious cases that we were able to be reasonably certain that the rules of intestacy had not been applied. Many more such cases might have come to light if we had been able to obtain more detailed information about the family structure at the time of the death.

The cases in which the family had apparently disregarded the legal rules for the distribution of the estate included the following:

'There was a verbal bequest of everything to my sister.' (A verbal bequest has no legal validity.)

'Everything went to my sister for looking after the deceased.' (Under the rules of intestacy, children share equally.)

'I got it for my younger brother.' (As above.)

'My sister looked after the deceased so the family let her have it all.' (As above.)

'Everything went to the deceased's common law wife.' (Under the rules of intestacy, a common law wife would not be entitled to anything.)

'The van went to his son, who said he was promised it verbally. Everything else went to the widow.' (The verbal bequest would have had no validity.)

'My sister took all.' (Children take equally.)

The wife and daughter took it equally. (Under the rules of intestacy, the surviving spouse has first claim on the estate.)

The deceased lived with the unmarried daughter. 'She had everything. It seemed right to us.' (Children take equally.)

'The daughter had everything as she looked after the deceased. There was no fuss about it.' (Children take equally.)

The daughter who looked after the deceased had everything. 'This was just natural.' (Children take equally.)

'Everything went to my sister who nursed the deceased.' (Children take equally.)

'The eldest son and his wife had the tailoring business; the other two sons did not want it.' (This would have been contrary to the rules of intestacy unless the other sons got assets of equivalent value.)

'Shared amongst the family, except one.' (This would be contrary to the principle that those entitled in the same class share equally.)

'Everything went to the son who lived with the deceased.'
(Children take equally.)

In one case the respondent said that the family 'All took what they wanted and the remainder was given away.'

In another case, 'There was a free-for-all; some of the family are still not on speaking terms.'

On the basis of this evidence it is impossible to be sure what proportion of cases represented distribution otherwise than in accordance with the rules of intestacy. But it was *at least* 12 per cent of the 208 cases in which the property was thought to be worth more than £50.

Making a Will

Making a valid will is a somewhat complicated operation and this question was designed to discover how many of the sample had made wills and whether these wills were likely to be valid. A valid will must be written; it must be witnessed by not less than two persons; the testator must either sign in the presence of the witnesses or acknowledge his signature in their presence; both witnesses must sign in the testator's presence; a beneficiary cannot take anything under the will if he is also a witness unless there are two valid additional witnesses. (These rules do not apply to a will made in the army on actual military service, which can be valid without these formalities being observed.) Will forms, which can be bought at many stationers, usually give detailed instructions on how to make a valid will but our survey showed that in a not insignificant proportion of cases the would-be will maker slips up in the formalities that have to be completed. Home-made wills are notoriously prone to be invalid because people fail to comply with the strict legal requirements. We decided that it would not be practicable to ask enough questions to find out in every case whether the will was valid or not. But we did ask whether the will was signed, whether it was witnessed and if so by how many witnesses.

All respondents were asked: 'If you were knocked down by a bus today and killed, who would get your belongings?' Surprisingly, no respondents answered that they did not know. All were asked whether their intention was expressed anywhere in writing. Out of the 1,651 respondents only 183 (11 per cent) had written anything down. This compares with 28 per cent in the total population who make wills.[1] In 50 cases of the 183 (27 per cent) the respondent had written his intentions in his own words; in 58 cases (32 per cent) it was written on a printed form; in 75 cases (41 per cent) it had been written by a lawyer. This contrasts with figures given by the Probate Registry taken from a study of all probate grants for a 13-week period from June to September 1966 where 77 per cent had been drafted by lawyers, 18 per cent were on will forms and 4 per cent appeared to be otherwise home made.[2] The much lower proportion in our sample who had not had their wills drafted by a lawyer may be due to the fact that our sample was predominantly very poor.

Of the 183 who had expressed their wishes in writing, there were 29 cases (16 per cent) where the document was said either not to have been signed or not witnessed by two witnesses, and was therefore apparently invalid as a will. (This figure excludes a number of cases where the document proved on further questioning to be either an army will which requires no formalities or a nomination of a close relative in an insurance policy.) The Probate Registry appear to reject only one will in 500 as invalid.[3] If our figures are representative this means that there must be a considerable number of invalid wills which never reach the Registry—presumably because they are seen to be formally defective before they get there. If they are not it would probably be because the poorest members of the community are those most likely to make invalid wills.

We identified as being in *need of advice* those who either tried to make their own wills or who did so with printed will forms—

[1] The Registrar General's figures show 579,000 deaths in 1959, and 163,000 wills admitted to probate. Wills therefore occurred in 28 per cent of total deaths. In addition there were a further 89,000 cases of letters of administration in the absence of any will. This represents 15 per cent of the figures for annual deaths. Totalling the percentages for wills and letters of administration there are therefore some 60 per cent of deaths which do not result in any attempt to get probate or letters of administration. It is also of interest to note that whereas 87 per cent of applications for probate were by solicitors, solicitors applied for letters of administration in 67 per cent of cases. (Information supplied by Registrar General's Department.)

[2] Justice, *Home-Made Wills*, 1971, p. 1.

[3] Ibid., p. 2.

excluding cases where the will was made in the army or was an insurance policy nomination, or was made by a solicitor. There were exactly 100 such cases.

Accidents

Anyone who has an accident and who is not wholly responsible for it may be entitled to damages. Whether he is entitled will depend on a variety of factors, of which the main one is whether there is someone who can be held wholly or partly to blame for the injury, who owed a duty of care to the injured person. It may be the employer who has a legal duty to provide his employees with a safe system of work, or a motorist who may be held responsible for injuries to other motorists, pedestrians, or fellow passengers caused by his negligence, or a householder who owes a duty of care to those who come on his property. Accidents which occur without fault on anyone's part do not normally give rise to claims for damages nor do those situations where it is rare to insure—for instance when a wife is injured in her own home through the negligence of her husband. (By contrast, spouses do sue each other for damages resulting from motoring accidents providing the driver's insurance policy covers his own passengers, which prior to 1972 was not legally compulsory.)

Damages for injuries caused by accidents fall under a variety of heads. One can claim for out-of-pocket expenses (taxis to the hospital, the cost of a child-minder to look after the children while their mother is in hospital, a new suit to replace one damaged in an accident.) Employees who are off work and who receive national insurance or industrial injury benefits often assume incorrectly that these benefits amount to full compensation. In fact, if the employer can be made responsible for any part of the responsibility for the injury, the employee can claim against his employer amongst other things for loss of earnings or wages. Half of any actual or probable industrial injury, disablement, or sickness benefit likely to be paid in the five years following the date of the accident is deducted from the damages payable for loss of earnings. But this deduction only applies to damages under this heading. It does not apply to any other type of damage—such as shock, medical expenses, or pain and suffering. Moreover, the fact that the injured workman is continued on full or partial wages does not reduce the damages at all unless the defendant is himself the employer. If A injures B in a road accident, the damages he has to pay include B's loss of wages while in hospital, even though B is continuing to receive his wages from the employer. (In such a case, however, B must hand over to the employer that part of the damages which represents the wages 'lost'.) Any impairment of earning capacity can be the subject of a claim and, in the case of the death of the breadwinner, a claim can be made by his dependants for their financial loss. In the case of death, a claim can also be made for the injured person's own pain and suffering, loss of expectation of life, medical and other (including funeral) expenses, and loss of actual (though not future) earnings.

It seems unlikely that the ordinary citizen has any clear notion of all the various heads of damages or of what compensation might be payable for different kinds of injuries. Even those who know that damages are payable for the loss of a leg or an eye, may be unaware of the fact that a separate payment can be exacted for continuing headaches, an inability to sleep after the accident, or for such loss of amenities of life as enjoyment of dancing, the ability to do gardening, or diminution in the sense of smell. Another common source of error is the assumption that a particular accident was entirely the fault of the injured person, when in law at least part of the blame can be attributed to the fault of someone else—usually the employer.

Respondents were asked whether they or their spouse or child then under 16 years of age had been injured in any kind of accident since 1960. A total of 243 respondents (15 per cent) said that they had. Of the 243, 19 (8 per cent) had been involved in a road accident while at work, 85 (35 per cent) in accidents in factories or other places of employment, 93 (38 per cent) in road accidents not at work and 46 (19 per cent) in accidents elsewhere.[1]

---

[1] According to the Report of the Winn Committee personal injury claims arising out of industrial accidents are about twice as frequent as road accidents. *Personal Injuries Litigation*, 1968, Comnd. 3691, para. 37.

When respondents were asked whose fault the accident was, 37 of the 243 (15 per cent) said that they themselves had been wholly to blame and 25 (10 per cent) said they did not know whose fault it was.

The 37 cases of those who said they were wholly to blame included the following eleven cases where the respondent's opinion was possibly wrong and where someone else may have been at least partly to blame:

(1) Hit by a van whilst crossing the road—8 days in hospital with cuts; 1 month off work. (This may in law have been partly the van-driver's fault.)

(2) Fell off a ladder at work—7 hours in hospital with an injured spine; spinal injury requiring use of a special belt, 10 weeks off work. (This may have been wholly or partly due to the employer's failure to provide a safe ladder.)

(3) Slipped on a floor at work—badly injured thigh; 6 weeks off work. (Again the employer might have been at least partly liable.)

(4) Injured while loading a lorry at work when a case slipped—cuts; 4 weeks off work. (Again the employer may have been partly liable for not providing a safe system of work.)

(5) Slipped on a greasy step at work—2 hours in hospital with sprained ankle; 3 months off work. (The employer might have been partly at fault.)

(6) Fell through a chair at work—1 hour in hospital with extensive bruises; 2 weeks off work. (The employer might have been partly to blame.)

(7) Injured by falling on a step at work—half a day in hospital with a sprained ankle; 1 week off work. (The employer may have been partly to blame.)

(8) Injured by fall into burning hot bitumen—2 weeks in hospital with severe burns; 3 weeks off work. (The employer may have been partly responsible.)

(9) Tripped on a raised pavement—shock, internal injuries. (This may have been due to failure by the highway authority to do repairs, for which the authority might be liable since the 1961 Highways Act, which came into effect on 3 August 1964.)

(10) Slipped on a stud in the road—badly bruised knee, which took over a year to heal, and fractured shoulder. (Again

the highway authority may have been at least partly liable.)

(11) Brakes failed on employer's van—broken rib, outpatient; 5 days off work. (Employee thought it was wholly his fault because he knew brakes were defective, but part of the blame might have attached to the employer.)

In many of these cases damages of some substance might have been awarded and in cases (2), (5), (9), and (10) these would probably have been considerable.

There were other cases where the respondent's assessment that the injury had been entirely his own fault or no one's fault was probably correct:

(1) Hit by a cyclist—concussion, 1 week off work; 1 week in hospital.

(2) Ran into the car in front on a wet road—broken nose; 1 week off work.

(3) Fell off bicycle—2 weeks off work.

(4) Fell off scooter—painful back injury; 1 week off work.

(5) Ran into a beam on a building site—1 hour in hospital.

(6) Hurt trying to jump onto a moving bus at traffic lights—6 weeks in hospital with broken knee cap; 2 years off work.

(7) Slipped on an icy road surface—broken wrist; 3 weeks off work.

(8) Slipped off a ladder on own lawn whilst painting the house—broken wrist; 8 weeks off work.

(9) Slipped on the stairs at the underground—no serious injury.

(10) Four-year-old child of respondent poured hot coffee over himself at home—burnt chest; few hours in hospital.

(11) Slipped while getting on a bus—extensive bruises, 2 hours in hospital; 4 weeks off work.

(12) Slipped in the snow—fractured left hand; 2 hours in hospital.

(13) Crashed firm's lorry as a result of failure of vision, recurrence of old army wounds, brain haemorrhage; 1 month in hospital, 2 months off work.

The 25 cases where respondents said that they did not know whose fault the accident had been included the following 16 cases, in which someone other than the injured person may have been partly to blame:

(1) Respondent slipped on potato peelings on stairs at place of work—became permanently unemployable with a back injury and was an out-patient in hospital for 5 years. (The employer may have been partly to blame.)

(2) Crane broke at work, injured trying to get away—broken leg; 1 week in hospital, 2 months off work. (This was almost certainly a case where the employer was wholly liable.)

(3) Respondent's husband killed in a road accident not at work—no details—parties separated.

(4) Knocked off scooter by car—bruises.

(5) Part of boiler fell on injured person at work—cracked toe bone; 4 weeks off work. (Again this sounds as if the employer could have been at least partly responsible.)

(6) Knocked down by car—concussion; 2 months in hospital.

(7) Fell down manhole, the cover of which had been cracked by a car—bruises; 3 days off work.

(8) Respondent's husband killed when his lorry crashed at work—nothing known about the cause of the accident. Respondent said she was too upset and bewildered to try to get compensation.

(9) Fall caused by employer's dog—injured back, cut leg, continuing back trouble; 6 months off work.

(10) Tripped over telephone wires at work—swollen knee; 3 weeks off work.

(11) Fell down a faulty step at work—broken vein in leg, injured foot; 6 weeks off work.

(12) Fell from tailboard of lorry at work—lacerated arm, 3 hours in hospital.

(13) Foot crushed by a beam at work—fractured bones in foot, regular out-patient; 8 weeks off work.

(14) Cut finger working as sheet metal cutter—6 weeks off work.

(15) Respondent's husband killed in a road accident not at work—he was knocked down by a lorry—considered to be an accidental death—'no one bothered to try to get compensation'.

(16) Respondent's husband injured when a lift moved and caught his hand at work—5 days in hospital, 38 stitches in hand; 6 weeks off work.

Cases (1), (2), (3), (5), (8), (9), (13), and (15) were all

cases of major injuries when damages could have been very substantial. We take the firm view that anyone who has had an accident other than one which is completely trivial needs advice on whether he has a claim for damages. This applies even where the injured person believes that he was himself wholly to blame for the accident or does not know who was to blame. As many of the cases just cited demonstrate, the layman is not equipped to form an adequate opinion on the question. For the purposes of this study, however, we decided to take a conservative view of the *need for advice* and thus we have not included respondents who reported cases of this kind among those with a need for advice. We have only counted cases where the respondent thought that someone else was at least partly to blame. There were 181 such cases.

Social Security Benefits

All respondents were asked whether since the beginning of 1960 they had applied for National Insurance or National Assistance (now Supplementary Benefits) for sickness, unemployment, injury, or any other reason and, if so, whether there had been an occasion when 'they had failed to give you what you thought you should have?' There were 90 such cases.

Out of the 90 cases, 16 had obtained what they thought was the right amount after taking the matter up with the officials concerned. We decided to count the remaining 74 as in *need of advice*.

Employment Problems

Respondents were asked whether they had ever been unfairly treated by an employer—whether they had been unjustly dismissed or denied holiday money, overtime, or a redundancy payment. A total of 89 respondents said that they or their spouses had had an experience of this kind. There were 37 cases where wrongful dismissal was alleged, and 22 cases of alleged failure to pay holiday money, overtime, or bonuses. In 13 cases the employee complained of not being promoted (which would not be the basis of a legal claim). In 9 cases the complaint was failure to pay insurance stamps. In 5 cases the employee thought that the employer had been unreasonable in refusing to allow time off work—which again would not normally be grounds for a legal claim. There were two miscellaneous complaints and one case in which the respondent did not make clear the nature of the complaint.

In 44 cases the respondent allowed the matter to drop without doing anything about it; in 32 he tried to get his employer to remedy the position—but without success; in 4 cases he got partial but not complete satisfaction from the employer. In 8 cases the employer put the matter right as a result of the complaint. There was one case in which the respondent would not answer this question.

We classified as in *need of advice* those respondents who had allowed the matter to drop without doing anything, those who had obtained some but not full satisfaction, and those who had obtained no satisfaction from their employer. There were 80 such cases. We recognize that in some of these cases advice would have revealed that there was no legal remedy but in a matter so central to a person's well-being as his job there would seem to be a strong argument that a felt grievance should be settled by reference to informed advice. Moreover the law in the field of employment is in a state of flux and employees will frequently not be in any position to know whether their complaint is or is not capable of solution by reference to law. In these circumstances competent advice is the more necessary.

Matrimonial Problems

Respondents who were or had been married were asked whether they had been involved in divorce proceedings since 1960 (14 had); if not, whether they had lived apart from their spouse (31 had); if not, whether they had ever wanted to know about getting a divorce (7 had). In all these 52 situations we thought there was a *need for advice*. A wife needs to understand her prospects of obtaining maintenance for herself (and her children) or interim relief pending divorce proceedings, quite apart from advice on whether a divorce can be obtained. But it is not only the wife who may need help. Matrimonial law, especially the law of divorce, is notoriously complicated and full of pitfalls for the unwary. For example, before the introduction of the Divorce Reform Act 1970 the husband who wrote to his wife after she had left him to say that he never wanted to see her again risked destroying his chances of taking divorce proceedings on the ground of desertion, even after the lapse of the then statutory three-year period. Properly advised, he would have written to tell her that he wanted her back—even when he knew that there was no real prospect of her return (and even when he had little real desire to see her back). There were (and remain) many similar difficulties in divorce law and any party to a broken marriage is normally in need of legal advice.

Other Court Proceedings

At the end of the list of specific situations, respondents were asked whether apart from any case already mentioned they or their spouses had been to court from 1960 onwards, excluding occasions when they were jurors or witnesses, and excluding also minor motoring cases. This question was the most tactful way which we could think of for finding out particularly about criminal cases. There were 31 respondents who said that they had had such a court case and a further 15 who said that their husband or wife had. Out of these 46 cases, 32 were criminal proceedings. We took the view that all 46 cases involving court proceedings showed a need for advice.

Juvenile Court Cases

Proceedings in a juvenile court are intimidating for the child and potentially serious both for the child and the parents. Even trivial offences can result in a child being detained for long periods in a penal institution. Advice as to what considerations should be urged before the court is therefore important even when the child pleads guilty to the offence. (There were no cases in our sample of a plea of not guilty.) We took the view that anyone whose child had appeared in a juvenile court had a *need for advice*. There were 37 such cases.

The Problem Analysed by Social Class and Resources

We analyzed by social class and income all those reporting each type of problem and show the results in Tables 29 and 30.

TABLE 29   PERCENTAGE REPORTING PROBLEM BY SOCIAL CLASS

	I	II	III 1	III 2	IV	V	Unclassified	Total	
Taking a lease	4	22	17	30	15	9	4	100	(54)
Repairs undone	1	5	9	45	22	15	3	100	(310)
Attempted eviction	—	7	7	32	33	15	7	100	(60)
Attempt to evict	6	22	11	28	11	17	6	100	(18)
Buying a house	11	26	19	20	9	9	5	100	(74)
Defective goods	3	10	10	41	17	14	5	100	(270)
Instalment arrears	—	1	4	51	18	18	7	100	(71)
Debtor would not pay	3	18	12	37	15	8	6	100	(124)
Taken to court for debt	3	6	6	51	9	15	9	100	(33)
Making a will	5	21	14	27	17	10	5	100	(183)
Accident	3	4	7	40	20	19	5	100	(243)
Social security benefits	1	7	16	42	17	14	3	100	(90)
Employment problems	2	9	12	54	10	7	5	100	(89)
Matrimonial problems	—	8	13	33	21	17	8	100	(52)
Other court proceedings	2	6	4	46	15	17	10	100	(46)
Juvenile court cases	—	3	5	38	24	27	3	100	(37)
Total sample:	2	8	11	37	20	15	7	100	(1,651)

Note: The question of death in the family does not appear in the analysis here and in Table 30 since the death was that of anyone in the near family and we had no means of discovering the social class, income or other characteristics of such family members.

The right-hand column in the tables also shows the proportion of the sample reporting each kind of problem. Some problems occur proportionately with about the same frequency in each social class. This is true of the purchase of defective goods, accidents, social security problems, and matrimonial problems. Others are clearly class correlated. Not surprisingly the higher social classes appear to have proportionately more problems with house buying, leases, and attempts to evict tenants. They also have more problems with wills and more people refusing to pay them the money they owe. Equally to be expected is the higher incidence of juvenile court cases in the lower social classes. Skilled manual workers reported disproportionately more cases of repairs which were undone, instalment arrears, and being taken to court for debts and employment problems. In some cases the numbers are small

TABLE 30   PERCENTAGE REPORTING PROBLEMS BY INCOME

	Over £500 above legal aid limit	Up to £500 above legal aid limit	Con-tributory legal aid	Free legal aid	Unclas-sified	Total	
Taking a lease	9	18	44	9	19	100	(54)
Repairs undone	5	23	50	16	7	100	(310)
Attempted eviction	7	25	47	13	8	100	(60)
Attempt to evict	28	22	28	6	17	100	(18)
Buying a house	28	26	23	4	19	100	(74)
Defective goods	8	30	44	10	8	100	(270)
Instalment arrears	4	30	51	13	3	100	(71)
Debtor would not pay	11	27	35	10	16	100	(124)
Taken to court for debt	9	33	42	6	9	100	(33)
Making a will	8	26	37	12	17	100	(183)
Accidents	6	28	42	13	11	100	(243)
Social security benefits	4	24	48	16	8	100	(90)
Employment problems	6	36	46	8	4	100	(89)
Matrimonial problems	2	15	48	23	11	100	(52)
Other court proceedings	6	23	44	19	8	100	(46)
Juvenile court case	—	24	51	19	5	100	(37)
Total sample:	5	23	44	16	11	100	(1,651)

and we cannot be sure how far skilled manual workers perceived as problems conditions or circumstances which would have been acceptable to less skilled workers. Semi-skilled workers reported most frequently attempts to evict them but again the total of cases reported was small.

Our categorization by income, as mentioned earlier, suffered from the fact that we were unable to obtain the data from 11 per cent of all respondents. The better off nevertheless had proportionately more problems with house purchase, leases, wills, and attempts to evict tenants. They also reported more problems with defective goods. Matrimonial problems were reported more often by the poorest and problems with instalments and debt by the middle income groups.

In this chapter we have shown the practical difficulties of defining precisely the circumstances in which advice is needed. We have had to draw a somewhat arbitrary line and decide that above it a loss or disadvantage is serious or important and just below it is not. The importance of a problem to an individual or family will inevitably depend on their financial and personal circumstances and we have ignored these aspects in the classification which we have used. We have also assumed that people do not go to law when debts are owed by friends or members of the family though in some such cases proceedings may actually be pressed with special relish. We have also assumed that no faults in consumer goods noticed over a month after purchase were faults in the goods and that no one would regard it as a waste of time to complain to any vendor. In the case of accidents we have assumed that our respondents were right when they said an accident was entirely their own fault. In all these respects we have therefore tended to understate rather than overstate the need for advice.

CHAPTER 9

The Use of Advisers

In this chapter we describe the various agencies and individuals to whom respondents went for advice with their problems, distinguishing those cases where by our criteria the respondent was in *need of advice*. We also show where the use of more than one adviser could be recalled. Finally we show the extent to which courts and tribunals were used and the extent to which clients were represented.

We asked what each adviser had done for the respondent and on this basis decided who was the Main Adviser. The coding of the Main Adviser was undertaken in the office. We divided the action taken by the adviser into five categories—(1) oral advice, (2) oral and written advice, (3) one or more letters written on the respondents' behalf, (4) drafted documents, and (5) handled the matter over a period (i.e. more than one of the last three categories). These categories broadly indicate an ascending order of work. The criteria applied was to classify as Main Adviser the person who had done most for the person seeking advice, as indicated by the action taken.

Taking a Lease
All 54 respondents who reported that they were private tenants who had signed a formal written lease were identified as being in *need of advice*. Eighteen of them (33 per cent) had taken advice. In as many as 16 cases the adviser was a solicitor, and in another it was a legal advice centre. In the last case the adviser was a bank manager.

Repairs Undone
Out of 310 respondents who said that landlord's repairs had been undone 123 were identified as being in *need of advice*, of

whom 83 (67 per cent) took no advice at all. The great majority of those who had taken advice (31 out of 40) had been only to the town hall or one of the council officials, such as the sanitary inspector, the medical officer, the borough engineer or the housing department. Four had been to a citizens' advice bureau, 1 to a legal advice centre, 1 to an M.P., 1 to a surveyor, and 1 to a medical social worker. Only 1 went to a solicitor.

Out of the 187 who had had the problem but did not by our definition need advice, 36 (19 per cent) had in fact taken it. The majority of the additional advisers (26 out of the 36) again were council officials or the rent officer or rent tribunal. The remainder were citizens' advice bureau (2 cases), legal advice centre (1 at the town hall, 1 run by a political party), the police (1), and miscellaneous (5). Thus most people having housing repair problems looked to their local authority for help and guidance. Private solicitors were not consulted at all, save for the one case referred to.

Attempted Eviction

We considered that anyone whose landlord tried to evict him needed advice. There were 60 respondents who reported this problem, of whom 41 (68 per cent) had taken advice. In 15 of these cases the main adviser had been a solicitor in private practice, in 12 the local authority, or rent officer or rent tribunal, in 8 a citizens' advice bureau, 5 a legal advice centre, and in 1 case the adviser was the police. Thus solicitors in private practice or lawyers in legal advice centres had together advised over a third of the total number of those who had been threatened with eviction, and half of those who took advice.

Attempt to Evict

Eighteen respondents had wanted to evict a tenant, of whom half had sought advice and half had not. Three of the 9 who had sought advice had been to a solicitor in private practice, 4 to a citizens' advice bureau, 1 to a rent officer or rent tribunal, and in one case information was not obtained. Again, all 18 respondents reporting this problem were considered to be in *need of advice*.

F

Buying a House

We considered that everyone needed advice when buying a house. All the 74 who had done so had taken advice and 71 had consulted a solicitor. One had obtained help from a son-in-law who was a solicitor's managing clerk. In 2 cases the type of adviser was not ascertained. These figures confirm what is generally understood to be the position—that solicitors have a virtual monopoly in this field.

Defective Goods

Out of 270 respondents who had bought faulty goods worth more than £5 we considered that 27 were in *need of advice*. In only two of these cases was advice taken—in one the respondent had been to a citizens' advice bureau and in the other to his father.

Out of the 243 cases which were not classified as needing advice, help was obtained in 17—from a citizens' advice bureau (5 cases), a solicitor in private practice (3 cases), a legal advice centre (4 cases). One respondent had complained to the Board of Trade and another had consulted a relative. In 3 cases the identity of the adviser was not ascertained.

The great majority of dissatisfied consumers had therefore taken no advice at all. Of those who had, over a third went to a lawyer—either to a solicitor in private practice or to a legal advice centre.

Instalment Arrears

Out of the 71 cases where instalment payments had fallen into arrears, we classified 28 as cases where the respondent was in *need of advice*. Only 5 of the 71 respondents had actually taken advice and only 3 of these were by our criteria in need of it. Two of these three had been to a solicitor and the other to a psychiatric social worker. The other two advisers were respectively a solicitor, and a doctor. In this field also therefore the great majority of those in need of advice had taken no advice at all.

Debtor Would Not Pay

Out of 124 cases where money was owed which the debtor

would not pay, we classified 47 as cases where advice was needed. In 13 of them (28 per cent) advice had been taken—from solicitors in 9 cases. Two respondents went to friends. One respondent went to an accountant who referred the case on to a debt collection agency, and another went to a dealers' association. In 2 of the 77 cases where we did not consider advice was needed, advice had been taken—from a solicitor in 1 case, and in the other the adviser was not ascertained. In so far as respondents had obtained advice, the majority therefore had been to solicitors.

Taken to Court for Debt

Thirty-three respondents had been taken to court for failure to pay a debt, of whom 21 were classified as being in need of advice. A total of 12 respondents had taken advice—all of them classified as needing it. Six went to solicitors in private practice, 2 went to a citizens' advice bureau, and the remainder went to miscellaneous sources—1 went to a court official, and 1 in each case went to 'the Q.C. for whom I work', to an accountant, 'a clerk in my office', and an insurance broker.

Death in the Family

There were 368 cases where some family member had died, leaving more than £50, or where it was not clear how much had been left. In 211 cases (57 per cent) no one had been asked for advice. In 37 cases (10 per cent) the family had consulted a solicitor in private practice. A variety of advisers had been used by the remainder. One case had been referred to a citizens' advice bureau, 1 to a legal advice centre, 2 to a bank which was acting as executor, 1 to the Personal Applications Department of the Probate Registry, and 2 to the deceased's employers. In 113 cases the respondent could not tell us to whom, if anyone, the family had gone.

Making a Will

There were 183 cases where the respondent said that he or she had made a written will. In 100 of these cases the respondent was classified as being in *need of advice*. Advice had been taken in 29 of these cases. In only 9 cases was the adviser a solicitor in private practice, though there was one further case where the respondent had copied a will drawn for another client by a solicitor. Three respondents had had help from a legal advice centre and in one case from a citizens' advice bureau. In 1 case the respondent had been to a bank manager. In 1 case the adviser was an accountant. In 2, he was an insurance broker and in several a relative—husband (2 cases), son (1 case), son-in-law (1 case), sister (1 case). In 1 case the adviser was an employer, in 7 cases 'a friend'.

In addition to the 100 cases where the respondent was classified as needing advice and the 8 cases where the 'will' was made in the army or was merely an insurance form nominating a relative, there were 75 further cases where the will had been written by a solicitor. Solicitors in private practice had therefore been consulted in a total of 84 out of the 183 cases in which respondents had made their wills and 3 respondents had been to a lawyer at a legal advice centre.

Accident

There were 243 respondents who reported an accident, of whom 181 were classified as needing advice, because they thought the accident was at least partly someone else's fault. Of these, 104 (57 per cent) had had advice. A solicitor had been the main adviser in 74 cases (71 per cent) of the 104 where advice had been obtained. The other main advisers were: trade union (10 cases), legal advice centre (4 cases), insurance broker or agent (5 cases), citizens' advice bureau (3 cases), surgeon (1 case), police (4 cases), London Transport official (2 cases), and a friend (1 case).

In this field therefore a large minority of 43 per cent had not had advice but of those who had been advised the great majority had gone to solicitors.

Social Security Benefits

A total of 90 respondents thought they had been entitled to more social security benefits than they had received, of whom 74 were classified as needing advice. Out of the 74 there were 60 (81 per cent) who had taken no advice. Seven had only had advice from the office responsible for the benefit. The remaining 7 who had advice went respectively to a solicitor (2 cases), a citizens' advice bureau (2 cases), a legal advice centre (1 case), an epileptic society (1 case), and a doctor (1 case). Out of the 17 cases not classified as being in need of advice, advice had in fact been sought in 4—in 1 case from a solicitor in private practice, in 1 from a tribunal, in a third case the respondent had been to a citizens' advice bureau. In the fourth, the source of advice was not ascertained.

In this field, therefore, as one might expect, very few respondents had been for independent advice and only 3 out of 90 had been to solicitors in private practice and 1 to a legal advice centre.

Employment Problems

There were 89 cases where respondents thought they had been unfairly treated by their employer. Out of the 80 cases where we thought the respondent had needed advice, there were 50 (62 per cent) where the respondent had not taken it. In the 30 cases where advice had been obtained the sources were: solicitor in private practice (3 cases), legal advice centre (1 case), citizens' advice bureau (3 cases), trade union (10 cases), tribunal (3 cases), Labour Exchange (8 cases), Board of Trade (1 case), manager or foreman (1 case).

In the remaining 9 cases where the respondent was not classified as in need of advice, respondents had taken advice in 5 cases—in 2 from a trade union, in 2 from a citizens' advice bureau, and in the fifth from someone at the hospital.

As might have been expected therefore, very few respondents had taken advice, and of those who had only 3 out of 35 had been to a private solicitor.

Matrimonial Problems

There were 52 respondents who said that they had either been divorced or separated or had wanted to know about getting a divorce, all of whom were classified as needing advice. Exactly half of them had taken it. In 21 cases the respondent had been to a solicitor in private practice, in 3 to a marriage guidance council officer, 1 to a citizens' advice bureau, and 1 to a doctor. In this field, therefore, solicitors played a major role.

Other Court Proceedings

There were 46 respondents who reported court proceedings (other than those ascertained in response to earlier questions). All of them were classified as needing advice. In 24 of these cases (52 per cent) the respondent had taken advice, in 20 of them from a solicitor in private practice. In 1 case advice had been obtained from a citizens' advice bureau, in another from a legal advice centre. In the 2 remaining cases advice came from a friend. Thus, in these circumstances also respondents who obtained advice went in most cases to a solicitor.

Juvenile Court Cases

Respondents reported 37 cases where a child had been involved in juvenile court proceedings. We thought that advice was needed in all such cases but it had been obtained in only 11 (30 per cent). In 4 of these cases the main adviser was someone at the town hall, in 3 cases the probation officer, in 1 a solicitor, and in another the respondent's brother who worked as a managing clerk in a solicitor's office. In 1 case the respondent had spoken only to the police. In the last case no clear answer was obtained.

In Table 31 we summarize the Main Advisers in cases where advice was needed and taken.

We looked carefully at the experience reported by those entitled to free legal advice on both the capital and income criteria at the time of interview. They reported fewer problems than the sample as a whole. This was not however surprising as they were less likely to have bought houses, had a formal lease, or had a tenant they wanted to evict. Moreover they had fewer cases of defective goods of sufficient value to constitute a need for advice under our criteria. For those problems which they did have, they were slightly less likely to have taken advice than the sample as a whole. But when advice was taken they were as likely as the sample as a whole to have had a solicitor in private practice as main adviser. The group, consisting of 211 respondents, reported 94 problems. Advice was taken on 38 of them—in 22 cases from a solicitor. In only one of these cases was the main adviser a citizens' advice bureau and in only one was it a legal advice centre.

TABLE 31 MAIN ADVISERS OF THOSE IN NEED OF ADVICE WHO TOOK ADVICE

	Solicitor in private practice	Legal advice centre	Citizens' advice bureau	Local auth-ority*	Other		Total
Taking a lease	16	1	—	—	1	[bank manager (1)]	18
Repairs undone	1	1	4	31	3	[M.P. (1), almoner (1), surveyor (1)]	40
Attempted eviction	15	5	8	12	1	[police]	41
Attempt to evict	3	—	4	1	—		9†
Buying a house	71	—	—	—	1	[son-in-law, managing clerk]	74‡
Defective goods	—	—	1	—	1	[father]	2
Instalment arrears	2	—	—	—	1	[psychiatric social worker]	3
Debtor would not pay	9	—	—	—	4	[debt collecting agency (1), dealer's assn. (1), friend (2)]	13
Taken to court for debt	6	—		—	4	[accountant (1), M.I.B. (1), court clerk (1), clerk in employer's office (1)]	12
Making a will	9§	3	1	—	16	[relative (5), friend (6), employer (1), insurance broker (2), accountant (1), bank manager (1)]	29
Accidents	74	4	3	—	23	[police (4), insurance broker (5), surgeon (1), London Transport official (2), Trade Union (10), friend (1)]	104
Social security benefits	2	1	2	—	9	[Ministry of Social Security (7), epileptic society (1), doctor (1)]	14
Employment problems	3	1	3	—	23	[trade union (10), labour exchange (8), tribunal (3), manager (1), Board of Trade (1)]	30
Matrimonial problems	21	—	1	—	4	[Marriage guidance (3), Doctor (1)]	26
Other court proceedings	20	1	1	—	2	[Friend]	24
Juvenile court proceedings	1	—	—	4	5	[probation officer (3), police (1), brother managing clerk (1)]	11†
Total:	253	17	30	48	98		450†‡

* Including Town Hall, Rent Tribunal, Rent Officer, Medical, Housing and Children's services.

† In one case the adviser was not known.

‡ In two cases the adviser was not known.

§ It should be remembered that the definition of Need for Advice was such as to exclude cases where wills were drafted by solicitors.

In Table 32 we summarize the proportion of cases in which in our view advice was needed but none was taken—even from a friend or relative who may have been able to give very limited help or may have given incorrect advice. Only in the case of house purchase was advice taken in every case reported to us. Advice was taken in about two thirds of cases when there was a threat of eviction or in debt cases and in just over two fifths of cases involving an accident. The proportion not taking advice was particularly high where instalments were in arrears (90 per cent), in social security problems (81 per cent), and where defective goods had been bought (92 per cent).

TABLE 32 NUMBER AND PERCENTAGE OF CASES WHERE ADVICE WAS NEEDED AND NOT TAKEN

Problem	Number of cases where no advice taken*	Percentage of cases where no advice taken	Total number of cases
Defective goods	25	92	27
Instalment arrears	25	90	28
Social security benefits	60	81	74
Debtor would not pay	34	72	47
Making a will	71	71	100
Juvenile court case	26	70	37
Taking a lease	36	66	54
Repairs undone	83	67	123
Employment problems	50	63	80
Attempt to evict	9	50	18
Matrimonial problems	26	50	52
Other court proceedings	22	48	46
Accidents	77	42	181
Taken to court for debt	9	42	21
Attempted eviction	19	31	60
Buying a house	0	0	74

* Including four cases where it was not known whether advice was taken.

In view of the common assumption that failure to take advice is due to inadequate income (or knowledge of the various schemes for obtaining free or cheap advice) or cultural barriers, it was of special interest to ascertain whether failure to take advice was correlated with income and social class. It was clearly of little value to aggregate every type of legal need for the testing of the hypothesis in view of the many different types of adviser used for different problems, the differing incidence of problems by income and social class, and the differing importance of particular problems to particular respondents. But once we came to analyse the data separately by each situation, the numbers became very small. To obtain the maximum value from our small numbers we divided our respondents into two broad income bands—those eligible for legal aid and those ineligible and into three social classes groups by adding classes I and II together and also classes III 2, IV, and V.

TABLE 33 PERCENTAGE OF THOSE NEEDING ADVICE WHO TOOK ADVICE BY INCOME GROUP

	Not eligible for legal aid		Eligible for legal aid		Unclassified	
	Number needing advice	Per-centage who took advice	Number needing advice	Per-centage who took advice	Number needing advice	Per-centage who took advice
Taking a lease	15	46	29	20	10	44
Repairs undone	35	32	82	30	6	50
Attempted eviction	18	72	35	66	7	80
Attempt to evict	9	55	6	50	3	33
Buying a house	40	100	20	100	14	100
Defective goods	5	—	18	11	4	—
Instalment arrears	18	—	8	11	2	—
Debtor would not pay	20	20	16	31	11	36
Taken to court for debt	11	73	8	25	2	100
Making a will	34	29	53	27	13	38
Accidents	54	65	106	50	21	76
Social security benefits	21	14	48	18	5	40
Employment problems	31	48	45	33	4	—
Matrimonial problems	9	66	37	40	6	83
Other court proceedings	13	61	29	44	4	75
Juvenile court cases	9	22	26	34	2	—
Sample	342	50	566	38	114	55

Our findings by income group are set out in Table 33. Faced with certain types of problem a substantially greater proportion of our higher income group reported that they had taken advice. This was the case with taking a lease, being taken to court for debt, employment and matrimonial problems, and other court proceedings—and to a slight extent with attempted eviction and accidents. But it was our poorer group which more frequently took advice of some kind when faced with juvenile court proceedings, problems of social security benefits, and debtors who would not pay. In the remaining needs for advice there was very little difference in the percentage taking advice in our two income groups.

TABLE 34 PERCENTAGE OF THOSE NEEDING ADVICE WHO TOOK ADVICE BY SOCIAL CLASS

	I, II, III 1		III 2		IV and V		Unclassified	
	Number needing advice	Percentage who took advice	Number needing advice	Percentage who took advice	Number needing advice	Percentage who took advice	Number needing advice	Percentage who took advice
Taking a lease	22	50	16	12	14	30	2	50
Repairs undone	12	17	59	29	48	43	4	—
Attempted eviction	8	75	19	60	27	59	6	66
Attempt to evict	7	28	5	80	5	40	1	100
Buying a house	41	100	15	100	14	100	4	100
Defective goods	6	17	8	—	12	8	1	—
Instalment arrears	1	—	14	7	11	9	2	50
Debtor could not pay	19	53	20	10	6	17	2	—
Taken to court for debt	4	50	13	61	4	50	—	—
Making a will	37	32	29	27	30	23	4	50
Accidents	28	64	74	51	70	60	9	62
Social security benefits	18	11	32	21	21	19	3	33
Employment problems	19	47	43	35	14	36	4	33
Matrimonial problems	11	63	17	53	20	40	4	50
Other court proceedings	6	83	21	57	15	33	4	66
Juvenile court cases	3	66	14	28	19	25	1	—
Sample:	242	54	399	39	330	42	49	51

Our findings for social class also showed no clear correlation for every type of problem (Table 34). In the case of attempted eviction, making a will, employment and matrimonial problems, and juvenile and other court proceedings there was a clear progression by social class with the percentages reporting that advice was taken increasing with social class. There was a clear progression in the reverse direction in the case of repairs left undone. In the other situations, no clear progression emerged.

The Use of Solicitors

Our analysis so far has included every type of adviser whether or not the adviser had any special competence to help the person seeking advice. The numbers would have been too small to analyse by income group and social class the use made of each type of adviser for each type of problem. We did however undertake this analysis for those taking problems to solicitors in private practice. This analysis is necessarily subject to the major limitation that the incidence of differing types of problems varied both by income and social class.

In total there were 361 respondents in the sample (21 per cent) who irrespective of need had been to a solicitor in private practice about one or more of the problems covered by our enquiry. Of these, 297 had been once, 47 had been twice, and 17 had been three or more times.

The great bulk of contacts with solicitors have been shown earlier in Table 31, where the respondent was classified as needing advice. There were seven types of case in which solicitors were seen by respondents who by our definition were not in *need of advice*. The most frequent example was that of making a will. There were 75 cases of wills drawn up by solicitors. These fell outside our classification of need where we included only those who had tried to make a home-made will. If these 75 cases are included in the need for advice category, the proportion taking advice in that situation would rise from 39 per cent to 66 per cent and the proportion in need of advice in that situation who saw solicitors would go up from 9 per cent to 48 per cent. This would mean that apart from house buying a higher proportion of respondents saw solicitors to have their wills drawn than in any other situation included in the study.

Apart from this case of making a will there were only six cases where respondents not classified as needing advice saw solicitors. Three were in cases of defective goods and one each in instalment arrears, debtor would not pay, and social security problems. The only other situation in which solicitors were consulted which was not included in our classification of need for advice was death in the family; respondents reported 37 cases where a solicitor had been consulted.

In Table 35 we show the proportion of those cases on which advice seemed to us to be needed where a private solicitor was consulted. We also show the proportion of those taking advice who consulted a private solicitor. Apart from house buying where, as mentioned earlier, the vast majority consulted

solicitors, solicitors were used in about 40 per cent of cases of
need for accidents and matrimonial problems and by over a
third of respondents with a need for help with leases. If we
exclude those who took no advice, solicitors were the chosen
source of advice for 80 per cent or more of cases involving
leases, matrimonial problems, or where money was owed and
for 71 per cent of accident cases.

TABLE 35 NUMBER IN NEED OF ADVICE WHO SAW A SOLICITOR IN PRIVATE
PRACTICE

	Total in need of advice	Percentage of those in need of advice who saw a solicitor	Percentage of those in need of advice and taking it who saw a solicitor
Buying a house	74	96	99
Other court proceedings	46	43	83
Accidents	181	41	71
Matrimonial problems	52	40	80
Taking a lease	54	30	88
Taken to court for debt	21	28	50
Attempted eviction	60	25	36
Debtor would not pay	47	19	69
Attempt to evict	18	17	33
Making a will	100	9*	19
Instalment arrears	28	7	66
Employment problems	80	4	10
Juvenile court case	46	2	9
Social security benefits	74	3	14
Repairs undone	123	1	2
Defective goods	27	—	—

* Seventy-five further cases where the will was drawn by a solicitor are excluded.

In Table 36 we show the number and percentage who had
seen a solicitor on one of the problems covered by our questionnaire by income, social class, sex, age, marital status,
economic activity, and educational achievement. When a
respondent had seen a solicitor in connection with more than
one matter, this is recorded only once in this table. We have
excluded from this analysis cases where it was the respondent's
spouse or other relative who had had the problem and then
consulted the solicitor.

TABLE 36 NUMBER AND PERCENTAGE WHO HAD SEEN A SOLICITOR IN
PRIVATE PRACTICE BY VARIOUS CHARACTERISTICS

Income	No.	%
No legal aid	135	29
Contributory legal aid	137	19
Free legal aid	34	13
Unclassified	55	29
Social class		
I	17	53
II	58	44
III 1	53	28
III 2	104	17
IV	67	20
V	39	16
Unclassified	23	24
Sex		
Male	180	23
Female	181	18
Age		
Under 65	312	23
65 or over	49	15
Marital status		
Married	269	24
Single	44	19
Divorced/separated	10	18
Widow(er)	38	15
Working		
Working	258	23
Not working	103	18
Educational achievements		
No educational qualifications	290	20
'O' or 'A' levels or equivalent only	39	36
Higher educational qualification (including teacher training or university degree)	16	76
Other	6	19
Unclassified	4	100

N.B. All results are signified at 1 per cent.

Contact with a solicitor was highly correlated with income and social class. While 13 per cent of those with an income which would make them eligible for free legal aid had had contact with a solicitor, the proportion among those not entitled to legal aid rose to 29 per cent. While 16 per cent of those in social class V had had contact with a solicitor, the proportion rose to 53 per cent in social class I.

While 24 per cent of those resident in Southwark had seen a solicitor, in the case of Islington and Tower Hamlets the proportions were 19 per cent and 20 per cent respectively. These proportions do not seem to correlate with the number of solicitors in the three boroughs: there was one firm per 7,000 of the population in Islington, one per 12,000 in Southwark, and one per 20,000 in Tower Hamlets.

The proportion of men who had seen a solicitor was higher than the proportion of women, and the proportion among those under the age of 65 was greater than among those aged 65 or over. Those who were married had had contact with a solicitor more than those who were not, and those who were working more than those who were not. Contact with a solicitor was highly correlated with educational achievement. Only 20 per cent of those without an educational qualification had had contact with a solicitor compared with 76 per cent of those with a higher educational background.

Numbers of References

Where appropriate to the type of case, respondents who said that they had taken advice were asked whether the adviser whom they had first seen had referred them on. If they had been referred on, they were asked whether they had taken up the reference and, if not, why they had not done so. The answers to this question must be treated with considerable reserve, as one would expect clients only to remember being advised to go and see someone else when they had taken this advice and to have forgotten when they had failed to take the advice. In the event, extremely few respondents could recall any advice to go elsewhere which they had not taken, the great majority of references which were remembered were taken up—91 out of 104. A further defect in this line of questioning is that some respondents may only have recalled the person whom they finally consulted. The fact that they had got there as a result of a suggestion by someone else may have been forgotten. For example, a respondent may have told us that his first adviser was the union's solicitor, forgetting that he went first to his foreman, then to the shop steward and only then to the union's solicitor. Another respondent with the same sequence may have told us that he had seen three advisers. The question was not asked in relation to leases, conveyancing, death in the family and making a will. The only situations in which a sizeable proportion of respondents recalled having more than one adviser were landlord's repairs, being evicted, and accidents.

Cases that went to a Hearing in a Court or Tribunal

We wanted to find out how many cases had involved a hearing either in a court or a tribunal. For some of the situations about which we asked, such a question was inappropriate; for example, the signing of a formal lease, landlord's repairs, the transfer of a house, a death in the family, and the making of a will. Two questions, on the other hand, were exclusively about court hearings—whether the respondent or husband/wife had been in a court as a principal if not already reported in response to earlier questions (there were 46) and whether a child had been in a juvenile court (there were 37). The total number of court hearings, apart from those in the last two questions, was 49 and there were 6 tribunal hearings—making a grand total of 132 court cases and 6 tribunal hearings. Apart from the questions specifically focussed on court cases, the largest single category of court hearings concerned matrimonial matters: there were 15 cases of this kind. The 181 cases of accidents where the respondent thought that it was at least partly someone else's fault resulted in a total of only 6 court hearings. The total numbers are set out in Table 37. There were 14 respondents who were unable to say whether there had been a hearing.

Legal Aid for Hearings

We asked respondents who had become involved in court

TABLE 37   NUMBER OF HEARINGS IN COURTS AND TRIBUNALS

	Court hearing	Tribunal hearing
Attempted eviction	8	3
Instalment arrears	6	0
Debtor would not pay	5	0
Taken to court for debt	7	0
Accidents	6	0
Social security benefits	0	1
Employment problems	2	2
Matrimonial problems	15	0
Other court proceedings	46	0
Juvenile court case	37	0
Total:	132	6

hearings whether they had applied for legal aid and whether it had been granted or refused (legal aid is not available for hearings in tribunals). In 14 cases legal aid had been granted, in 7 refused, and in 107 it had not been applied for. The details are shown in Table 38.

We analysed those who did not apply for legal aid by

TABLE 38   NUMBER OF APPLICATIONS FOR LEGAL AID FOR COURT HEARINGS

	Not applied for	Refused	Granted	Unclassified	Total number of court hearings
Attempted eviction	4	3	0	1	8
Instalment arrears	5	0	0	1	6
Debtor would not pay	5	0	0	0	5
Taken to court for debt	6	1	0	0	7
Accidents	5	0	1	0	6
Employment problems	2	0	0	0	2
Matrimonial problems	5	1	9	0	15
Other court proceedings	39	2	4	1	46
Juvenile court cases	36	0	0	1	37
Total:	107	7	14	4	132

reference to the eligibility for legal aid on income and capital combined as at the time of our interview. It was found that one third were outside the legal aid limits, 10 per cent were eligible for free legal aid, and 47 per cent for contributory legal aid. In 9 per cent of cases the position was unclear. The categories of legal aid refused and legal aid granted were too small to justify further analysis. (Their financial circumstances may also have been different at the time at which they would have had to apply.)

The cases where legal aid was not applied for included the following cases where the respondent was eligible financially at the time of our interview and where legal aid might have been granted:

Attempted eviction—'Trumped-up case by landlord, eventually the landlord dropped it but I had to pay half his costs.'

—'Court order for eviction, went to Housing Department, got into Nazareth House. No proper home for years and nobody gives me much help. They just shove you on from one place to another. They don't usually care. I owed £40 in rent arrears and refused to pay because the repairs were not done. I don't know who spoke for me in court. I went to the wrong court room.'

Instalment arrears—£90 dining room suite: 'I left it to the discretion of the judge who ordered me to pay for it.'

—£295 car which didn't work. 'I didn't know you could get help without money. I paid it all in the end.'

Debtor would not pay—Husband was defaulting on his maintenance payments. 'I took him to court. Couldn't ever get a solicitor. Knew I couldn't afford it. The court ordered him to pay 10s. a week. I would have done better with a lawyer to speak for me.'

Taken to court for debt—Washing machine not working. 'Boss's secretary said we wouldn't have to pay. So I thought it would be all right. Spoke for myself but I had to pay. Would have done better with a lawyer.'

Matrimonial problems—Separated. 'I would like to divorce him but cannot afford it as the maintenance is useful. The magistrates were very unfair and wouldn't pay any attention to me. Husband told them a pack of lies about his income.'

Other court proceedings—Theft case (three months' sentence).
—Assaulting a police officer (fine).

Juvenile court proceedings—Out of 36 cases there were no applications for legal aid: taking away and driving a motor car (3 months' approved school); truancy and stealing from handbag (3 weeks in remand home, 2 years' probation); driving without insurance and licence (5 years' driving ban); stole from work (sentence not disclosed); broke into store and stole (sentence not disclosed); broke into meter and stole contents (sentence not disclosed).

Representation at Hearings

Respondents who had been involved in either court or tribunal hearings were asked who, if anyone, had spoken for them and, in cases where respondents had not been represented by lawyers, they were asked, 'Do you think you would have done better if you had had a lawyer?'

Out of a total of 132 court and tribunal hearings, there were 50 cases where the respondent said he represented himself and 42 cases where he was represented by a lawyer. In the remaining cases the respondent either did not know or mentioned a variety of other persons who represented him. Three quarters of respondents who had not been represented by lawyers did

TABLE 39   REPRESENTATION IN COURT HEARINGS

	Lawyer	Other	Self	Not ascertained	Total
Attempted eviction	2	0	5	1	8
Instalment arrears	0	1	4	1	6
Debtor would not pay	2	0	3	0	5
Taken to court for debt	1	0	6	0	7
Accidents	4	1	1	0	6
Social security benefits	0	0	1	0	1
Employment problems	1	0	1	0	2
Matrimonial problems	10	0	5	0	15
Other court proceedings	20	3	19	4	46
Juvenile court proceedings	2	19	6	10	37
Total:	42	24	50	16	132

Respondent represented by — column headers: Lawyer, Other, Self, *Not* ascertained, Total not think they would have done better with a lawyer to speak for them.

In these three boroughs, we found substantial unmet need for legal advice. While everyone took advice when buying a house and the majority when court action was facing them or there had been an accident or they were faced with eviction, in most of the other types of case the taking of advice from any source was the exception rather than the rule. In the case of court actions for debt and accidents it was only a bare majority which took advice. Moreover, whereas some who took advice went to the local authority, a CAB or a variety of other professional people, some went to agencies and friends who were unlikely to have any special competence to help. There were variations in the proportion taking advice by income and social class but the direction and extent of the variation differed according to the type of problem. People who took advice generally went to solicitors when leasing or buying a house, when faced with court proceedings, accidents, matrimonial or debt collection problems. They generally went elsewhere with other problems. Solicitors were used less by women than men, and less by the poorer, the aged, the less educated, and those of lower social class. Only a minority of people were represented by lawyers in court or tribunal hearings.

CHAPTER 10

The Failure to Take Advice

In Chapter 9 we showed that a substantial proportion of people had failed to take advice when in our view they needed it. But as explained in Chapter 8, it is hard to draw any hard and fast line between circumstances where advice is needed and circumstances where it is not. So much depends on the details of the case, the legal knowledge of the person who has the problem, and his financial circumstances. For example, a man with high earning capacity may reasonably decide to devote his time to earning more rather than to disputing a small claim.

Thus in this chapter we examine more closely the details of the particular problems which had faced our respondents. Did those who took advice seem to fare better than those who did not? Were the cases on which no advice was taken those in which there was little prospect of success or where the possible gain was small? Were those who did take advice satisfied with the service they received or were they likely to discourage others from seeking advice? What reasons did people give for not taking advice? These are the questions we attempt to answer in this chapter. In the next chapter we explore the more general question of knowledge of the advisory services, the actual costs and expected costs of taking advice, and the general attitude to the local advisory services.

Was the Adviser Useful?
Did those who took advice fare better than those who did not? In some types of case on which we had collected information we found no way of answering this question. For example, four of the situations about which we asked involved, or if they were pursued would have involved, court or tribunal hearings—

matrimonial cases, criminal cases, juvenile court cases, and cases when the respondent was taken to court for debt. Other cases could have led to a court or tribunal hearing, though one would expect most to be settled out of court. From the information collected for this study however we were unable to say whether those who had had advice fared better in a court or tribunal hearing than those who had not.

Nor were we able to make any test of the effectiveness of the service provided in the case of leases or house purchases. It would have been difficult to find out how far leases were improved as the result of representations made by our respondents' advisers; therefore we did not try to ask this question. In the case of house purchase, all our respondents for whom we had information obtained professional advice.

Two of our situations involved eviction—either attempts to get the respondent out or attempts by the respondents to get their tenants out. Was there any evidence that those who took advice obtained any real advantage other than the ability to plan with full knowledge of their legal rights? In the case of those who were under pressure to leave, there were 41 who took advice and 18 who did not. In one case this information was not obtained. Ultimately 34 of them left. While 72 per cent of those who had not taken advice left, among those who had taken advice only 52 per cent left. This suggests that advice may have been helpful but the numbers are too small for any firm conclusions to be drawn.

We attempted to identify tenants who had probably been protected under the Rent Acts to see whether they were more (or less) conscious of their legal position than those who had not been protected. We therefore asked tenants whether the tenancy had begun before November 1957, the date from which all new, unfurnished tenancies were decontrolled by the Housing Act 1957, or after that date but before December 1964 (when the Protection from Eviction Act 1964 restored the protection of the Rent Acts to most unfurnished tenancies). There were 14 cases of unfurnished tenants threatened with eviction whose tenancies had begun before November 1957 or after December 1964 and who were therefore probably protected. Thirteen of these (93 per cent) had taken advice and only one (7 per cent) had not. Six had left, but 5 of the 6 had taken advice, which suggests either that they were not in fact protected (because for instance the landlord wanted the premises for his own occupation) or that they preferred to leave even though they were protected—or that they were not well advised.

In the case of the 15 furnished tenants threatened with eviction, we asked whether the respondent had been to the rent tribunal, which can give limited security of tenure. Three of the 15 had taken their cases to the tribunal and 1 was intending to do so. When advice was linked to whether the tenant stayed or left, there were 8 who stayed up to the time of interview, as against 5 who had left. In 2 cases it was not clear what had occurred. Seven of the 8 who left had had no advice. By contrast 4 of the 5 who stayed had had advice. Thus in the case of furnished tenancies, advice did appear to have been advantageous, but again the numbers were very small.

Only 18 cases were reported to us of respondents who wished to get their tenants out. In 9 of these advice was taken and in 9 it was not. In 4 cases the tenant stayed: in only 1 of these cases had the landlord taken advice. In 1 of the 3 cases where no advice was taken and the tenant stayed, the tenancy was unfurnished and began sometime between November 1957 and December 1964 and was therefore unprotected by the Rent Acts; in the second case the tenant bought the landlord out; in the third, which was furnished, the landlord thought there was no point in getting advice as the tenant was rent controlled. This was partly mistaken since the rent tribunal only gives limited security of tenure to furnished tenants for some months. Thus this landlord would have discovered, if he had obtained the correct advice, that he could eventually evict his tenant.

Out of the 14 cases where the tenant left, the landlord had taken advice in 8 of them and failed to take advice in the remaining 6. So 8 out of 9 landlords who had taken advice, but only 6 out of 9 landlords who had not taken advice succeeded in getting rid of their tenant. The numbers are, however, again too small for us to be able to conclude that these differences are significant.

There were two questions which concerned goods—the first concerned the purchase of defective goods and the second cases where the respondent was unable to keep up instalments. In only 2 of the 27 cases defined as in need of advice had the purchasers of defective goods taken advice. The numbers are too small to examine how far they had obtained better results than those who had not. Similarly there were only 3 respondents who had taken advice among the 28 in need of advice who had been unable to keep up their instalments. Two of these three paid up in the end and one did not pay. Among those who did take advice, 5 did not pay and in 18 payment in full was made or was still being made. (In two cases the question was not answered.) It was not possible to find out enough about these transactions to form a view as to whether those who lacked advice would have fared better if they had had it.

There were 47 cases which we defined as needing advice where money was owed to the respondent. Advice was obtained in 13 of them and some money was recovered in 7 of these (54 per cent). Among the 34 cases where no advice was taken only 12 (35 per cent) had recovered some money by the time of the interview. The cases where no advice had been taken consisted of 26 business debts, 1 matrimonial matter, and 7 other types of debt. The cases where advice was taken consisted of 7 business debts, 3 matrimonial debts and 3 other kinds of debt. Advice had therefore been taken in 75 per cent of the 4 matrimonial debts and in only 21 per cent of the 33 business debts. Advice seemed to be associated with better results.

The most common need for advice which we identified in this survey was in connection with accidents. In 104 (57 per cent) of the 181 cases the injured person took advice; in 77 (42 per cent) no advice was taken. We then separated those where the injured person had either died (5 cases), been in hospital (129 cases), or had been off work (169 cases). Counting each case once only there was a total of 138 cases. Advice was obtained in 94 of those cases (68 per cent). This means that in 44, almost a third of cases when the injured person died, went to hospital, or was off work, no advice was taken.

In Table 40 we show whether compensation was obtained by those who did and those who did not take advice. The table also shows the breakdown between the different types of accident.

Over two-thirds (45 out of 66) of those who had taken advice received compensation compared to only one-eighth of those who had not taken advice. The majority of those involved in road accidents took advice. The proportion taking advice was

TABLE 40   NUMBER OF ACCIDENT CASES BY WHETHER ADVICE TAKEN AND COMPENSATION PAID (EXCLUDING CASES STILL PENDING AND WHERE THERE WAS NO INFORMATION)

	Advice taken			No advice taken			
	Compensation	No compensation	Total	Compensation	No Compensation	Total	Grand Total
Factory accidents	15	6	21	6	25	31	52
Road accidents at work	4	3	7	0	3	3	10
Road accidents not at work	24	7	31	3	22	25	56
Other accidents	2	5	7	2	27	29	36
Total:	45	21	66*	11	77	88*	154

* These totals are for cases completed and are therefore lower than figures given elsewhere for advice or no advice in accident cases.

N.B. The results are significant at 1 per cent.

highest (7 out of 10) where the road accident occurred during a work situation. While a minority of those with factory accidents took advice (21 out of 52), 15 of the 21 who did take advice obtained compensation. Those with other accidents were least likely to take advice and least likely to obtain compensation when they did so. These figures, therefore, showed a strong association between advice and success in the form of compensation. They also showed that the common view that those injured at work normally would take advice is mistaken.

In the few cases where compensation was obtained without advice the amount received was small in nearly every case. In 2 cases sums of between £250 and £500 were received: the remaining 9 amounts were under £50. Only 8 of the 45 who had taken advice and received compensation obtained less than £50. There were 17 who received between £50 and

£249, 6 who received between £250 and £999, 3 up to £2,000, 4 up to £5,000 and 1 over that amount. Thus 82 per cent of those without advice received under £50, compared with 18 per cent of those who had taken advice.

At first sight it appears that taking advice greatly increased both the chance of obtaining compensation and the amount received. But this would only be true if those who did and those who did not take advice had suffered similar injuries and had equally strong cases. To test the effectiveness of advice we needed to know what compensation could have been obtained by the two groups if they had had the best advice.

The assessment of damages for personal injuries is a complicated affair involving detailed investigation of many factors. It was impossible in an inquiry such as this to assemble all the information needed to make a precise estimate. Nevertheless we did collect the main facts as seen by our respondents and we asked an expert, a partner in one of the country's leading firms of solicitors with long experience in the field of personal injuries litigation, to review the cases to see if there were any in which the amount of compensation appeared to be seriously inadequate. In many cases our consultant expert said the information available was insufficient to enable him to form any judgement but in 116 cases he was able to give an opinion.

The expert's evaluation of the potential of some of these claims is given in brackets after the description in the following cases.

Wife was injured when the bus she was on moved away. The bus conductor rang the bell too soon as she was alighting. She suffered bruising and shock, and had since developed a hernia which was aggravated by the fall. Her husband said that he had not made any attempt to get compensation or even advice—'I didn't think the expenditure of time and money would be worth it.' (*£250.*)

His brakes failed, causing collision with another car at traffic lights. His wife was injured and off work for two months. The wife would have had a claim against her husband for damages, which would have been met by his insurers, but no claim was made or advice sought. The husband said, 'I didn't want to bother.' (*£200.*)

Finger smashed and off work for five weeks when a piano fell on his hand as a result of faulty wheels. He considered that the fault was either that of his workmates or of his employer, but did not try to obtain compensation because, as he put it, 'It wasn't worth it. I was financially O.K. at the time.' (*At least £100.*)

Husband had an eye caught and ripped by a concrete girder through the fault of other employees and the employer. In addition to several days in hospital and three weeks off work, this man lost the sight of his eye, became partially deaf, and suffered shock. He did not seek advice about a possible claim for compensation until the three-year period within which an action for personal injuries must be brought had expired. He therefore got nothing. (*A claim in time might have brought him £3,000–£5,000.*)

Fell off a plank at work and twisted his knee. He considered it partly his fault, partly that of a fellow employee. In addition to two weeks in hospital, having his cartilage removed, he was off work for four months. He made no claim for compensation 'because it was partly my own fault'. (*With contributory negligence worth £450 general damages.*)

Husband lost his thumb in an accident at work, for which he and the employer were both to blame. He was in hospital for four days and was off work for two months, but made no claim for damages—because he received a disability payment from the National Insurance of £1·50 per week. Only half of this would have had to be taken into account if a claim for damages had been made. (*On the assumption that the respondent's husband was 50 per cent to blame, such a claim might have been worth some £750.*)

Injured when a machine blew up, whilst he was loading it. He had burns on his face, was in hospital for one day and off work for three weeks. He did not take any advice and accepted £5 a week for the three weeks from the employer. (*If he had been properly advised, the claim could have been worth £75, apart from loss of wages.*)

Husband was hit by rubber waste thrown to him, knocked unconscious, and subsequently had headaches. He thought that the accident was caused by the employer's faulty system of unloading, but 'it never crossed my mind to claim any-thing'. (£50.)

Treated as an out-patient and off work for six weeks with an injured foot and broken blood vessel in leg when fell down temporary steps, which were defective owing to the employer's fault. No advice was taken and no compensation claimed. (£120.)

Off work for three weeks with a deep cut in a leg caused when he fell from a loose rung on a ladder. He considered that the fault was that of his employer, but did not take advice or make a claim because he had been with the firm for twenty-five years and 'didn't want the sack'. (£50.)

Husband was off work for six weeks with broken toes when a steel plate fell on his foot through a fellow employee's error. No advice was taken and no claim made—'there was no need to claim'. (£100.)

A G.P.O. worker was injured when a van overturned which was driven by his mate. The accident was the latter's fault. He was in hospital for two nights suffering from shock and concussion and was off work for three weeks. No advice was sought ('No need. No one seriously hurt'). (*Good case. Should have recovered damages of about £100 assuming recovery on return to work.*)

Respondent was injured in an accident in the employer's van when a fellow worker panicked and threw a can of petrol. He suffered from burns on his hands and face and was off work for a month. He went to a legal advice centre but was told that he did not have much chance of a claim. (*Seems good case. Worth perhaps £150.*)

Broke his wrist when he fell over a trestle at work owing to a fellow employee's fault. No advice was taken because 'it wasn't worth it; the employer found me other work'. (*£100 general damages.*)

Wife was injured at work when a gas oven exploded after the gas had been left on by a fellow employee. She received cuts on her leg, was an out-patient for two weeks, and was off work for the same time. She did not take advice about compensation as she was working for her son and didn't want to claim against him. (*Good case, would probably be paid for by son's insurance, worth £75.*)

A container fell off a truck on top of him. He suffered severe back strain and was off work for three months. The accident was a fellow employee's fault. No compensation was claimed because 'I was getting full wages while sick'. (*Good case. £500 if good recovery.*)

There were also cases where the expert commented adversely on the terms of the settlement, although the injured person had received some compensation. (The amount received is stated before the details; the figure in brackets was suggested by the expert as the amount which, in his view, could probably have been obtained.)

£185: thirty-nine stitches in leg and five-inch skin graft on head; two months as an out-patient and off work. Car failed to stop at double white line and knocked respondent off moped —advised by solicitor. (*£275.*)

£100: one day in hospital and ten weeks off work after respondent was knocked off his bicycle by a motorist's open car door—advised by solicitor. (*£150 plus loss of wages.*)

£35: broken bone in hand, out-patient for six weeks, after respondent was knocked off bicycle by car door opening— advised by solicitor. (*£75.*)

£400: six weeks in hospital with broken leg and ten weeks off work when car jumped lights and collided with respondent's car—advised by own insurance company. (*'Very unsatisfactory.'*)

£100: suffered bruising and had difficulty in walking; out-patient for two months after being hit by car while crossing road—advised by citizens' advice bureau. (*'Seems far too low. If difficulty in walking was permanent, even on a fifty-fifty basis for fault, would be worth £1,000.'*)

£500: injured arm muscle, out-patient for six months; respondent's son slipped and his arm went into unguarded machine—advised by firm's solicitor. (*'Dubious to be advised by firm's own solicitor.'*)

£40: one week off work, minor bruises, cut hand, caused when car hit respondent who was driving a moped—no advice. (*'Seems low.'*)

£125: husband (a policeman) in hospital eight days, off work for three months with severe lacerations on both legs and fractured facial bone; knocked off cycle by motorist turning without giving a signal—advised by Police Legal Department. (*'Seems very low—£250 general damages.'*)

£415: two weeks in hospital, two weeks off work, two joints off index finger when finger went through rollers whilst cleaning machine—advised by citizens' advice bureau and legal advice centre. (*'Seems low.'*)

£50: hospital in-patient for four days, off work for three weeks and had to have twenty-two stitches in his scalp. Was advised by the insurance broker. (*Must be worth more—£100 at least in general damages.*)

£60: fell and suffered shock when the bus on which he was a standing passenger swerved to avoid a car accident. London Transport paid the £60. (*If London Transport paid anything they must have thought they were liable and their offer was probably insufficient.*)

£40: wife was in hospital a few hours and off work for three months with a slipped disc and strained back after the bus she was in stopped suddenly and she was thrown off. Advised by the 'woman in the laundrette' and by a legal advice centre. (*If London Transport paid, it was probably worth much more.*)

£160: off work for two months with shock and bruising after injury in a head-on collision with another car whose driver caused the accident—the claim was 'settled between the parties'. (*Seems low. £250–£300.*)

£211: daughter was in hospital for a week but off work for two years with a back injury after a car jumped the lights and ran into her car. Advised by a solicitor. (*Sounds much too low. Worth at least £1,000.*)

£25: off work for three weeks with a bruised leg after being dragged along by a bus. The accident was the bus driver's fault—no claim made, 'I took the £25 offered to save more trouble.' (*Worth a lot more. Probably £100 at least.*)

£25: off work for three weeks when a bus braked sharply and threw him on to a bar at the front of the bus. 'The gentleman from London Transport came and I filled out a form and they gave me £25.' (*You can be sure it was worth more, perhaps £100.*)

£5 a week from employer whilst off work: in hospital for one day, in-patient for one night, and off work for three days

with burns on his face after the machine he was working at
blew up whilst he was loading it. The fault was that of the
firm's engineers—no advice taken and no claim made. (*Ridicu-
lous figure. Should have got at least £75 general damages.*)

£35: off work for three weeks with a broken toe after a bale
of rubber fell on his foot in the docks—no advice taken or
claim made. 'Who could I have gone to?' (*Probably worth at
least twice as much.*)

£40: two bones in the foot were fractured and he was off work
for five weeks, after a girder fell on his foot—would have taken
advice and made a claim 'if the insurance people hadn't settled
with me'. (*If the insurance company paid it was undoubtedly worth
more—probably at least double.*)

The total picture which emerged from this evaluation is
given in Table 41.

TABLE 41   PERCENTAGE OBTAINING 'CORRECT' COMPENSATION IN ACCIDENT
CASES

	Took advice %	Took no advice %	Total %
'About right'	22	2	12
'Got too little'	22	11	16
'Got nothing, should have got something'	6	37	22
'Got nothing, right' (e.g. no claim)	2	26	14
'Got something, worth investigating further'	1	5	3
Not enough information or case still pending	47	19	33
Total:	100 (87)	100 (94)	100 (181)

In 90 per cent of the cases where the amount of compensation
was considered 'about right' the respondent had had advice.
In 65 per cent of the 29 cases where the expert thought that too
little compensation had been obtained the injured person had
taken advice—in 12 cases from a solicitor! In one case where

a solicitor had advised the injured person had got £211, though the expert thought the case might have been worth £1,000. In another the amount obtained was £200, though the expert thought it might have been worth £600–£700. In a third case where the adviser was a solicitor the amount received was £125 though our consultant thought that the injuries deserved £250. This suggests that an expert in the assessment of personal injuries may frequently secure more for his client than another lawyer with less expertise. In one case where advice had been taken from a citizens' advice bureau only £100 had been paid for an injury which left the respondent with difficulty in walking. Our expert thought the claim would have been worth £1,000 even if the respondent had been 50 per cent responsible for his own injury.

The ten cases of respondents getting 'too little' in which no advice had been taken included the following:

Respondent obtained	Expert's evaluation of claim's worth
£300	£600
50	100
50	350
25	100
25	100
20	50
15	75
2	50

In addition to the 29 cases where the respondent got something but in our consultant's view not enough, there were as many as 40 cases in which no compensation at all had been obtained and the expert considered that a claim could have been successful. In five of these cases (12 per cent) advice had been taken; in 35 (88 per cent) it had not. In four of the five cases where advice had been taken our consultant thought the claims were worth amounts of £500, £150, £100, and £50. In the fifth case he was unable to put a figure on the claim.

Out of the 35 cases where no advice had been taken there were 25 where he felt able to put a figure on the claim. The amounts in these cases were:

£750	1 case	£75	3 cases
£500	1 case	£50	7 cases
£450	1 case	£40	1 case
£250	1 case	£35	1 case
£200	1 case	£25	1 case
£150	1 case	£20	1 case
£120	1 case	£10	1 case
£100	3 cases		

The cases in which he found it not possible to put an actual figure on the injuries included one where the claim was said to be worth 'several hundred pounds', one where there was 'obviously a claim' and three where it was said to be 'worth claiming'.

We can therefore summarize the main conclusions on the accident cases identified in the survey. First, compensation was obtained much more frequently where advice had been taken. Second, larger amounts of compensation were obtained by those who took advice. Third, although there were cases where our consultant thought the respondent did not obtain enough although advice was taken, there were far more such cases where no advice had been taken. There were ten cases where no advice had been taken and no compensation recieved and the consultant thought the claim worth £100 or more.

The Importance of the Matter
One possible reason for not taking advice is because the matter does not seem of sufficient importance to warrant the effort. The importance is most clearly indicated where an amount of money is at stake. As has already been seen, people are not always in a position to know in what precise circumstances compensation might be obtained, nor are they well placed to estimate the amount. But where goods or debts are involved, our respondents knew how much was at stake. There were 18 cases where the goods which were defective were worth over £25 and in none of them advice was taken. The only 2 cases of need for advice in which advice had been taken involved amounts of under £25. There were 7 further cases involving goods worth under £25 where no advice was taken.

There were 12 cases where the respondent was unable to

keep up instalments and owed £100 or more. In only one of these cases was advice taken. In 2 of the 12 cases where the amount owed was between £25 and £100 advice was taken. In the case of money owed to our respondents, 7 of the 11 who were owed £100 or more took advice.

As mentioned earlier, 32 criminal cases were reported to us: in only 13 of them had advice been taken. The charges and decisions in these 13 cases were as follows:

Indecent exposure (£25 or three months);
Larceny (not guilty);
Pilfering lead (one year suspended sentence);
Motor offence (case dismissed for lack of evidence);
Taking a car (£25 fine and one year disqualification);
Theft (two years' imprisonment);
Dangerous driving (£10 fine, endorsement of licence);
Driving while disqualified (twelve months' imprisonment);
Driving without due care and attention (licence endorsed);
Assault of spouse (penalty not stated);
Assault on wife (bound over);
Driving without due care and attention (penalty not stated);
Dangerous driving (disqualified for one year and £30 fine).

There were thirteen criminal cases where no advice had been obtained:

Receiving charge (£25 fine);
Shoplifting (£3 fine);
Drunken driving (£15 fine);
Theft—three (one three months' imprisonment; one a £200 fine and one a fine of unspecified amount);
Assaulting a police officer (a fine of unspecified amount);
Assault of neighbour (bound over);
Asault of aunt (£5 fine and bound over);
Cheating London Transport (£1 fine);
Not having T.V. licence (£10 fine);
Assault and battery (bound over);
Drunk and disorderly (£1 fine);
Civil disobedience (bound over for twelve months).

There were six cases where we did not have full information.

G

Thus advice was not obtained in one case which led to three months' imprisonment and in another which led to a £200 fine. In all the cases where no advice was taken the respondent had been found guilty, while there were 2 out of 13 cases for which advice was taken where the respondent was found not guilty.

Most of the penalties were relatively minor—conditional discharge, fines of £1, 30s., £2, £15, £20, or probation. But there were a number of cases which were more serious. In one case a child was sent to an approved school for three months for taking away and driving a motor car. The parents had obtained advice from the probation officer. In another case where a child had been sent to a remand home for three weeks and then put on probation for two years for truancy and stealing from a handbag, the parents had had no advice at all.

Satisfaction

In the attempt to ascertain whether respondents who had had advice were satisfied with the advice they ultimately received, we asked, 'Did you think you had all the advice and help you needed?' Where the answer was in the negative, respondents were asked to specify in what way they had had less help than they thought they needed. The replies are set out in Table 42. A clear majority (66 per cent) of respondents thought they had had all the help they needed. Excluding those unable to answer the question, most of those who were less than satisfied complained either about the result achieved or about the competence of the adviser. Out of 117 cases of complaints, 81 (69 per cent) related to the competence or performance of the adviser. Slowness was a cause of complaint in only 19 cases and price in 9 cases. There were so few complaints that it was not possible to ascertain whether there were significant differences in the proportion of dissatisfied clients according to the type of adviser or the type or class of respondent.

When we analysed the cases where respondents complained of the competence of their advisers we found that in 25 cases they were complaining about the local authority (in 22 of these cases the complaint related to repairs undone); in 18 cases the complaint was about a solicitor in private practice (in 11 cases this concerned an accident); and in 12 cases the complaint was

TABLE 42   PERCENTAGE SATISFIED AND DISSATISFIED WITH ADVISER

	Satisfied or reasonably satisfied	Dissatisfied: complained of						
		Price	Speed	Com-petence	Price and slowness	Other	Don't know	Total
Repairs undone	31	0	7	32	0	1	10	81
Attempted eviction	34	0	1	4	0	0	2	41
Attempt to evict	7	0	1	0	0	0	1	9
Buying a house	62	4	2	3	0	1	2	74
Defective goods	13	0	0	2	0	0	3	18
Instalment arrears	3	0	0	0	0	0	2	5
Debtor would not pay	10	0	1	1	0	0	2	14
Taken to court for debt	10	1	0	2	0	0	0	13
Accident	71	0	3	17	0	3	10	104
Social security benefits	10	0	0	5	0	0	3	18
Employment problems	16	1	0	8	1	2	5	33
Matrimonial problems	18	0	1	3	0	0	4	26
Other court proceedings	18	1	1	4	1	0	1	26
Juvenile court case	10	0	0	0	0	0	1	11
Total:	313	7	17	81	2	7	46	473

against a citizens' advice bureau. The remaining complaints were spread amongst a variety of advisers.

Reasons Given For Not Taking Advice
Where appropriate, we asked respondents why they had not taken advice and recorded the answers. Many respondents gave more than one reason and the reasons given in the interview may not necessarily have been the most important, even assuming that they could have recalled precisely why they had acted or rather not acted in cases some of which had occurred several years before. Nevertheless the answers are of some interest in indicating attitudes to the advisory services and to the legal system.

The following were some of the reasons given for not taking advice in particular situations.

Landlords' Repairs Undone
'No. I did not want to cause trouble, as they were very good to me.' (Ceiling collapsed in three rooms; house due to be demolished.)

'No. They told us this was temporary for another year.' (Serious damp and faulty plumbing.)

'No. Did not want to cause trouble and be evicted.' (Ceiling needed replastering.)

'Danger of being evicted.' (Damp in kitchen, leaky outside toilet.)

'Do not know where to go.' (Leaking roof.)

'No. Do not want to aggravate landlord.' (Leaking roof.)

'No. What can you do anyway?' (Dry rot in bedroom.)

'No. Would not know where to go.' (Sink coming away from wall, all windows and doors fit badly.)

'Do not know who to go to.' (Waterpipes from above leaking.)

'No. I would not know what to say.' (Ceiling falling down.)

'I did not know where to go and I did not want to get thrown out again.' (Falling ceiling and walls.)

'I do not know where to go. We leave it to the superintendent.' (Damp.)

'I do not know where to go.' (Very damp.)

'Been too ill—78 years old.' (Rotten floorboards.)

'No. Did not know where to go.' (Damp roof.)

'Did not have the time.' (Leaking roof.)

'No. They are too slow.' (Leaking roof.)

'No. Nothing gets done.' (Extreme damp—walls, ceiling falling in one room.)

'I don't know where to go.' (General dilapidation.)

'Do not know where to go.' (Plaster peeling off.)

'No point. He won't do it—his son's a lawyer!' (Dampness.)

'No. The place might be condemned if I did.' (General damp.)

'No time to get off work.' (Draughts, damp.)

Defective Goods

'Not worth the trouble.' (£28 record player bought new, defective sound, seller promised to repair it but never did.)

'No, didn't know where to go.' (£40 second-hand washing machine, faulty, taken away after buyer stopped paying instalments.)

'Bailiff threatened to take furniture if we didn't pay, so we did.' (£80 washing machine, useless, repaired three times under guarantee but didn't work.)

'Didn't know where to go.' (£29 new radiogram, not working properly.)

'No, too expensive.' (£75 new T.V. set, bad picture.)

'What's the use.' (£13 new fanheater, did not work.)

'Didn't know where to go.' (£36 new radiogram, bad sound, returned and forfeited previous H.P. payments.)

'No, we were too busy with other things.' (£40 new vacuum cleaner, never worked.)

Making a Will
Respondents whose wills were apparently invalid gave reasons for not taking advice including:

'No. Never entered my mind.'

'Not worth it.'

'A friend who worked in a lawyer's office said it was all right to do it as a letter.'

'Thought it would be all right.'

'I didn't go into it properly—not much to leave.'

'It never worried me.'

'Not necessary. It's automatic when someone dies.'

'Nothing worth leaving.'

'No need with the forms you get.'

'Not worth while.'

'Mum concerned about that.'

'Never thought about it.'

'Not thinking of dying.'

These were all cases where the purported will was not signed or not witnessed by two witnesses and was therefore apparently invalid.

Accidents
There were 77 accident cases where advice was needed but not obtained. The reasons for not taking advice included the following. (The comments in brackets are those of the expert to whom we referred the cases):

'No need—no one seriously hurt.' (Good case. Should have recovered damages of £100 or so.)

'Not seriously hurt. Rider very young and didn't want to take action.' (Possible case; bad shaking up worth perhaps £50.)

'Ignorance. Couldn't afford time and money.' (Bad case.)

'Didn't think expenditure of time and money worth it.' (Reasonable case worth £250.)

'No one to take action against.' (Motor Insurers Bureau would possibly have made an ex-gratia offer.)

'No point because of age. I've had a good innings. I'm too old to get compensation.' (Would probably have got something.)

'Passenger in friend's car.' (Good case against driver—on the face of it worth several hundred pounds.)

'Didn't want to bother.' (Good case—£200 general damages.)

'Only a bruise. I didn't think I'd get any.' (Obviously a claim should have been made.)

'Did not think it was worth it.' (Worth claiming.)

'Did not want to bother.' (Unfortunate that no claim was made.)

'No witness.' (Pity no advice sought. Usually can get something when a scooter is involved—respondent had been knocked down by a scooter.)

'No one bothered. We were too upset. Accidental death.' (Most unfortunate that no advice taken—respondent's dead husband knocked down and killed by lorry.)

'Was not serious. Had sick pay.' (Worth about £50.)

'Was told he didn't have much chance, so left it at that.' (Seems good case, worth perhaps £150.)

'Not worth it. Financially O.K. at that time.' (Good case. £150 general damages.)

'Wasn't worth it. Employer found me other work.' (£100 general damages.)

'Working for son, so didn't want to claim.' (Good case— £75.)

'Partly own fault.' (Despite the contributory negligence £400 general damages.)

'Worried about scar so didn't follow it up.' (£50 if small scar.)

'Never crossed my husband's mind.' (Possible case—£50.)

'Getting full wages while sick.' (Good case for £500 if good recovery.)

'With firm 25 years and didn't want the sack.' (Probably wouldn't have got the sack—insurance company pays, not employer, £100 general damages.)

'No point—assessor didn't take it up.' (Seems good case—£500 general damages.)

'Culprits not caught.' (Could have gone to Criminal Injuries Compensation Board.)

'Wasn't worth it.' (£25 general damages.)

Social Security Benefits

In the case of dissatisfaction with social security benefits, the reasons given by respondents who had not taken advice included the following:

'There's no citizens' advice bureau round here.' (Sickness benefit.)

'No. They only make a fool of you.' (National Assistance.)

'No. Where can you complain?' (National Assistance.)

'The National Assistance said ignorance was no excuse.' (Sickness benefit claim: the respondent had said that the doctor's certificate had arrived too late.)

'I was ill. Didn't think anything could be done.' (Sickness benefit.)

'No. Didn't think about it.' (Lost pension contributions unfairly.)

'No. Who can you go to?' (Supplementary benefit.)

'No. You don't get anywhere.' (Supplementary benefit.)

'Husband doesn't like going up there.' (National Assistance when husband came 'out of the nick'.)

'Didn't know what to do.' (National Assistance.)

'Don't know how.' (Unemployment benefit.)

'Didn't know where to go.' (National Assistance.)

'No. Felt it was useless.' (National Assistance.)

'I didn't want to waste time.' (Unemployment pay after dismissal.)

'Wasn't short of money.' (Unemployment.)

'Not worth it.' (Sickness.)

'Waste of time.' (Sickness.)

'Didn't bother.' (Sickness.)

'No point.' (Sickness.)

'Didn't understand. Too much bother.' (National Insurance.)

'No point. Ministry of Social Security hopeless.' (Sickness.)

'Didn't know which way to turn.' (National Assistance.)

'No use.' (Unemployment.)

'No. They are the crowd who are supposed to help.' (National Assistance.)

'No. You don't get anywhere.' (Sickness benefit.)

Employment Problems

Those who were dissatisfied by the actions taken by their employer and had not taken advice included the following:

'Thought there was nothing we could do.' (Employer went bankrupt.)

'No. Too costly.' (Only got half holiday pay.)

'Don't know who to go to.' (Redundancy pay.)

'Had only been in the country for one year and didn't know, where to go.' (Dismissed for no reason.)

'Nothing could be done about it.' (Sacked with no reason.)

'Don't want to think about it.' (Disagreement about wages.)

'Not worth the bother.' (Not paid holiday pay as promised.)

'No. There's no union.' (Less holiday pay than expected.)

'No. Shop steward never bothers, he gets £20 a week from the firm as bonus.' (Dismissed while sick.)

'No. I don't belong to a union.' (No holiday pay.)

'No. Didn't want any fuss.' (Cleaner dismissed after twelve years without any reason.)

'No one to go to. Union doesn't help.' (Reorganized job; I wasn't suitable for new job.')

'Didn't bother.' (Wrongful dismissal.)

'No. It wouldn't do any good.' (No holiday pay.)

Other Court Proceedings

Reasons for not taking advice in the criminal cases included:

'I had an idea the goods were knocked off.' (Receiving.)

'Didn't know where to go—too upset and my mother was dying.' (Shoplifting.)

'No. I was guilty.' (Drunken driving.)

'No use.' (Assaulting a police officer.)

'It's no good is it once they find you and you plead guilty. (Driving offence.)

'Not worth it.' (Cheating London Transport.)

'Didn't know where to go.' (Prosecuted by neighbour for assault.)

Juvenile Court Cases

The reason for not taking advice when children were before the juvenile courts included:

'Didn't think it necessary.' (Son sold bicycle he had 'found' to a friend.)

'No point.' (Son driving untaxed and uninsured moped.)

'No point in police courts.' (Taking and driving a motor car.)

'No—he was guilty.' (Driving stolen scooter with no licence and insurance.)

'No—he was in the wrong.' (Broke into a store and stole goods.)

'Impossible—not enough time.' (Driving abandoned scooter.)

'Didn't bother.' (Riding motorcycle without speedometer.)

'No—minor matter.' (Stole microphone in gang.)

'No—he was in the wrong.' (Noisy motorcycle, no insurance.)

'No—police helped us.' (Riding on back of stolen scooter.)

'Not thought necessary.' (Receiving stolen cycle.)

While the numbers are not sufficient to warrant an attempt at systematic coding, among the reasons which stand out for not taking advice are apathy, a general acceptance of misfortune, and a lack of confidence that advice can be helpful. This contrasts with the findings earlier in the chapter that people seemed to have benefited from advice where we could test for this, that the losses due to lack of advice were often substantial, and that people who took advice were on the whole satisfied with the help which they obtained.

CHAPTER 11

Knowledge of the Advisory Services

In this chapter we examine the extent to which limited knowledge of the advisory services may have proved a barrier to their use. How many people know of the services offered by citizens' advice bureaux or where to find one? How many people know of a solicitor? How many people know about the statutory and voluntary legal advice schemes and the facilities for legal aid?

Knowledge and Use of Citizens' Advice Bureaux
Respondents were asked whether they had ever visited a citizens' advice bureau. Unlike the questions described in the last three chapters, there was no time limit on when such a visit might have occurred. A total of 1,322 (80 per cent) said they had not and a further 60 (4 per cent) said they had never heard of them. No reply was given in three cases. The remaining 266 (16 per cent), who said that they had visited a bureau, included 73 who said that they had already mentioned the fact earlier in the interview.

Only 14 per cent of respondents resident in both Islington Southwark had visited a citizens' advice bureau compared with 20 per cent of respondents resident in Tower Hamlets. (This result is significant at 5 per cent.) While Islington and Southwark had two and one citizens' advice bureaux respectively, there were six in Tower Hamlets. This suggests that an increase in the number of citizens' advice bureaux does lead to an increase in the proportion of the population who use them, though not perhaps as large an increase as might be expected.

We next analysed those respondents who had visited a citizens' advice bureau by income and social class. We found that bureaux had been used about equally by all income groups and social classes, with a slightly higher usage by skilled manual workers.

All respondents, except those who had never heard of the citizens' advice bureaux, were asked whether they knew where there was a citizens' advice bureau which they could get to within an hour's journey. If they said they did know, they were asked where it was. The answers were divided into those who said they knew precisely and those who said they knew imprecisely; all others were classed as 'don't know'. There were 572 (36 per cent) who said they knew precisely, 339 (21 per cent) who said they knew imprecisely, and 669 (42 per cent) who did not know. In eleven cases the respondent gave no coherent answer.

Out of the 911 who said that they knew where there was a citizens' advice bureau (precisely or imprecisely), 11 did not answer the second half of the question and indicate the address at which they thought there was a citizens' advice bureau. We were anxious to verify the answers of the 87 per cent who did give an address and were fortunate in securing the help of Miss Joyce Parkinson of the Family Welfare Association, who kindly undertook the laborious task of checking all the answers by hand. Answers were placed into one of six categories. If the address given by the respondent was that of a citizens' advice bureau, it was marked as 'correct'; if the address was not that of a citizens' advice bureau but was recognizable as that of the town hall, it was marked as 'local authority'; in cases where the address represented some other agency such as a legal advice centre or an advice office run by one of the political parties or a settlement house, it was put into a category of 'other agencies'. Where the respondent did not give enough information to classify ('somewhere in Stepney', 'Kennington', 'Finsbury Park', etc.) it was marked 'vague' and in a few cases where Miss Parkinson was unable to discover what the respondent thought he was referring to, it was marked 'not known'. The final category was 'wrong'. The results appear in Table 43.

Surprisingly, only one respondent gave a totally wrong answer. Ninety-one out of 797 (11 per cent) gave answers that were too vague to be checked. A substantial number—304 of the 796 (38 per cent)—gave answers which showed that they had confused the citizens' advice bureau with some other agency, but in all these cases they did at least indicate an agency which offered advice. Most of these agencies would themselves either have been able to help, or might have referred the caller to a citizens' advice bureau. So this kind of error may not be important.

TABLE 43 NUMBER AND PERCENTAGE THINKING THEY KNEW WHERE THERE WAS A CITIZENS' ADVICE BUREAU, BY BOROUGH

	Right (No.)	(%)	Too vague (No.)	(%)	Local authority (No.)	(%)	Other agency (No.)	(%)	Wrong (No.)	(%)	Not known (No.)	(%)	Total (No.)	%
Islington	81	39	11	5	88	43	19	9	0	0	7	3	205	100
Southwark	116	32	72*	20	48	13	117	32	1†	—	10	3	364	100
Tower Hamlets	186	82	8‡	3	22	10	10	4	0	0	0	0	226	100
Total:	383		91		158		146		1		18		797	

* Including forty-eight who gave Walworth Road, which might have referred to a citizens' advice bureau which is just off Walworth Road, or to the Town Hall Information Centre which is on Walworth Road, or to Cambridge House, which is just off Walworth Road.

† Respondent gave Tower Bridge Police Station.

‡ Including one respondent who said Bethnal Green Road, which is equidistant from the citizens' advice bureau and from the local authority information centre.

We show in Table 44 the percentage knowing precisely or imprecisely of a citizens' advice bureau by income and social class and the age of the respondent.

In the highest income brackets there was little to choose between the knowledge of the older and the younger respondents, whereas in the lower income brackets the younger were

TABLE 44 PERCENTAGE KNOWING WHERE THEREIS WAS A CITIZENS' ADVICE BUREAU BY INCOME AND SOCIAL CLASS AND AGE

Income group	Percentage knowing of citizens' advice bureau within 1 hour's journey		Social Class	Percentage knowing of citizens' advice bureau within 1 hour's journey	
	Over 65	Under 65		Over 65	Under 65
No legal aid	66 (15)	64 (287)	I	0 (—)	42 (13)
			II	29 (5)	58 (67)
Contributory legal aid	47 (57)	57 (341)	III 1	53 (15)	57 (89)
Free legal aid	40 (64)	59 (63)	III 2	50 (46)	62 (315)
			IV	53 (40)	58 (148)
Unclassified or won't say	41 (5)	48 (79)	V	45 (28)	57 (100)
			Unclassified	33 (7)	53 (38)
Total:	44 (141)	58 (770)	Total:	44 (141)	58 (770)

more likely to know of a citizens' advice bureau. Among the under 65s the proportion knowing of a citizens' advice bureau varied little by social class.

Next we analysed the same data by reference to period of residence in the area to see whether those who had lived in the area longer had a greater knowledge of local advisory facilities than more recent arrivals. There was, however, no difference. Among respondents who had lived in the borough for three years or more the proportion who said they knew of a citizens' advice bureau within an hour's journey was 58 per cent—precisely the same proportion as in the total sample.

We also looked to see whether knowledge of citizens' advice bureaux varied between boroughs, in view of the different number of bureaux in the three boroughs (one in Southwark, two in Islington, and six in Tower Hamlets). As we expected, when there were more bureaux, the service was better known. In both Islington and Southwark exactly 50 per cent of respondents said they knew of a citizens' advice bureau, but in Tower Hamlets 74 per cent of the respondents knew of a citizens' advice bureau.

Knowledge and Use of Solicitors
In the next series of questions we asked respondents whether they knew of a firm of solicitors to whom they could get within an hour from their place of work or home and, if so, how they had come to hear of them. A total of 488 respondents (30 per cent) gave sufficient information about a firm of solicitors for the interviewer to put them into the category of 'knew precisely'; 348 (21 per cent) gave information which resulted in their being put into the category of 'knew imprecisely'. The remaining 815 (49 per cent) did not know of a firm even imprecisely.

A check of the questionnaires where respondents had named a firm showed that a very large number of firms were mentioned, including many outside the three boroughs. While 56 per cent of respondents in Southwark knew of a solicitor, the proportions for Tower Hamlets and Islington were 49 per cent and 44 per cent respectively. There were 38 firms in Islington, 24 in Southwark, and 10 in Tower Hamlets, so these figures suggest that there is not a clear connection between knowledge of a firm and the number of firms in the borough. This is the more likely since many firms mentioned were outside the three boroughs.

The next step was to analyse respondents who said they knew of solicitors by income, capital, and social class groups. Knowlege of a firm of solicitors increased significantly with rising income, capital, and social class. Thus, whereas only 33 per cent of those in the free legal aid income group knew of a firm of solicitors and 49 per cent of those in the contributory legal aid income group, the comparable proportion for those whose income was above the legal aid limits was 63 per cent. While 46 per cent of those without disposable capital said they knew of a firm of solicitors, the proportion for those with disposable capital of over £500 was 75 per cent. While 75 per cent of those in Social Class I knew of solicitors, 67 per cent of Social Class II and 63 per cent of Class III (non-manual), the proportion was 48 per cent in Class III (manual), 44 per cent in Social Class IV, and 46 per cent in Social Class V. (These results were significant at 1 per cent.)

All respondents who said that they knew of a firm of solicitors within one hour's journey were asked, 'How did you first get to hear of them?' The largest single group consisted of 261 (31 per cent) who said that they had noticed the plate while walking by. The next largest category consisted of 252 (30 per cent) who said that they had got the name from a friend, relative, or neighbour. A further 92 (11 per cent) said that the firm was the family solicitor or had acted for them before, 39 (5 per cent) got to hear of the firm from their employer, 31 (4 per cent) from their union, 24 (3 per cent) from a citizens' advice bureau, 8 from a legal advice centre, and 5 from the police. There were 109 who reported miscellaneous other sources and 15 who could not recall how they had first heard of the firm.

A detailed analysis of these answers by income showed that the increasing knowledge among the better off came about primarily because solicitors' plates were noticed more often and because more solicitors were heard of through friends. Only slightly more of the better off had family solicitors. The analysis by social class indicated a different picture. Family solicitors were much more common in Social Class I and to a lesser extent in Social Class II. Where these social classes did not have family solicitors, they knew of firms through friends and employers. Only 6 per cent of Social Class I and 13 per cent of Social Class II had got to know of solicitors by seeing the plate as compared with 16 per cent of Social Classes III manual and IV, 17 per cent of Class V and 20 per cent of Class III non-manual.

Respondents who knew (precisely or imprecisely) of a firm of solicitors were asked whether they had spoken to them within the previous 12 months and, if not, whether they had spoken to them within the previous 7 years. A total of 128 (8 per cent of the total number of respondents and 15 per cent of those who knew of a firm) said that they had spoken to a firm within the previous 12 months and another 170 (10 per cent of the whole sample, or 20 per cent of those who knew of a firm) said they had spoken within 7 years. A total of 538 (64 per cent) had not spoken to the solicitors within 7 years, if at all. It will be recalled that a total of 815 (49 per cent of all respondents) had said they did not know of any firm of solicitors.

The responses to this question were analysed by reference to the income, capital, and social class of the respondents. It showed that the richer and higher social class respondents were significantly more likely to have actually seen a solicitor in the last seven years than those who were poorer and in the lower social class groupings. Twenty-four per cent of those whose income was above the legal aid limit had seen a solicitor, as compared with 12 per cent for those entitled to free legal aid, and 15 per cent for those entitled to aid subject to contribution. The same picture emerged from the breakdown by reference to capital. Fourteen per cent of those with no disposable capital had spoken to a solicitor, as compared with 19 per cent of those with disposable capital of up to £500, and 38 per cent of those whose capital was over £500. Similarly, whereas the percentage of those in the Class I and Class II category who had spoken to a solicitor was 35 per cent and 32 per cent respectively, the equivalent proportions in the Class III non-manual and manual groups were 20 per cent and 16 per cent respectively and in the Class IV and Class V were 15 per cent and 12 per cent respectively.

Knowledge of Legal Aid Facilities

We were anxious to discover how much respondents knew of the legal aid scheme and its various facilities. The first question we asked was, 'Can people who don't have much money get free or very cheap legal advice from a lawyer in private practice, e.g. in a solicitor's office?' The object of this question was to see whether respondents knew about either of the two official means of getting advice free or for low fees—the statutory scheme and the voluntary scheme.[1] It was also designed to discover whether respondents appreciated that the service was offered in the solicitors' own offices. Our question was phrased to avoid referring specifically to these schemes. Indeed, they had only been mentioned earlier in the questionnaire to those few respondents who had had a court hearing. A total of 415 respondents (25 per cent) said that a poor person could not get free or cheap advice in a private solicitor's office and another 298 (18 per cent) said that they did not know; nearly half, therefore, gave the wrong answer or none at all; the remaining 938 (57 per cent) said that a poor person could get such help.

The replies to this question were again analysed according to the income and social class of respondents. The results are shown in Table 45. Knowledge about free and cheap advice was slightly higher in the higher income groups. On the other hand, the proportion not answering was much larger in the two lower income groups than in the higher one—27 per cent and 24 per cent as compared with 9 per cent. The social class table, by contrast with the income table, shows that the higher social classes seem decisively more knowledgeable than the lower: 78 per cent of Class I, 65 per cent of Class II, and 56 per cent of Classes III manual and non-manual, but only 54 per cent of Classes IV and V knew that one can get free or cheap advice in a solicitor's office.

The 938 respondents who thought that free or cheap help was obtainable from a solicitor in his office were asked, 'What does one have to do to get such advice or where should one go?' The correct answer to this question is that one goes to the

[1] See Chapter 2, pp. 24-5.

TABLE 45   PERCENTAGE BELIEVING THAT A POOR PERSON CAN GET FREE
OR CHEAP ADVICE

Income	Yes	No	Don't know	Total	
No legal aid	68	23	9	100	(465)
Contributory legal aid	66	10	24	100	(732)
Free legal aid	64	9	27	100	(266)
Unclassified	52	19	28	100	(188)
			(significant at 1%)		
Social Class					
I	78	9	12	100	(32)
II	65	20	14	100	(138)
III 1	56	32	11	100	(187)
III 2	57	24	19	100	(615)
IV	54	25	21	100	(339)
V	54	28	18	100	(243)
Unclassified	52	26	22	100	(97)
	57 (938)	25 (415)	18 (298)	100	(1,651)
		(significant at 1%)			

solicitor's office and asks for it provided the solicitor is on the
legal aid advice panel. Only 86 respondents (9 per cent) of
those who said they knew such advice was obtainable and
5 per cent of the total sample gave this as their answer. The
largest number 269 (29 per cent), said they would ask at a
citizens' advice bureau. The next largest number, 190 (20 per
cent), said they would go to a legal advice centre. (This
answer was correct in so far as many such offices would give
free advice to the poor, but it was wrong in so far as the question
specifically referred to advice given in a solicitor's private
office.) Sixty respondents (6 per cent) said they would go to a
'Legal Aid Society'. Possibly they had in mind some kind of
legal advice centre, or possibly the administrative buildings or
offices of the Legal Aid Scheme, which do not normally dispense
legal advice, but which do provide the necessary forms to
enable an application to be made to a solicitor. Twenty-five
(3 per cent) said they would go to the courts—which do not
officially give advice at all, though some do so unofficially.
Ten respondents thought they would go to the police (presumably for direction as to where to go, rather than for the

advice itself) and 92 (10 per cent) respondents specified a variety of other places. A total of 206 (22 per cent) respondents said they did not know where one should go. The proportion who knew did not vary significantly when analysed by the combined or strict legal aid criteria.

Next we asked whether the respondent had heard of the legal aid and advice scheme before the interview. In total, 985 (60 per cent) respondents said they had previously heard of the scheme. But 185 of the 985 (19 per cent) who said they had heard of the scheme *also said that a poor person could not get free or cheap advice in a solicitor's office.* These people, in other words, appeared to know of the free or cheap advice scheme, but did not associate it with solicitors' private offices. This may be one of the reasons for the failure of the legal advice scheme to make as much impact as had been hoped.

We analysed in Table 46 these answers by reference to income, capital, and social class. There was a clear and significant correlation between lack of means and lower social class with lack of knowledge about legal aid. On the income

TABLE 46   PERCENTAGE WHO HAD HEARD OF THE LEGAL AID SCHEME

Income		Capital			Social Class		
No legal aid	71 (332)	Above £500	70	(113)	I	90	(28)
Contributory legal aid	59 (426)	Under £500	65	(200)	II	67	(91)
Free legal aid	45 (118)	None	57	(576)	III 1	66	(123)
Unclassified	59 (109)	Unclassified	59	(96)	III 2	60	(370)
					IV	54	(183)
					V	54	(132)
					Unclassified		
						60	(58)
Total	60 (985)	Total	60	(985)	Total	60	(985)

Strict legal aid eligibility

No legal aid	72	(352)
Contributory legal aid	57	(395)
Free legal aid	43	(91)
Unclassified	57	(147)
Total	60	(985)

N.B. These results are significant at 1 per cent.

test, only 45 per cent of those entitled to free legal aid had heard of it as compared with 59 per cent of those entitled to contributory legal aid, and 71 per cent of those above the legal aid limit. On the capital test 57 per cent of those with no disposable capital had heard of legal aid compared with 65 per cent and 70 per cent of the two higher groups with some disposable capital. When we analysed the results by the combined income and capital test the results were virtually the same as for income and capital separately. On the social class breakdown, 90 per cent of Social Class I had heard of legal aid, 67 per cent of Class II, 66 per cent of Class III non-manual, 60 per cent of Class III manual and 54 per cent of Classes IV and V.

We next asked, 'Where does one go to get help under this scheme?' There are several equally correct answers to this question. One can go to a solicitor in private practice and ask him to give one help in filling out the relevant forms, or one can send in a form to one of the Legal Aid Offices run by the Law Society in different parts of the country. This applies to all civil work, including matrimonial proceedings in the magistrates' courts. It does not apply to any criminal cases—since these are technically not dealt with as part of the Legal Aid and Advice Scheme administered by the Law Society. Instead criminal legal aid is provided by the courts themselves. We recognized that the ordinary person would not be likely to distinguish between the Legal Aid and Advice Scheme for civil cases and legal aid for criminal cases and that the answers to this question might therefore be confused. The replies are shown in Table 47.

The great majority of respondents (74 per cent) did not know or had not heard of the scheme. Just under a fifth said they would go to a solicitor or to a court. There were 4 per cent who said that they would go to a citizens' advice bureau. Analyses of these replies by reference to the combined income and capital legal aid least revealed considerable differences between respondents' replies according to their means. The better off were better informed. Conversely knowledge of the scheme was least among those for whom it was mainly designed.

The final question in this series regarding knowledge of

TABLE 47   PERCENTAGE SPECIFYING WHERE LEGAL AID PROVIDED

	No legal aid	Combined legal aid criteria Contributory legal aid	Free legal aid	Unclassified	Total
Solicitors	12	8	5	9	9 (145)
Court	11	8	5	8	9 (145)
Citizens' advice bureau	5	3	2	6	4 (67)
Free legal advice centre	2	2	2	1	2 (32)
Other	4	2	1	3	2 (34)
Don't know where provided or had not heard of scheme	67	77	85	73	74 (1,228)
Total:	100 (492)	100 (693)	100 (211)	100 (255)	100 (1,651)

legal aid was, 'How can you get a solicitor to speak for you in court under the legal aid scheme?' The correct answer to this question is that in criminal cases one should ask the court, and in civil cases one should apply to the office of the local legal aid committee. A solicitor commonly makes both kinds of applications. The answers given by respondents, excluding those who had never heard of legal aid, are shown in Table 48.

TABLE 48   PERCENTAGE ANSWERING HOW LAWYER OBTAINED FOR COURT WORK UNDER LEGAL AID

	No legal aid	Combined legal aid Contributory legal aid	Free legal aid	Unclassified	Total
Would go to a solicitor	17	14	12	15	15 (145)
Would go to or ask at court	16	15	12	14	15 (145)
Would ask at a citizens' advice bureau	7	6	4	10	7 (67)
Would ask at a legal aid society or poor man's lawyer	5	3	4	1	3 (32)
Miscellaneous: town hall (12), political parties (3), other (19)	3	4	2	5	3 (34)
Don't know	53	58	66	55	57 (562)
Total:	100 (352)	100 (395)	100 (91)	100 (147)	100 (985)

As many as 57 per cent said they did not know. There were 15 per cent who said that they would go to a solicitor and another 15 per cent who said that they would go to a court.

When these figures were analysed by reference to the combined income-capital test to estimate eligibility for legal aid, the results suggested that whereas the proportion of Don't Knows rose as the financial resources of the respondent decreased so the proportion mentioning solicitors increased with the financial resources of the respondents. The richer the respondent the more likely they were to mention solicitors.

CHAPTER 12

Opinions and Expectations

Payments for Advice

One reason why people may hesitate to take advice is because of the cost or expected cost of obtaining it, particularly if they have no knowledge of the statutory and voluntary schemes. We asked those respondents who had visited a solicitor on one of the specific matters included in our questionnaire what they had been charged for initial advice.

As explained in Chapter 2, a client on supplementary benefit, provided he does not have disposable capital of more than £125, is entitled under the statutory legal advice scheme to receive advice for a maximum of an hour and a half for nothing. A client who qualified by virtue of the rather strict means test requirements could, at the time of the survey, obtain advice for 2s.6d. (12½p) per half an hour for a total of one hour and a half. A person not entitled to statutory legal advice may still obtain advice relatively cheaply if the solicitor to whom he goes operates the voluntary scheme under which solicitors give advice for half an hour on payment of £1. Otherwise, he pays whatever the solicitor charges—if anything, as many solicitors are prepared to give advice without payment.

In 82 cases out of 88 where the respondent could separate and knew the precise amount charged for initial advice, that advice was given without charge. In 25 of these 82 cases the applicant was receiving supplementary benefit. One half of the 88 cases were accident cases. There appeared to be only two cases in which the solicitor had charged over £1. When a charge was made it was usually part of a composite bill and respondents were unable to separate it.

Solicitors sometimes ask for money on account of work to be done. Occasionally they may ask for more than the client can afford. In criminal cases, especially those which are likely to result in the imprisonment of the client, it is probably the rule rather than the exception. In accident cases, where the solicitor can expect to obtain his costs from the insurance company, it is rare. We asked all respondents who said that they had been to a solicitor in private practice whether they had been asked for anything on account. The great majority had not. Out of the 144 respondents who were able to give a definite reply, 129 (89 per cent) had not been asked for any payment on account. Of the 16 respondents who had been asked for something on account 8 had been asked for £10 or less, 6 for sums of between £10 and £20 and 2 for more than £20. Both the latter cases involved court proceedings.

We asked all respondents a question designed to ascertain what they expected solicitors would charge. It is often said that one of the reasons for reluctance to consult solicitors is the fear that the cost would be more than could be afforded, but no one has previously tried to ascertain what level of charges people would expect to be asked to pay. The question was not easy to frame in a meaningful way. For example, there would have been little purpose in asking how much the respondent thought an average conveyancing or accident or matrimonial problem might cost. Those who have not been faced with these problems could not be expected to know what was involved. Moreover, an average transaction would have been a useless standard of measurement, as it would have conveyed varying impressions to different respondents. We therefore settled on a question which simply asked how much a solicitor would be expected to charge for half an hour's advice. Though the question was narrowly framed, at least it required all respondents to think relatively precisely about the work involved for the solicitor.

The question asked was, 'Suppose you were to go to a solicitor as a private client, about how much do you imagine he would charge for half an hour's advice?' We looked at the answers of those who had not seen a solicitor in the previous seven years and who, therefore, had no basis of actual experience. The answers are set out in Table 49.

There was a wide spread of answers. While $16\frac{1}{2}$ per cent

TABLE 49   NUMBER AND PERCENTAGE ESTIMATING CHARGES FOR HALF AN HOUR'S ADVICE FROM A SOLICITOR

	Respondent not having spoken to solicitor for past seven years	
	(No.)	(%)
Nothing	16	1
2s.6d.	6	·5
Over 2s.6d. under £1	69	5
£1	127	10
Over £1 but under £2	203	15
Over £2 but under £3	239	18
Over £3 but under £5	219	17
Over £5 but under £10	147	11
Over £10 but under £20	46	3
£20 or over	18	1
Don't know	228	17
Total:	1,318*	100

* Excluding those who had spoken to a solicitor in the previous seven years and 36 cases in which we had no information.

thought a solicitor would charge up to £1, 15 per cent thought the charge would be £5 or more. We also analysed the answers for those who had seen a solicitor during the previous seven years. There was, once again, a wide spread of answers, but 51 per cent gave figures within the range of £1 but under £5 compared with 42 per cent of those who had not seen a solicitor.

We analysed the answers for those who had not seen a solicitor in the previous seven years by reference to the income and social class of the respondents. The category of those who did not know was larger in the lower than the higher income groups—31 per cent and 16 per cent, as against 9 per cent. But the lower income groups expected solicitors to charge significantly less than the higher income groups. For example, 44 per cent of those entitled to free legal aid expected a solicitor to charge under £3 compared with 54 per cent of those not entitled to legal aid. There was no significant difference by social class.

One limitation on the availability of solicitors is the fact that they are generally open only in normal office hours during the week. They rarely open on Saturday mornings and virtually never in the evenings. Thus a further cost of visiting a solicitor may be loss of working time. To ascertain how important this was, we asked respondents who were normally at work, 'Would you have any difficulty in getting to see a solicitor during working hours?' and, 'Would it cause you to lose pay?' Although about three-quarters of working respondents said that they would not have had difficulty in seeing a solicitor, just under a quarter would have some difficulty and 28 per cent thought they would lose pay.

The income and social class classification showed no marked differences in the difficulty of getting off work to see a solicitor, but there were significant differences in the likelihood of losing pay. The percentage likely to lose pay in getting off work to see a solicitor varied on the income scale from 25 per cent for those not entitled to legal aid to 14 per cent for the contributory group and 19 per cent for those entitled to free legal aid. On the social class scale the pattern was clearer. It rose from 4 per cent for Class I and 15 per cent for Class II to 35 per cent for Class III non-manual, 35 per cent for Class III manual, 34 per cent for Class IV and then fell to 27 per cent for Class V.

The Perceived Role of Solicitors
Respondents were asked, 'In what kind of situations (other than any of which you have already told me) do you think you would go to a solicitor?' Respondents were asked to give two examples. This was, therefore, a question which, in effect, invited respondents to give their instinctive association with the concepts 'legal problem' or 'solicitor'. The answers are set out in Table 50 in the order of the number of times they were mentioned.

There are a number of aspects of this list which are of special interest. One of the most striking is that of the 2,146 positive responses (omitting the cases where the respondent said he would never go and those where no reply was given), the four categories of accidents, property and landlord-tenant problems, debt-business-hire purchase, and matrimonial and family problems accounted for 1,334 or 62 per cent of the total. Secondly, only one respondent mentioned complaints

TABLE 50   SITUATIONS IN WHICH SOLICITOR WOULD BE CONSULTED

Accidents	388
Property problems and landlord/tenant	387
Debt/money/business/hire purchase/when cheated	312
Matrimonial and family	247
Criminal	202
General advice and legal documents	183
Wills/estates/death	169
Proceedings or claims in court	102
Trouble with neighbours/nuisance	44
Employment	43
Miscellaneous, extortion, unfair treatment, libel (35), slander (24), defective goods (2), professional negligence (1), bad workmanship, insurance, passport, betting, cruelty, finding someone, negligence—one each	69
No responses or don't know, counting each respondent twice if he did not answer at all and once if he gave one answer but not two, as required by the question	780
Would never go—188 respondents, each counted twice for this purpose	376
Total 1,651 respondents:	3,302

about defective goods and only 24 respondents mentioned hire purchase problems, though 52 did say, 'When cheated', which may have included problems of this kind. Not a single respondent seemed to associate solicitors with problems arising in the social security system—injury, sickness, unemployment, or other national insurance benefits.

From the legal profession's point of view perhaps the most disturbing finding is that 188 respondents, over 11 per cent of the total, said they would never go to a solicitor for anything. (Seven of these had been to a solicitor in the seven-year period.) One went so far as to say, 'I would have to be going to the gallows before I'd go near one.' There was a striking progression by social class in this strong negative feeling, which was felt by 3 per cent of Class I, and 5 per cent of Class II, 6 per cent of Class III 1, 11 per cent of Class III 2, 14 per cent of Class IV and 17 per cent of Class V.

Preference For a One-sided Lawyer

We asked respondents, 'If you went to a lawyer as an ordinary citizen, would you prefer a lawyer who *only* represented people like yourself or one who was also prepared to represent the other side—for instance the landlord, the hire purchase company, or the police? The purpose of this intentionally loaded question was to try to find out if the same importance is attached by laymen as by lawyers to the principle of lawyers holding themselves out as willing to act for either side. Most lawyers do not act wholly for landlords or wholly for tenants but sometimes for one and sometimes for the other. They believe that such variety of work increases their usefulness to all their clients. The same applies to lawyers who practise in the criminal courts, many of whom sometimes act for the prosecution and sometimes for the defence. This applies more to the barrister than to the solicitor but to some extent it is true of solicitors as well. The lawyer regards it as advantageous to avoid becoming too closely identified with one side. Some clients may however have greater confidence in a lawyer who only acts for their kind. They may regard the uncommitted lawyer who shifts from side to side as unreliable, or in a sense even untrustworthy.

In reply to our question, 743 (45 per cent) said that they preferred the lawyer who acted only for one side and 501 (30 per cent) said that they preferred the lawyer who acted for either side: 392 (24 per cent) said that they did not know and 15 gave no reply to the question. When these responses were analysed by reference to borough no differences emerged.

The high proportion unable to answer the question were not evenly distributed among different economic and social classes. It was the poorer and those of lower social class who were least able to give an answer to the question. Those who favoured a lawyer who acted for both sides were, as might be expected, the richer and those in higher social classes. The picture for those favouring a 'one-sided' lawyer was much less clear cut. A higher proportion of richer respondents preferred the 'one-sided' lawyer than of the poorer respondents, but in regard to social class it was Social Classes III manual, IV, and V which had the highest proportion preferring the 'one-sided' lawyer. It should be added that the answers to attitude questions of this kind must be treated with some reserve. The problems of attitude questions are explored in more detail in Appendix III.

Adequacy of the Local Advisory Facilities?
We invited respondents to express a view about the advisory facilities in the area. All respondents were asked, 'What do you think of the range of advisory services in your neighbourhood? Is it adequate?' In total, 636 (38 per cent) said that the services were adequate and 227 (14 per cent) said that they were inadequate (Table 51). The largest single group—782 (48 per cent)—said that they did not know. There were six respondents who gave no reply to the question. The highest proportion of satisfied respondents was in Tower Hamlets, which has the fullest facilities (see Chapter 1). There was little variation in the answers given by social class or by income.

TABLE 51 PERCENTAGE OF RESPONDENTS THINKING THE ADVISORY SERVICES WERE ADEQUATE, BY BOROUGH

	Adequate	Inadequate	No View	Total	
Islington	34	13	52	100	(484)
Southwark	36	14	50	100	(701)
Tower Hamlets	47	13	40	100	(466)
Total:	38	14	48	100	(1,651)

N.B. The results are significant at 1 per cent.

Next we asked, 'If you were in charge of advisory facilities in your neighbourhood, what do you think you would do to improve them?' The largest category by far—1,052 (64 per cent)—said they did not know and another 29 said they did not need improving. Of the 570 who had any suggestions, 276 (48 per cent) suggested more advertising; 76 (13 per cent) said more services were needed; 74 (13 per cent) said improve the quality of the staff; 63 (11 per cent) said have more outlets and the remainder put forward miscellaneous suggestions, including longer hours of opening (12 cases) and home visits (11 cases).

Respondents were then asked, 'Where do you think is the best place for the ordinary citizen to go when he wants legal advice?' The answers are given in Table 52 in the order of frequency of mention. The citizens' advice bureau was mentioned more than twice as frequently as any other source including solicitors or legal advice centres.

TABLE 52   NUMBER AND PERCENTAGE SELECTING BEST PLACE FOR LEGAL ADVICE

	No.	%
Citizens' advice bureau	561	34
Solicitor	237	14
Town hall	182	11
Legal Advice Centre at Toynbee Hall, Cambridge House, Mary Ward, etc.	145	9
At Town Hall	12	1
Police	58	4
Solicitor if you can afford it, otherwise legal advice centre	28	2
Tenant's association	24	1
M.P.	23	1
Trade union	13	1
Miscellaneous: Labour Party Rooms (6); other political advice offices (3); court (10); National Assistance (7); library (4); the Welfare Office (4); church or priest (4); Labour Exchange (4); probation officer (3); legal aid scheme offices (3); doctor (1); disabled persons' club (1); A.A. (1); a friend (2); other (32)	85	5
Don't know	283	17
Total:	1,651	100

We analysed these results by borough, income, capital, and social class for the three largest categories—citizens' advice bureau, solicitors (including all legal advice centres), and the town hall. The analysis by reference to the respondent's borough showed that the proportion selecting solicitors as the best form of advice was not related to the number of solicitors' firms per head in the borough. In Islington, where there were 38 firms (1 firm per 6,000 of the population), 19 per cent mentioned solicitors; in Southwark, where there were 24 firms (1 firm per 12,000), as many as 36 per cent mentioned solicitors; but in Tower Hamlets, where there were 10 firms (1 firm per 20,000), only 18 per cent mentioned solicitors. The proportion who selected citizens' advice bureau as the best source of advice was however more related to the availability of citizens' advice bureaux in the boroughs. In Islington, where there were two citizens' advice bureaux for a quarter of a million inhabitants, 31 per cent of respondents mentioned citizens' advice bureau compared with 26 per cent in Southwark, where there is one bureau for 295,900, and 47 per cent in Tower Hamlets, where there is one for 31,000.

The breakdown by income (Table 53) showed a steady increase in the percentage selecting solicitors with increase in

TABLE 53   PERCENTAGE SELECTING BEST SOURCE OF LEGAL ADVICE BY BOROUGH, INCOME GROUP, AND SOCIAL CLASS

Borough	Citizens' advice bureau	Solicitor in private practice	Legal advice centre	Town hall	Police	Other	Don't know		Total
Islington	32	15	5	16	5	10	19	100	(484)
Southwark	27	22	14	11	4	9	14	100	(701)
Tower Hamlets	47	9	8	6	2	6	21	100	(466)
Income									
No legal aid	38	20	10	10	4	8	9	100	(465)
Contributory legal aid	33	15	9	11	4	11	19	100	(732)
Free legal aid	31	9	11	12	2	12	26	100	(266)
Don't know/won't say	34	20	8	10	4	8	19	100	(188)
Social Class									
I	32	44	—	3	3	6	12	100	(32)
II	41	22	12	9	1	5	10	100	(138)
III 1	36	20	11	12	2	9	9	100	(187)
III 2	36	14	9	12	5	12	15	100	(615)
IV	31	16	10	11	3	8	20	100	(339)
V	32	12	9	10	3	8	25	100	(243)
Unclassified	29	12	10	12	5	8	24	100	(97)
Total:	34 (561)	16 (265)	9 (157)	11 (182)	3 (58)	9 (145)	17 (283)	100	(1,651)

N.B. The results are significant at 1 per cent.

income. Thus, solicitors were mentioned by 9 per cent of the lowest income group, by 15 per cent of the middle income group, and by 20 per cent of the highest income group. The proportions who referred to citizens' advice bureaux showed a similar progression; conversely the Don't Know category was much greater in the lower income groups—26 per cent in the lowest group compared with 9 per cent in the highest group.

In the social class classification there was little difference in the proportions who mentioned citizens' advice bureaux. The percentage mentioning solicitors was much the highest in the three top social classes, 44 per cent, 22 per cent, and 20 per cent compared with 14 per cent, 16 per cent, and 12 per cent in the three lowest categories. The percentages mentioning the town hall were lower in the Class I and II groups than in the other four. The Don't Knows were greatest in the lower social classes—ranging from 15 per cent, 20 per cent, and 25 per cent in the three lowest groups to 12 per cent, 10 per cent, and 9 per cent in the three highest.

CHAPTER 13

Conclusions

In this final chapter we relate the findings from the two surveys and summarize the main conclusions. In many ways the two surveys are complementary to each other. While the agency survey was extensive, the population survey was intensive. The main aim of the agency survey was to find out how much advice was sought, on what, and from whom. We particularly wanted to know how much advice of a legal or quasi-legal character was needed and to what extent such questions were referred to lawyers.

The main aim of the population survey was to examine the more serious legal problems which people had encountered and to see how they had managed with such help as they had obtained. The emphasis was as much on needs which went unmet as on needs which were met in whole or part. We wanted to see who got what help, the means by which people came to use particular agencies and services, and why some of them were not used more—particularly the voluntary and statutory provisions for legal aid and advice. Were the barriers to greater use of these services unfavourable attitudes towards them, inadequate use of referrals made to them by other agencies, ignorance of what services are available and how services can be mobilized, or costs or fears about costs, however misguided? How great was the problem of unmet need, how serious were the consequences, and who suffered them? How far was it due to financial obstacles, the limited availability of services in the immediate locality, ignorance of available legal remedies, or deeper cultural barriers? Could it simply be resolved by making more services available and publicising what was on offer?

We selected the three London boroughs for our study because they had a high proportion of semi-skilled and unskilled manual workers. They proved to be boroughs with wide areas of housing stress and marked education deprivation. Only 14 per cent of our sample had left school later than the age of fifteen, only 2 per cent had any full-time education beyond the age of eighteen. On the other hand, they were, by national standards, relatively well endowed with advisory services. Though there were less solicitors per head than in the country as a whole, there was a relatively well developed citizens' advice bureau service—both in quantity of outlets and in the generosity of their staffing. Tower Hamlets was particularly well equipped in this respect with no less than six bureaux serving a population of just under 200,000. By national standards the boroughs were also well provided with legal advice centres, either in or near them. Again Tower Hamlets was at that time particularly well favoured in this respect. There was, indeed, probably as extensive a range of advisory services (except for solicitors in private practice) in that borough as anywhere else in the country, particularly in view of the comparatively small population of Tower Hamlets.

The local authority services were also relatively well developed: two of the local authorities provided information services, but they joined with other inner London boroughs in financing many of the voluntary agencies. There were, moreover, active Members of Parliament and local political parties, and a wide variety of other small and informal advisory services, some aimed primarily at particular religious or other communities and others offering a more general service. By any standard, Tower Hamlets was well endowed with helping agencies and so was Islington, though to a lesser extent. The area with the least services was Southwark—particularly northeastern Southwark.

We were fortunate in the cooperation given to the survey by the agencies in the boroughs. As a result, we were able to obtain a comprehensive picture of the work done over short periods by the citizens' advice bureaux, legal advice centres and probation service, and a nearly comprehensive picture of the work done by some other types of agency. We were, however, unable to randomize the periods for which the information was collected. The main gap in our survey of providers was caused by our

H

failure to persuade no more than a few firms of solicitors to record information for us. This was partly due to our inability to overcome their suspicion of our intentions—to which we had ourselves probably contributed from our other work. We were very disappointed that we were only able to persuade a fifth of the firms providing statutory free advice or advice under the voluntary scheme to record information for us. Other research workers might well have been more successful in this part of the survey.

The response rate to our population survey was somewhat disappointing. The main defect in our sample was the failure to make contact with all but a handful of persons who had changed their address between the compilation of the electoral register and the interview, which took place a year or more afterwards. Apart from the virtual omission of this important category of respondent, our sample corresponded well to the census data from the checks on sex, marital status, housing tenure, country of origin, and social class, which we were able to make. It may be that the incidence and type of problems on which advice was needed by those who had moved their homes in the previous year or more would have proved different from that in the population as a whole. In particular one would have expected them to have had more housing problems. This was one reason why it would have been misleading to attempt to gross up our sample to give estimates of the incidence of problems in general or of certain types. A second reason was the rarity of the more serious type of legal problem. We asked respondents to recall problems over a seven-year period and to tell us about the most recent problem of each type. We could not assume that the number of incidents or needs were correctly stated for a period of seven years or that respondents correctly attributed a particular incident or need to a particular year. The likelihood of errors in recall and the bias in the sample towards those who had not recently changed their address needs to be borne in mind when interpreting the findings from this survey.

The survey of agencies, though incomplete, gives us the best indication of the minimum use of advice and information services, even though we can only express this in terms of visit rather than of persons making visits. We estimated that 36 visits per 1,000 were made in a twelve-week period in Tower Hamlets, 17 per 1,000 in Islington, and 14 per 1,000 in Southwark. Nearly half the visits we recorded were to citizens' advice bureaux, over a quarter to local authority departments, and 15 per cent to legal advice centres.

In total the agencies which recorded for us had an average of nearly 1,300 visits a week or nearly 70,000 per year. All these figures exclude the work done by solicitors. The ten firms which recorded for us (out of fifty-two providing legal advice) between them saw nearly fifty clients in the recording week free or under one of the schemes. Possibly these firms on average provided more advice of this kind than others. It would be too hazardous to estimate the amount of this advice given by all solicitors from such a small and probably unrepresentative sample.

We looked to see how far the provision of services in the three boroughs affected the extent to which they were used. The rate of demand made on Members of Parliament and local authorities was similar in the three boroughs. But we estimated that twenty-two visits per 1,000 were made over a twelve-week period to citizens' advice bureaux in Tower Hamlets, which had six bureaux, five per 1,000 in Southwark, which had one, and seven per 1,000 in Islington, which had two. Similarly there were nine estimated visits per 1,000 in Tower Hamlets with its four legal advice centres and only two visits per 1,000 in Southwark, which had one legal advice centre. (We have no statistics for Islington as the legal advice centres operating at that time were unable to record for us.)

The greater utilization of these facilities by the residents of Tower Hamlets was also found in our population survey. In that borough, 20 per cent of the population had ever visited a citizens' advice bureau compared with 14 per cent in the other two boroughs. Moreover, 74 per cent of the population of Tower Hamlets said they knew where there was a citizens' advice bureau compared with 50 per cent of the population in both Islington and Southwark. We also examined the relationship between the number of firms of solicitors and contact with them, even though a considerable proportion of the population used firms outside the three boroughs. There were thirty-eight firms in private practice in Islington, twenty-four in Southwark, and ten in Tower Hamlets. In Southwark 24 per cent of the population had seen a solicitor concerning one of the problems we asked about and there was one firm per 12,000 persons. In Tower Hamlets 20 per cent had seen a solicitor and there was only one firm per 20,000 persons. In Islington, on the other hand, with one firm per 7,000, 19 per cent had seen a solicitor. Thus, the number of firms per person in the borough did not correspond with the proportion of the population which had used solicitors (including those outside these boroughs) during the last seven years.

Our total of nearly 70,000 visits to advisory agencies during the year for the three boroughs does not indicate the number of people in need or the number of different problems. A proportion of the visits recorded were made by people resident outside the three boroughs and no doubt the residents of the boroughs also used facilities outside them. Multiple visits made by the same person to the same agency or to another agency on the same problem were recorded separately. A number of people 'shopped around' among different agencies on the same problem without necessarily telling each agency what help they had had from others.

Our survey of the population gave us virtually no help in establishing the pattern of referral. Very few people reported that they had been to more than one adviser. If we had accepted these findings at face value, we would have been seriously misled. But our survey of agencies showed that nearly a third of those who visited legal advice centres were referred by the citizens' advice bureaux, and 7 per cent by local authorities. About a quarter of the visits to Members of Parliament, legal advice centres, citizens' advice bureaux, and certain local authority services were as the result of recommendations by friends and relatives. Over a tenth of visitors to probation officers were referred by court officials. Bearing in mind that between a quarter and a half of those who visit legal advice centres, citizens' advice bureaux, and the probation service have been there before, referral by others is the main way by which people find their way to agencies.

This picture is confirmed by examining the pattern of

referrals made by the different agencies. About a half or more of the visits we recorded at citizens' advice bureaux, local authorities, and the probation service led to referrals elsewhere. Over a fifth of visits to legal advice centres led to referrals. Both the citizens' advice bureaux and the probation service referred about 15 per cent of their clients to private solicitors, and a further 9 per cent and 4 per cent respectively of clients to legal advice centres. A major task of the main agencies we studied was to identify the service which was best able to help, to explain about the services and encourage their use, and perhaps make an introduction.

We attempted to establish what proportion of the visits recorded by the agencies were on legal problems. Cambridge House and Toynbee Hall had nearly 100 visits per week based on our recording periods, or nearly 150 per week according to their own administrative statistics. A high proportion of these visits were repeat visits, but virtually all of them were on legal matters. In addition, there was the contribution made by the legal advice centre in Islington which did not record for us, and the work done for the population of the boroughs by Mary Ward and by other agencies. When one of us (Rosalind Brooke) sat in on the work of citizens' advice bureaux, she classified two-thirds of the work seen as legal in a wide sense of the term—nearly half of it involving major legal problems. If the small observed sample was representative, nearly 200 visits a week (excluding telephone calls) were on questions where legal advice was given or required, or much more if our recording periods understated the annual work load as the administrative statistics suggest. In about a third of the roughly 180 consultations per week with probation officers, it was thought that the client would be wise to see a solicitor. Thus, we know of over 350 consultations per week, or nearly 20,000 per annum, on legal matters with legal advice centres, probation officers, and citizens' advice bureaux in the three boroughs.

We were unable to make a similar classification for the other agencies. It should be pointed out in this connection that some of the Members of Parliament were qualified lawyers and others had considerable technical knowledge of housing legislation—a subject on which they were frequently consulted.

This minimum of some 20,000 consultations on legal questions for a combined population of about 730,000, excluding consultations with private solicitors, can be set against the then total of 72,619 consultations under the statutory legal advice scheme in the year 1967–8 for the whole of England and Wales[1]—which the Prices and Incomes Board suggested should be multiplied by five to get the true amount of free or virtually free legal advice given by solicitors to persons who were not their ordinary clients.[2]

In so far as we were unable to record information for every agency in the borough, all the figures derived from our survey of agencies understate the utilization of services. Moreover, they exclude information and advice given outside an agency setting by persons with or without some legal knowledge, or the use made of trade unions or of services provided by newspapers—such as the John Hilton Bureau of the *News of the World*. The use of agencies which did not record for us and informal advisers is undoubtedly large, as indicated by our population survey. On a number of our specific legal need questions, a considerable proportion of the main advisers for those classified as needing legal advice was not a person with legal training or such training as is provided to citizens' advice bureaux personnel. This was the case particularly with problems of employment, making a will, and debt problems. Moreover, nearly a quarter of those with accidents of a seriousness to warrant legal advice had their main advice from a union official, the police, an insurance broker, or some other such person not specifically trained to act in this capacity.

Nevertheless, it seems useful to bring together these figures from the agency survey to compare the picture which they suggest with the data collected from the population survey. There we found that, while 16 per cent of our respondents had at any time visited a citizens' advice bureau, 18 per cent had spoken to a solicitor during the last seven years, and 21 per cent had been to a solicitor about one or more of the problems covered by our survey (including wills which may have been

---

[1] *Legal Aid and Advice: Report of the Law Society, 1967–68*, H.M.S.O., 1969, p. 12, Appendix 3.
[2] National Board for Prices and Incomes, *Remuneration of Solicitors*, 1968, Cmnd. 3529, para. 39.

made at any time). Thus from this survey it appeared that a higher proportion of the population had had contact with solicitors than with citizens' advice bureaux.

When we classified the main advisers of those in need of advice who took it, in only one case (attempts to evict) did the citizens' advice bureau emerge as the most common main adviser. House-purchase, leases, evictions, debt problems, wills, accidents, matrimonial problems, and court proceedings concerning adults were most commonly dealt with by lawyers as the main adviser. Housing repair problems were mainly dealt with by local authorities and employment problems by trade unions. This is again a very different picture from that suggested by the agency survey. But the two findings can be reconciled when it is recalled that the citizens' advice bureaux and some other agencies are to a considerable extent problem sorters. Moreover, other agencies, whose main function is not the provision of advice, also sort and refer to more appropriate agencies. Thus, where advice is obtained on a traditional legal problem, it is most commonly given ultimately by a lawyer, though the citizen may have arrived there by a complicated route.

Our study does, nevertheless, show the important role which citizens' advice bureaux and similar agencies play in the current legal system, and in the administration of the social and other services. In proportion to the number of their outlets, they had a high caller rate—probably considerably higher than that of solicitors. There were remarkable variations between different bureaux in the precise function which they performed and in what they did for their visitors. But on average they made telephone calls for over a quarter of their visitors, particularly helping those who were not accustomed to phoning public authorities or others with status and authority. They wrote letters for 14 per cent of their visitors, particularly for those who were ill-equipped to write them themselves. They also filled in forms for 6 per cent of their visitors. Specific services of this kind were most commonly performed for the lower social classes. In this capacity, they acted as an independent channel of communication between government and governed, between employer and employee, between manufacturer and consumer.

They were the general practitioners of the advisory system, channelling legal problems to lawyers and other problems to those agencies which could make a decision or review a decision which had been already made. The local authority social service departments (children's, welfare, information and advice centres, maternity and child welfare) also made telephone calls for about a quarter of their visitors and wrote letters for 7 per cent. The other local authority services which we examined (legal, housing, and rent officers) wrote letters for 17 per cent of their visitors. The most extensive letter-writers were Members of Parliament and the political parties, which wrote letters for 73 per cent of their visitors.

When we looked at the problems upon which advice was sought, our survey of agencies indicated that over a quarter of the consultations with the agencies which recorded for us (excluding our limited data for solicitors) were on landlord and tenant related matters. Local authority departments and citizens' advice bureaux provided between them 85 per cent of the consultations on landlord and tenant questions in roughly equal proportions. Legal advice centres dealt with 13 per cent. Although Members of Parliament only dealt with 3 per cent of these visits, housing matters in general were a high proportion of their work for constituents. Matrimonial problems and associated problems of custody of children, affiliation, and family relationships accounted for 18 per cent of the visits recorded in the agency survey, and about 40 per cent of these were to citizens' advice bureaux, 27 per cent to probation officers, 20 per cent to local authority departments, and 14 per cent to legal advice centres. Employment and redundancy problems constituted 8 per cent of consultations, personal injuries 7 per cent, debt 6 per cent and social security 5 per cent. At least 40 per cent of the visits on these problems were to citizens' advice bureaux. At legal advice centres 46 per cent of the visits were about personal injury problems and 25 per cent about debt problems.

Out of the list of seventeen legal problems which we put to the respondents of our population survey, the problem which was reported to us most frequently was that of personal injuries. It is not, however, possible to use our population survey to gauge all the types of legal problem upon which people sought advice, as the data collected was restricted to seventeen defined situations of need.

But the population survey with its specific questions did enable us to get an impression of the extent of unmet need for legal advice which we defined to exclude all but relatively serious needs. In interpreting the figures it should be borne in mind that we enquired only about the most recent incident of need and then tried to discover whether any advice had been taken from anyone—even a friend or relative. Only in the case of house purchases had all those who needed advice taken any. The only other problems upon which advice had been taken in a clear majority of cases was when people had been threatened with eviction, needed a debt collected, or when an injury was suffered for which someone else was thought to be responsible. Only about half had taken advice when wanting to evict a tenant, when taken to court for debt, when faced with matrimonial problems or other court proceedings. Over 60 per cent of those with employment problems had taken no advice and about two-thirds of those who made wills, signed leases, had a child taken before the juvenile court, or had repairs which the landlord had failed to make. Only about one in ten had taken any advice when they had purchased defective goods, got into arrears with their instalments, or felt they had been denied their rights by the Ministry of Social Security (if we exclude the obvious action of taking it up with the local office of the Ministry itself). The extent of unmet need, even by the crude standard of advice from *anyone*, was therefore substantial despite the number of available services.

In total our 1,651 respondents told us of 1,022 cases where, in our view, legal advice was needed. Advice of any kind had been taken in only 450 cases and in only 270 cases was a lawyer the main adviser: lawyers in private practice dealt with 253 cases and lawyers at legal advice centres with 17. The main adviser in 48 cases was the local authority (mainly cases of housing repair). In 30 cases the main adviser was a citizens' advice bureau. Thus, not much more than a quarter of the cases which in our view needed an independent lawyer's attention received it.

The cases which did not reach a lawyer were not confined to the type of problem which lawyers do not normally handle—such as employment problems and social security problems. There were 181 cases of personal injury involving time off work, hospital care, or death, but only 78 of them were dealt with by private solicitors and legal advice centres. In a third of these cases the injured person had taken no advice at all. Thus, one household in sixteen reported a case of personal injury which had not been handled by a lawyer. Less than half of the fifty-two respondents with matrimonial problems had consulted a lawyer. Neither had the same percentage of sixty families threatened with eviction seen a lawyer. No one had gone to see a lawyer about any of the twenty-seven cases of defective goods, although in two-thirds of these cases the items were worth £25 or more.

Only 42 of the 132 respondents who had been in court were represented by a lawyer. Less than a third of those threatened with a court case for debt had legal advice about it and only one of the seven actually taken to court for debt was represented by a lawyer. In only 13 out of 32 criminal cases was legal advice obtained. Over half of those who had taken no advice were found guilty. One respondent was sent to prison for three months and another was fined £200: neither had had any legal advice. One child was sent to an approved school for three months and another to a remand home for three months. In neither case had the parents had legal advice. All these cases of unmet need were found in our sample of only 1,651 families.

There was evidence that those who took advice fared better than those who did not. This was clearest in the case of those who had suffered personal injuries. Not only did a much larger proportion of those who took advice obtain compensation, but they obtained more. Advice was of proven efficacy. On the assessment of our expert adviser, a higher proportion of those who took advice received about the right amount and a much lower proportion received too little or nothing when something should have been paid. Moreover, in many cases no advice was taken in cases where the expert thought a claim was warranted and in other cases the respondent appeared to have made an inaccurate diagnosis of whose fault the accident had been. There were a great many cases where no advice had been taken out of doubt about the value of doing so.

Of those who did take advice on any of the problems, two-thirds were wholly satisfied with the help they received. Those who had complaints concentrated not so much on cost or delay but on the competence of their advisers. Thus, the sense of apathy or hopelessness which often emerged when we asked why no advice was taken was unlikely to have been based on the reported experiences of people who had taken advice. Nearly three-quarters of those few who felt able to express a view were satisfied with the local advisory services.

Nor did fear of cost appear to be a major consideration, possibly because the more costly services were so little sought after. Only 14 per cent of our respondents thought that a private solicitor was the best place to go for legal advice, though 17 per cent did not express an opinion. The majority thought that the best place to obtain legal advice was somewhere where it would have been obtained free—particularly citizens' advice bureaux. On the other hand, two-fifths of our respondents did not know where there was a citizens' advice bureau. About 40 per cent had not heard of the legal aid scheme and over 40 per cent thought that a poor person could not get free or cheap legal advice or did not know where he could.

About half of our respondents thought that a solicitor would charge £2 or more for half an hour's advice given in ordinary private practice, a third thought that the charge would be over £3, and 15 per cent thought the charge would amount to over £5. Possibly more important than the prospective charge was the fact that 28 per cent of working respondents expected to lose pay if they took time off work to see a solicitor. This problem on the whole affected disproportionately respondents who were poorer or in the lower social classes. While the fear of high legal charges, lost earnings, and the difficulty of getting time off may have deterred some from going to a solicitor for advice, most people seemed to know where to obtain advice elsewhere, albeit if less skilled, without charge. If they had visited one of these agencies, they would in many cases have been directed to a solicitor, and been told about the legal advice scheme and legal advice centres.

Only 13 per cent of those with an income which at the time of interview would have entitled them to free legal aid who had had one of the legal problems about which we asked had seen a solicitor, compared with 19 per cent of those classified as entitled to contributory legal aid and 29 per cent classified as above the legal aid limits. A similar pattern emerged from the social class analysis. Whereas over half the professional class and nearly half the intermediate class had had contact with a solicitor on one of the legal problems, this was true for less than a fifth of manual workers. Whereas 76 per cent of those with higher education had taken their problems to solicitors, this was only true of 20 per cent of those without educational qualifications. The younger, the men, the married, and the better educated were more likely to see solicitors than the aged, the women, the single, and the less well educated. The poor with legal need made very little use of solicitors, despite the legal aid and advice scheme. This was partly due to the fact that their legal problems were those in which lawyers have hitherto played little part. But this only shows that the legal aid and advice system was not yet functioning on any scale in these areas. But it was also true to a significant extent in areas where the legal aid scheme is thought to be working well, such as accidents and matrimonial problems.

When we probed deeper, we found that detailed knowledge of local facilities and statutory services was thinly spread. Less than a quarter of our respondents knew precisely where to find a citizens' advice bureau and only 30 per cent knew precisely where there was a firm of solicitors. Half the respondents did not know even imprecisely of a firm. Only 5 per cent knew that one simply went to a lawyers' office to obtain legal advice under the statutory scheme. Only 18 per cent knew how to apply for legal aid—either criminal or civil. Of those who knew a firm of solicitors, the largest single category of response to the question of how they had come to know of them was that the name-plate had been noticed. In so far as knowledge of what is available is a prerequisite to any solution to the problem of unmet legal need, much more needs to be done to increase the extent of public awareness of available facilities and how to use them.

Knowledge of the services—how to use them and where to find them—was greater in the higher social classes and among those with greater financial resources. They were much more likely to know of a solicitor and to have been in contact with one during the last seven years. In the case of knowledge of citizens' advice bureaux, there were no significant class and income differences. But only 12 per cent of those classified as entitled to free legal aid had spoken to a solicitor in the last seven years. Only 5 per cent of this group knew that one went to a solicitor to get legal aid, though a further 5 per cent thought one went to a court, which would be a correct answer in the case of criminal legal aid. While 64 per cent of this group said that they knew that a poor person could get free or cheap advice from a solicitor in his office, only 5 per cent of the total sample knew how to obtain it. In general, extremely few of those for whom the statutory schemes were designed knew how to use them.

This ignorance about how to use the services no doubt contributed to the limited use actually made of them. This was particularly serious in the case of court hearings. Out of a total of 132 court hearings reported to us in our population survey, no legal aid was applied for in the case of 105 hearings, in some of which it appeared from the facts reported to us that legal aid might have been granted. On the other hand, in only 16 out of 85 cases where no lawyer represented the client in court did the respondent consider that a better result would have been obtained with the help of a lawyer. This may have been a realistic assessment or alternatively may have been the result of ignorance of what a professional advocate can achieve.

If all the specific needs for advice recorded in our population survey are added together, we found that, among those entitled to legal aid at the time of interview, advice of any kind had been taken on 38 per cent of the problems we had recorded and 50 per cent in the case of those not entitled to legal aid. We found that advice had been taken on 54 per cent of the problems reported by professional and non-manual workers, 39 per cent by skilled manual workers, and 42 per cent by semi-skilled and unskilled workers. Thus, as expected, the poorer and those in the lower social classes were less likely to have taken advice, but the figures show that unmet need is by no means confined to these groups.

Part of the problem is one of perception of need. Some respondents clearly did not look to the law to remedy situations for which legal remedies were available. Lawyers were seen as people who should primarily be consulted on housing, accidents, and money problems, and to a lesser extent on matrimonial, criminal, and probate matters.

But also important is the attitude of people to lawyers and the legal system. As many as 11 per cent of our respondents said that they would never to go a lawyer. This attitude was to be found more frequently among the lower social classes. Eleven per cent of skilled manual workers, 14 per cent of semi-skilled manual workers, and 17 per cent of unskilled manual workers said they would never go to a solicitor, but the number also included 3 per cent of professionals. It may be relevant to note in this connection that 45 per cent of our respondents would prefer a lawyer who normally acted for people like themselves, compared with 30 per cent who preferred a lawyer who was prepared to act for either side—landlord as well as tenant, retailer as well as consumer. The better off respondents and those in the higher social classes were much more likely to prefer the 'two-sided' lawyer.

One conclusion which could be drawn from this study of three boroughs, which, especially in the case of Tower Hamlets, were relatively well endowed with services, is that the advisory services were not only ineffective but inefficient. That they were ineffective is indicated by the substantial extent of unmet need. That they were inefficient is suggested by the extensive sifting or referral function performed by the citizens' advice bureaux, local authorities, probation officers, and others. If, with better knowledge and more favourable attitudes, people found their way to the right agency first, not only could there be a substantial manpower saving in the advisory services as a whole, but there could be a substantial saving in the time people devoted to trying to meet their legal needs. One key point which has failed to get across is that the first step in obtaining statutory legal aid or legal advice is simply to walk into a solicitor's office who is listed as offering the service. Nearly a fifth of the respondents who said that they knew about the legal advice scheme did not associate it with solicitors in their private offices.

If these deficiencies were to be remedied much more would be needed than the display of more or better posters in post offices. Part of the problem is probably the image of solicitors in the eyes of those who have not previously used their services. Citizens' advice bureaux appear to be readily approached by all social classes, while not all are willing to approach solicitors. If some means were found of presenting solicitors to the public —particularly to those with manual occupations—as more approachable, just as bank managers have been presented in advertisements over the last few years, more people might go directly to solicitors—though whether all solicitors would be able to meet their needs is another question.

But it is much easier to portray in a television or film insert the precise services which a bank manager offers than those which a solicitor offers. It is not easy to explain precisely where the law provides a remedy. Thus, what at first sight appears to be inefficiency in the advisory services may need to be not only tolerated but provided for. It is the citizens' advice bureau staffs and the receptionists and duty officers in a whole range of public services who sift the citizens' problems and pilot them through the growing maze of services. The more varied the channels of information and advice, the more of those who need pointing in the right direction may find their way to the right destination. Thus, sorting services may have a permanent, indeed critical, role to play in the advisory system. How effective they are in this capacity will depend on the extent of recognition that this is one of their explicit functions for which their staffs need careful training. It will depend also on the scale of financial provision for services of this kind. It may also be affected by the proximity or otherwise to each other of the facilities such as solicitors' firms, legal advice centres, and citizens' advice bureaux. Further research may reveal that lawyers are best placed if they are in or very close to citizens' advice bureaux, but it is also possible that much the same effect can be achieved if they are spread in the community and appropriate mechanisms are developed for steering the client to the right lawyer. Research may also show the value of simple procedures such as ensuring that anyone who comes into hospital after an accident automatically receives a leaflet about legal advice and how it can be obtained.

It seems certain that if the legal advisory services are to fulfil their intended function, they will need to have much closer links with the communities which they are serving and much better channels of communication with all their potential users. There are experiences in the United States as well as in Britain which could be valuable in developing new and experimental schemes to meet this objective. This is not the place to set out the various alternative solutions which are currently being canvassed or to describe the different experimental services which have been set up or are being planned. But what seems to be needed is research into the various ways of reaching into the community to educate people in their legal rights, to help them identify legal problems, and to inform them of what action can be taken with appropriate advice.

Our survey has shown substantial unmet need particularly among those with low incomes and of low social class in three London boroughs which were relatively well provided with services. We have indicated some of the barriers to the fuller use of these services. We would be surprised if the extent of unmet need were less in the country as a whole. Solutions will need to be found to these problems if the legal system is to be used by all those whom it is intended to serve.

APPENDIX I

Method of Research for the Agency Survey

Introduction: the 'ideal' method

All the agencies in the three boroughs described in Chapters 2 and 3 which appeared to play some part in advising or referring to advisory agencies were visited or contacted. Ideally we would have liked to observe all these agencies in action and obtain systematic data about the use made of them, the characteristics of those who used them, the services which they received, and details about referrals to other agencies. Such information would have been collected on purpose-built forms drawn up by the research workers in consultation with the agencies, under the supervision and guidance of the research team.

The problems presented to agencies vary in complexity: some calls may be for information, other visits may require skilled advice over weeks and months. Some agencies act as referring agencies (for example the police and hospitals), while others may advise someone over a period of time and possibly conduct correspondence. Thus in addition to collecting crude statistics about how many people come to an office with certain types of problems, it would have been desirable to refine such information by using some uniform criteria based on seriousness, importance to the client, and legal complexity. Moreover all this information about the use of agencies' services would need to be collected at random intervals over a period of a year to allow for fluctuating periods of demand.

We were not, however, able to undertake this 'ideal' programme of research for all the agencies operating within the borough or providing services to people living within the three boroughs. Our resources did not permit us to gather anything other than impressionistic material from many of the national organizations. Moreover it would have been extremely difficult to collect systematic data for the three boroughs from trade unions owing to the administrative structure which has already been described in Chapters 2 and 3, and the large number of trade union officials who may be consulted by members. Similarly, in the case of newspapers which provide advice by post and receive large volumes of letters from all over the country it would have been an enormous task to examine their correspondence systematically to identify the writers from the three boroughs we were studying.

Confidentiality

Confidentiality was another barrier to the collection of data based on the ideal method described above. Some agencies—for example, the police—refused altogether to provide us with information for this reason. For other agencies the issue of confidentiality had two aspects. Some agencies were worried lest the survey would damage the confidence of clients in the service provided. For example, citizens' advice bureaux regard it as particularly important that clients should know that their private affairs are not divulged to others without their consent. Some citizens' advice bureaux are for this reason careful not to ask for information (e.g. name, address, or marital status) which is not relevant to the problem. Other agencies, like the probation service, were particularly concerned that the presence of a worker at an interview might have an inhibiting effect on client/worker relationships. The Inner London probation service, despite a very heavy burden of work, nevertheless agreed to record certain information for us. The citizens' advice bureaux, for their part, were prepared to allow us to be present during interviews. This had never been permitted before for research purposes. In a busy citizens' advice bureau this meant considerable disruption of the office. We are extremely grateful to the organizers and helpers for their unfailingly helpful co-operation with the survey.

Use of Agencies outside the Three Boroughs

We were not able to discover the use made of agencies outside the three boroughs. Some agencies are unevenly distributed in the three boroughs so it is probable that some residents visit agencies which are convenient to their place of work. For example, to what extent do Southwark residents use citizens' advice bureaux outside that borough, and to what extent do Tower Hamlets residents go to solicitors elsewhere? Some national services like the probation service in Inner London do not operate on a borough basis, so we included all offices which covered any part of the Borough. For example, two of the three probation offices covering Islington were not situated within the borough boundaries and had clients from

Hackney as well as Islington. The police, county, and magistrates' courts' boundaries are not generally identical with borough boundaries. Police and courts' experience and practice may differ, therefore, within London boroughs as well as in different areas of the country.

In the case of local organizations only those units located in the three boroughs were studied. The one exception was Mary Ward Legal Advice Centre which was known to be used by a number of referring agencies including citizens' advice bureaux and probation officers north of the river. We decided to include Mary Ward not only for this reason but also because it was one of the three full-time legal advice centres in the Inner London boroughs. The only individuals working partly outside the boroughs were one or two of the Members of Parliament, whose constituency boundaries were not coterminous with borough boundaries. The greater proportion of those in the constituency of Shoreditch and Finsbury live in the borough of Hackney. Other national organizations like the courts, hospitals, and Ministry of Social Security operate through many offices and units. No doubt the volume of advice varies among the different units, moreover different courts and hospitals have no uniform policy on the questions covered by this survey. With our limited resources it was not possible to visit all the hospitals and Ministry of Social Security offices in the three boroughs, though we did visit most of the county courts and magistrates' courts.

For the reasons already outlined, we were not able to collect systematic data for all local and national agencies. In addition we decided, after visits of observation, not to ask some departments to record information for us. The public health departments would have presented special problems in the collection of data: many enquiries come by telephone and letter (which we excluded early on in our survey). There might be as many as fifty people in the office who would handle requests for advice. Other agencies, like housing departments, received few enquiries that were not in connection with their normal work.

Data Collection
Our data was collected in two ways. Firstly there were interviews with a senior official supplemented by visits of observation to a few agencies. Some data was collected exclusively by interview, most of it in person but some by telephone. Secondly, more systematic data was collected by asking agencies to record for us (or to allow us to record on their behalf) certain information.

We wanted systematic and uniform information from all agencies. As our forms would be filled in by a large number of staff in several of the agencies, we had to restrict the information requested to a basic minimum. Some of these forms had to be filled in at public counters, or in rooms where more than the member of staff and enquirer would be present, so we could not ask for any details about income. Nor did we feel it tactful to ask questions about age, though in the employment question we could discover if a person was still at school or was retired. Another major difficulty was caused by the confidentiality issue: we could not ask for the caller's exact address, which would have been the only sure way of discovering whether he lived in the borough or not. Instead we asked for the caller's postal district, knowing that London postal districts do not exactly coincide with borough boundaries. Because the agencies were busy, we could not ask them to collect information for us on the previous history of the client's problem, beyond discovering who had referred him to the agency.

Copies of the recording schedules used for the survey are filed in the British Library of Economics and Political Science. Answers to nearly all our questions were obtained by most agencies during the interview with the client—sometimes with the help of the survey workers. There were greater difficulties where the research workers had to fill in the forms themselves from records and files. In the two children's departments information was recorded only for those people entered in the office day book (which is primarily designed to record applications for receptions into care). Any other callers to the department who were referred elsewhere or who had an interview with a child care officer were not recorded. In this case our information was almost entirely derived from office files which the departments were kind enough to make available. Information was not obtained about other casual callers whom child care officers saw during the recording week.

Some agencies, however, did not record the information during the interview, either because the agency was not willing to let the client know that the survey was being undertaken, or because it would take too much of the staff's time. At Mary Ward Legal Advice Centre there was the special problem of large numbers of voluntary lawyers who attended on Wednesday evenings who it was thought could not all be briefed and persuaded to co-operate in the survey. Information for some agencies was therefore collected by the survey workers either from office files exclusively or from oral information supplied by an agency worker, sometimes supplemented by office files. Tables 1 and 2 show the methods used for collecting data at the different agencies.

TABLE I COLLECTION OF DATA: AGENCIES FOR WHICH SYSTEMATIC INFORMATION WAS COLLECTED

Agency	No. of visits by clients recorded	Method of recording	Period of study
Legal Dept., Islington	58	Survey worker during interview	1 consecutive week
Members of Parliament			
Islington S.W.	1	do.	1 do.
Bethnal Green	8	do.	1 do.
Islington North	12	do.	1 do.
Toynbee Hall Legal Advice Centre	179	Agency during interview with survey worker present	4 evenings
Citizens' Advice Bureaux			
Finsbury	39	do.	1 consecutive week
Islington	104	do.	1 do.
Southwark	122	do.	1 do.
St Margaret's House	45	do.	1 do.
Toynbee Hall	95	do.	1 do.
Poplar House	123	do.	1 do.
Pilgrim House	44	do.	1 do.
Dame Colet	38	do.	1 do.
Jewish Institute	66	do.	1 do.
Legal Dept., Tower Hamlets	22	do.	1 do.
Housing Section of Legal Dept., Islington	24	Agency during interview	1 do.
Maternity and Child Welfare Clinics, Islington	126	do.	1 do.
Information Centre, Southwark	110	do.	1 do.
Welfare, Southwark	52	do.	1 do.
Welfare (Homeless), Tower Hamlets	15	do.	1 do.
Family Advice Centre, Isle of Dogs	22	do.	2 do.
Rent Officer, Southwark	19	do.	1 do.
Rent Officer, Islington	65	do.	1 do.

Table 1—*contd.*

Agency	No. of visits by clients recorded	Method of recording	Period of study
Stepney Tories, Legal Advice Centre	6	do.	6 evenings
University House, Legal Advice Centre	78	do.	1 consecutive week
Bernhard Baron, Legal Advice Centre	34	do.	6 evenings
Dame Colet, Legal Advice Centre	47	do.	4 do.
Probation Service			
3 Islington and Hackney offices	128	do.	1 consecutive week
3 Southwark offices	54	do.	1 do.
3 Tower Hamlets offices	22	do.	1 do.
Peckham Conservatives	9	do.	4 evenings
Cambridge House Legal Advice Centre	54	Survey worker from records	1 consecutive week
Family Advice Centre			
Southwark	21	Survey worker from records + agency information	2 consecutive weeks
Shadwell	38	do.	2 do.
Toynbee	24	do.	2 do.
Children's Dept., Southwark	21	Survey worker from records	1 do.
Children's Dept., Tower Hamlets	11	do.	1 do.
Mary Ward Legal Advice Centre	107	do.	1 do.
Total Schedules:	2,043		

TABLE 2 COLLECTION OF DATA: AGENCIES FOR WHICH LESS SYSTEMATIC INFORMATION WAS OBTAINED

Agency	Methods of Collecting Data Interview (personal or telephone)	Visit of observation
Courts—County	X	
Courts—Magistrates	X	
Hospitals	X	
Legal Advice Centres		
Leysian Mission	X	
Poor Man's Lawyer, Islington	X	
Friends House, Islington	X	X
Local Authority Departments		
Children (Islington)	X	
Housing (Southwark)	X	
Housing (Tower Hamlets)	X	X
Information (Tower Hamlets)	X	
Legal (Southwark)	X	
Public Health (Tower Hamlets)	X	X
Welfare (Islington)	X	
Members of Parliament		
Shoreditch and Finsbury	X	
Islington East	X	
Peckham	X	
Bermondsey	X	X
Dulwich	X	
Poplar	X	
Stepney	X	
Southwark	X	
Ministry of Social Security	X	
Police	X	
Political Parties		
Conservative candidate for Southwark	X	
Liberal candidates	X	
Rent Tribunals	X	
Rent Officer, Tower Hamlets	X	
Trade Unions	X	

Briefing Procedures

We tried to brief as many members of staff in the organizations which were recording for us, though obviously in big local authority departments we could not expect a meeting to be called to enable us to do so. We were not able to brief staff in the maternity and child welfare clinics in Islington, and the two welfare departments. In other local authority departments (information services, housing and rent officers) we had discussions with the staff who were doing the recording, while in the legal departments a survey worker was present in Tower Hamlets on the first day and in Islington for the whole week, which enabled us to answer queries on the procedures. All but two of the citizens' advice bureau organizers came to a conference of citizens' advice bureau organizers held to discuss the survey at the London School of Economics. The draft form was discussed and subsequently amended. A survey worker was present on the first and third day of the recording weeks for citizens' advice bureaux, and thus was able to demonstrate the use of the schedule and to answer any queries that arose. Briefing procedures for probation officers were less comprehensive. About half of the senior probation officers attended a meeting at the Inner London Probation head office where the draft recording schedule was discussed. There were no meetings with probation officers in the nine offices, nor was the research worker present during the recording week, although she had talked to at least one senior probation officer in each office. We did, however, write an explanatory letter for all officers.

There was no need for briefing procedures at two of the legal advice centres (Cambridge House and Mary Ward), as the survey workers filled in the forms themselves. At Toynbee Hall the survey workers acted as interviewers during the recording weeks, and could thus answer queries or fill in gaps where items had been overlooked. At University House and Bernhard Baron we had discussions with the organizers and the forms were filled in by only one person at each of these agencies.

Classification and Coding

Although we had tried to brief as many people as possible, and despite our general notes for agencies on the schedules, there was still some difficulty over the classification of problems. We excluded as 'departmental' any problems coming to a department because one of its functions was to deal with them. For example, visits of clients on probation, supervision, or after-care were considered to be 'departmental' and also visits made to local authority legal departments in connection with compulsory purchase orders of houses. This latter type of enquiry created difficulties of definition and may not have been uniformly classified. There were other problems of classification in other agencies: for example, in one citizens' advice bureau many problems were categorized as being social security problems though all the client wanted was to have a pension book signed because he was illiterate or could not read English. There may have been other errors in classifications of which we were not aware because we were not always present in the agencies during the recording.

All the recording schedules were processed in the survey office. In this way the differences in the various schedules could be allowed for in the programming and codes allocated to parts of the schedules which were not pre-coded. In our coding schedule we had a possible range of 31 types of problem about which the client consulted the agency, and 26 possible places to which the client might have been referred as a result of his visit.

The agencies were asked to record only personal visits, not telephone or written requests for information and help. The agencies were recording visits during a specific period. Thus, in the case of agencies open every day, if a caller came twice in a week he would have been recorded twice. But when a caller was sent away on the same day to get further information (as happened at one citizens' advice bureau on one occasion) he was only recorded once. In other words we were recording visits made during the recording period, not cases or problems dealt with during that period. If a person came with multiple problems, then the agencies recorded all of them, but in the survey office such schedules were amended so that only the most 'legal' problem was included in the analysis. For example, if a woman came to consult the worker about difficulties over supplementary benefit and a divorce or separation, then the divorce was the problem coded.

Ideally we would have liked to be able to gauge the seriousness of every problem recorded on every schedule. We would also have liked to assess the seriousness by some standard of legal complexity and the need to consult a lawyer. Some problems might have been legally complex but not normally thought of as being suitable for a lawyer; for example, questions of social security law. The best way of doing this would have been for the survey workers to assess the seriousness on an agreed basis. But as has been seen most of the agencies could not agree to our being present at interviews. It was not possible to ask agencies to gauge the seriousness, as very elaborate briefing procedures would have been needed to ensure that the coding was standardized. For these two reasons it was only possible to get any assessment of seriousness and legal complexity when a survey worker was present. The citizens' advice bureaux agreed to allow us to be present in the bureaux and thus we were able to make this assessment ourselves. Inevitably opinions about seriousness (from the clients' or from an 'objective' point of view) will vary, but at least we were able to be consistent in making our assessments. We show in Table 3 the main criteria used. The probation officers made their own individual assessment as to whether the caller's problem was legal in the sense of requiring the services of a lawyer.

Fieldwork

The main part of the fieldwork was completed between July 1967 and March 1968. During these nine months the headquarters of each organization had to be contacted to obtain permission to do the research. Then further consultation and briefing meetings had to be held, and recording schedules drafted. In addition, the actual period of recording the work had to fit in with the organization's own arrangements, e.g. citizens' advice bureaux take students during the vacations and could not undertake the further work of the survey at the same time. For all these reasons, the visits of observation and recording periods were not always at times convenient for the research. For example, we were only able to attend each citizens' advice bureau for two days during the two weeks they were recording for us, because we were arranging the recording of the work of the probation service at the same time.

Some field work was carried out in August 1968 when a few visits to agencies were made, e.g. to one newly set up legal advice centre in Islington and to those agencies which had proved difficult to contact earlier. The remaining fieldwork was carried out in October and November 1968. Interviews with solicitors on the legal advice panels were carried out during those two months. The solicitors who agreed to record information about new clients did so during that period.

Recording Period

For all these reasons it was not possible to collect our information over periods chosen on a wholly random basis spread over a sufficient period to allow for seasonal variations. This could not be arranged partly because of the need to fit in with the convenience

TABLE 3 MINOR AND MAJOR LEGAL PROBLEMS IN CITIZENS' ADVICE BUREAUX

Type of Problem	Minor legal	Major legal
Landlord and tenant	No rent book Notice to quit Bad state of repair	Harassment Eviction notice Very bad state of repair Rent Tribunal or Rent Officer proceedings
Debt	Under £5	Over £5
Wills, Winding up estates	Under £5 estate Letters of administration Make will Considering dispute over will	Over £5 estate Dispute will
Personal Injuries	Hospital 1–4 days Minor injuries (i.e. not broken limbs) Pain and suffering	In hospital over five days Major injuries: broken limbs Death Unable to work for six months or more
Employment	Holiday pay dispute Bad working conditions	Dismissal without notice Dangerous working conditions Redundancy
Matrimonial	Variation of maintenance orders Access to children	Divorce, separation and maintenance proceedings Custody of children
Affiliation	Tracing putative father Variation of affiliation order	Proceedings for order Proceedings for order to be quashed

TABLE 3—contd.

Type of Problem	Minor legal	Major legal
Social Security	Delays for 2–3 weeks in payments of benefits Suspension from unemployment benefit	Appeals to tribunals and committees
Criminal	Larceny proceedings	In custody Drug charges Receiving charges
Neighbour	Assaults Slander Disputes about access to house/garden	
Legal Aid	Make application	Appeal to Area Office

of the agencies and partly because of the difficulty of providing proper supervision to so many agencies at the same time. Some of the agencies we were studying operated daily, others opened part of the week, while yet others opened one or two evenings a week.

Agencies were asked to record clients for one week, if they were open daily. Part-time organizations (those open 2–3 days per week) recorded clients for a fortnight, while those open one evening a week recorded clients for four evenings. We decided on the one week because in some busy organizations like citizens' advice bureaux, the probation service, and solicitors' offices, a week was the maximum period we could expect them to tolerate this extra burden. As the research worker did the recording during M.P.s surgeries, it was not possible to record more than one evening's work for each of the three Members of Parliament who consented to allow this.

The statistical data for all agencies except solicitors was collected from the first week in October 1967 to the third week in March 1968. The probation officers recorded their callers for the same week, except for two offices which recorded during the succeeding week. Citizens' advice bureaux recorded their clients during different weeks falling between 1 January to 20 February 1968. Legal Advice Centre clients were recorded mainly in October 1967 at daily centres, while the one-evening-a-week centres recorded their clients from October to December 1967. One extra recording session at Toynbee Hall legal advice centre was undertaken on 21 February 1968 because the number of schedules we had obtained did not tally with Toynbee's figures and we suspected that forms for quite a number of clients had not been completed.

Data to Represent Three Months' Work by Agencies
To show the data on a common time basis, we multiplied all of it to represent twelve weeks' work by each organization. This assumes that the recording period was representative, which may not have been the case. We might have chosen to multiply the work recorded to represent six or twelve months' work. But as some agencies close completely for the summer (for example some of the legal advice centres and some Members of Parliament's surgeries) this would have exaggerated their volume of work. Many agencies—in local authority departments in particular—told us that the number of callers dropped from July to October. On the other hand, we may have minimized the work done by some other organizations. During the two-week period when Islington citizens' advice bureaux were recording visits, there was snow and ice on the streets and it was extremely cold: this may have reduced the number of callers to below the average. In order to make all our data represent the same length of time of twelve weeks, we multiplied by twelve the work recorded for us by the seven citizens' advice bureaux, local authority departments, and Members of Parliament. We multiplied by six the data collected by the family advice centres and by two citizens' advice bureaux. We multiplied by two the work done by Bernhard Baron and the Stepney Tories Legal Advice Centres. It would be possible therefore to compare our figures if multiplied by four, with each organization's statistics for the year. It is important to remember, however, that our survey was not able to take account of any seasonal variations in the use made of each agency. Moreover some agencies' statistics are collected on a different basis, e.g. citizens' advice bureaux record the number of problems raised rather than the number of visitors. Moreover telephone calls and letters are included in their statistics but not in ours.

Comparison of Survey Data with Agencies' Statistics
Table 4 shows the agencies' own statistics compared with figures, 'blown up' to represent a year. Some of the agencies are not included in this table because they do not keep routine statistics: for example, University House Legal Advice Centre only started to do so at the

Table 4 Comparison of work done [agencies' own statistics and our estimates]

		Agency statistics	Estimated figures based on recording schedule*
Legal Advice Centres			
Cambridge House		4,330 (1967–8 interviews)	2,592
Mary Ward		7,272 (1967 interviews)	5,136
Toynbee Hall		2,790 (1967–8 interviews)	2,148
	Total:	14,092	9,876
Citizens' Advice Bureaux†			
Finsbury		4,196 (1967–8 total calls)	1,872
Islington		10,139 do.	4,992
Southwark		14,127 do.	5,856
St Margaret's House		4,040 do.	2,160
Toynbee		5,860 do.	4,560
Poplar House		10,777 do.	5,904
Pilgrim House		3,397 do.	2,112
Dame Colet		1,065 do.	912
Jewish Institute		1,702 do.	1,584
	Total:	55,503	29,952
Probation Service			
Islington (and Hackney)		5,435 (1967 returns)	6,000
Southwark		2,148 do.	2,592
Tower Hamlets		2,137 do.	864

* Our figures do not include telephone and letter enquiries.
† Citizens' advice bureaux statistics count number of problems, and include those made by telephone and letter.

time of our recording week. We have used the most up-to-date figures we could obtain from the agencies: those for the probation service were for 1967, and those for other agencies were for 1966–7 or 1967–8.

The records of two of the three legal advice centres show sub-tantially more work done in a year than our estimates indicate. Their figures were based on total number of interviews rather than cases or new cases. There is also some considerable difference between our estimated figures and the citizens' advice bureau's own figures. As mentioned earlier, their figure for 'Total calls' included enquiries made by telephone or letter, which we excluded from our survey.

The probation service figures for 1967 were compiled from confidential tables supplied by the service and estimated for the five court areas: North London and Old Street for Islington and Hackney, Tower Bridge and Southwark Juvenile Court for Southwark, and Thames Court for Tower Hamlets. These figures include miscellaneous work (other than home contacts and escort duties), and matrimonial enquiry work (other than social enquiries, enquiries under the Guardianship of Infants Act 1925, and adoption enquiries). The figures for Southwark and Islington and Hackney based on our schedules show a greater volume of work than the returns for 1967.

The Sample Used for the Population Survey

Drawing the sample from the electoral register inevitably involved omissions when the respondent had never been on the register and losses where respondents had moved during the time which elapsed between the collection of the particulars for the register and the survey. Some moved outside the three boroughs and we lacked the resources to try to track them down in their new addresses, even in the rare cases where we were able to obtain them. The register we used was that in force from 16 February 1967 to 15 February 1968 and was based on information collected on 10 October 1966. The main survey was launched in October 1967 and interviewing was completed by March 1968. This was much later than we had planned when we drew the original sample, owing to the large number of pre-pilots and the many different drafts of the questionnaire. In the event, the proportion of respondents who were not available for interview was higher than we had anticipated or would have wished.

Using a sampling fraction of 1/170 we obtained a total of 2,827 names—853 in Islington, 1,168 in Southwark, and 806 in Tower Hamlets. (In drawing up the sample we excluded those on the electoral register marked with an 'S' (Service Voters), an 'L', or 'LC' (not entitled to vote at a Parliamentary election), and a 'Y' (entitled to vote only after October 1967). We used 161 of these names in the pre-pilots and the pilot, leaving us with a total of 2,666 names for the main survey—807 in Islington, 1,096 in Southwark, and 763 in Tower Hamlets.)

We recruited forty-two interviewers, most of whom had extensive experience in commercial surveys. We paid 30s. (£1·50) for each completed interview and 10s. (50p) for cases where there was no contact after four attempts except for cases where the first or subsequent attempts established that contact was impossible—for instance because of death or removal from the boroughs. A total of three days were devoted to briefing and training for the pilots and the main survey. Not only was the questionnaire explained and discussed at length, but dummy interviews were demonstrated and conducted under supervision.

Partly no doubt because of the interval of a year or more between the preparation of the electoral register from which the samples were drawn and the interviewing, there were 408 ineffective addresses: 52 respondents had died, 48 houses had been demolished, 40 were empty, and 266 respondents had moved outside the three boroughs. Two respondents were in prison.

We interviewed 1,651 respondents out of the remaining 2,258—73 per cent. We were refused interviews by 362 respondents: in 51 cases the reason given was disability or severe illness. A further four respondents failed repeatedly to keep the appointments which they had made with our interviewers. No contact was made with 241 respondents, despite four attempts at different times of the day; of these 67 were said to be away. The full position regarding the sample was therefore as follows:

Total sample drawn		2,827
Less: *those used in pre-pilots and pilot*		161
		2,666
Less: *Ineffective addresses*		
Died	52	
House demolished	48	
House empty	40	
Moved	266	
In prison	2	
		408
		2,258
Less: *Not interviewed*		
Refusals	362	
No contact	245	
		607
Respondents interviewed		1,651

The ineffective addresses and non-respondents are analysed according to borough in Table 1. There were no major differences in this respect between the three boroughs.

I

TABLE I　Non-response rate by borough

	Islington		Southwark		Tower Hamlets		Total	
Respondents	484	60%	701	64%	466	61%	1,651	
Non-respondents	323	40%	395	36%	297	39%	1,015	
Total:	807	100%	1,096	100%	763	100%	2,666	
Non-respondents	323	32%	395	39%	297	29%	1,015	100%
Total:	807	30%	1,096	41%	763	29%	2,666	100%

As a check on the representativeness of our respondents, we show in Table 2 those characteristics of our respondents which can be compared with data from the 1966 sample census of population for the three boroughs.

The slightly lower proportions of male and single people among our respondents is consistent with the greater mobility to be expected in these two categories. The lower proportion of Commonwealth immigrants may also be due to higher mobility but also partly due to under representation on the electoral role, though some of our respondents may have been erroneously classified as foreign. As would be expected, the proportion of respondents in private rented accommodation was lower than found in the census. Again those in private rented accommodation are likely to be more mobile.

Table 2 also shows a comparison of the social class composition of our sample with that from the 1966 sample census. No breakdown of social class III into manual and non-manual for the census was available. There was a higher proportion in our sample than in the census who could not be classified either because of a refusal to provide the information or because the information provided was not precise enough for coding. The comparison indicates an over-representation in our sample of social classes I and II—particularly the former—and a slight under representation of the other social classes—particularly social class V. This again is likely to be due to the greater mobility to be expected in these social classes.

We obtained further data on the education of our respondents which could not be compared with information collected in the 1966 sample census. A total of 86 per cent of our respondents had left school at the age of 15 or earlier including 3 per cent who had left school before age 12. Eight per cent had left school at the age

Table 2   Characteristics of respondents and census population

		Respondents	Sample Census 1966*
Sex	Male	46	48
	Female	54	52
Marital Status	Married	71	71
	Divorced	2	1
	Widowed	14	11
	Single	14	17
Country of Origin	British Isles	87	84
	Ulster and Ireland	5	5
	Commonwealth	4	8
	Foreign and at sea	4	3
	Visitor and not stated	—	1
Housing tenure	Owner occupied	10	10
	Council rented	41	37
	Private rented	47	50
	Other or not stated	2	3
Social class			
All males	I		2·0
	II		8·0
	III		49·4
	IV		21·6
	V		15·8
Unclassified			3·3
Economically Active Males	I	3·3	2·1
	II	8·7	8·3
	III	49·8	51·0
	IV	21·5	21·8
	V	13·0	15·6
Unclassified		3·9	1·2

* For age and marital status data, the figures given are for persons aged over 22. To allocate persons to marital status in the age group 20–24, it is assumed that no one under 22 was widowed or divorced and that half of those married in this age group were aged over 22.

of 16, leaving 5 per cent who continued their education beyond this age. Only 2 per cent had had any full-time education beyond the age of 18. As a result 90 per cent had no educational qualifications, 4 per cent had only one or more 'O' levels or the equivalent, 2 per cent some form of technical school qualification, 1 per cent had one or more 'A' level, 1 per cent had passed a University examination and the remainder had other post-school qualifications.

When asking respondents about their legal problems and what they had done about them we tried to discover whether the information given related to problems they had had whilst living at their present address or elsewhere in the three boroughs covered by the survey. The overwhelming majority of the problems reported (88 per cent) occurred while the respondent was living at his present address. In another 7 per cent of cases the problem occurred while living elsewhere in the three boroughs and in only 5 per cent was the respondent living outside the boroughs.

A total of seventy of the people interviewed told us that they were unable to give the full particulars of the income of themselves and of their husbands or wives. No doubt some preferred to say that they were unable when in fact they were unwilling. Out of the 70, 10 were men (8 of them married) and 60 were women (55 of them married). In most cases, the problem seemed to be that wives did not know their husbands' earnings, but there were also cases where the husband did not know his wife's earnings. There were 38 who said they were unable to tell us the family savings: again the majority were married women.

There were 115 respondents (roughly an equal number of men and women) who refused to say what the family income was and 118 who refused to give us information on the family savings. As expected, refusals were greatest in social classes I and II.

In Table 3 we show income by social class. While the higher social classes contained higher proportions in our higher income group, 7 per cent of families in our highest income category were in the lowest social class and a few families in the highest social class were entitled to free legal aid. In Table 4 we separate respondents 65 or over and under 65. Half the respondents aged 65 or over were in our free legal aid income group. About half of those under 65 were entitled to legal aid subject to contribution. Of those over 65, 5 per cent were above the legal aid limits whereas of those under 65 the proportion was 33 per cent. (See Table 5.)

The older respondents had a higher proportion in the two lower social classes.

Our respondents appear from such checks as were practicable and from other information about the three boroughs to be broadly representative of the population of the boroughs given the fact that our sample was drawn from an electoral register which was over a year out of date.

TABLE 3   INCOME GROUP OF RESPONDENTS BY SOCIAL CLASS

	I	II	III non-manual	III manual	IV	V	Unclassified		Total
More than £500 over legal aid limit	11	19	18	30	8	7	8	100	(90)
Up to £500 over legal aid limit	2	10	13	40	16	14	4	100	(375)
Contributory legal aid	1	5	12	38	23	16	5	100	(732)
Free legal aid	1	4	8	32	25	20	10	100	(266)
Don't know	—	19	4	51	19	4	3	100	(70)
Won't say	4	19	9	30	20	10	7	100	(115)
Unclassified	—	—	—	—	—	—	100	100	(3)
Total:	2	8	11	37	20	14	7	100	(1,651)

TABLE 4   INCOME OF RESPONDENTS BY AGE

	Over 65	Under 65	Total	
More than £500 over legal aid limit	1	6	5	(90)
Up to £500 over legal aid limit	4	27	23	(375)
Contributory legal aid	38	46	44	(732)
Free legal aid	50	8	17	(266)
Don't know, Won't say	7	12	11	(188)
Total:	100	100	100	(1,651)

TABLE 5   SOCIAL CLASS BY AGE

	I	II	III non-manual	III manual	IV	V	Unclassified		Total
Under 65	2	9	12	39	19	13	6	100	(1,332)
Over 65	—	6	9	30	26	21	7	100	(319)
Total:	2	8	11	37	20	14	7	100	(1,651)

Attitudes to the Legal System

In the attempt to probe our respondents' views on law, lawyers, the courts, and the legal system generally, we asked a series of thirty-five questions at the very end of the interview.[1] The answers to the questions are set out in Table 1 in the order in which they were put.

Most of the statements were strongly worded. Since most of them were leading questions which suggested the appropriate answers, we put in most instances the converse proposition so as not to bias the results. Thus, a statement asserted, 'The laws are made for the people and stand for what the people want', but also, 'The people never get a chance to say what sort of laws they want.' The statements were provocative and were intended to get a response.

However the proportion of respondents who expressed no view was never very low and in the case of some questions very large. It was lowest in answer to Question 13, where 16 per cent of respondents had no view. At the other end of the scale, 47 per cent were unable to express a view in answer to Question 26. There were three questions where over 40 per cent of respondents gave no answer. One was about the relative approachability of lawyers as compared with trade union officials. The other two were both about solicitors' charges. Question 1 suggested that 'Lawyers charge fair prices.' Almost twice as many respondents agreed as disagreed, but 46 per cent had no view. Question 27 suggested the reverse—that 'Lawyers often overcharge.' The results were strictly comparable. Almost 40 per cent disagreed. Just over 10 per cent agreed and just under half had no view. In most other questions the Don't Know category accounted for between 20 and 35 per cent of the total. Extreme

---

[1] The interview schedule instructed the interviewer to say: 'I would now like to ask you some questions about your attitude to lawyers, to the law, and to the courts. Would you prefer to read them for yourself? Please mark the box which best expresses your feeling about each question. There are no right or wrong answers and no catch questions. Everyone has different answers to the questions and we just want to find out what people think.'

TABLE I ATTITUDES TO THE LEGAL SYSTEM

				Percentages		
	Dis- agree strongly	Dis- agree	No view	Agree	Strongly agree	Total
1. Lawyers charge fair prices	3	16	46	33	1	100
2. Lawyers help rich and poor alike with equal energy	6	33	22	37	2	100
3. Lawyers are dishonest	6	49	33	11	1	100
4. Lawyers have their offices in convenient places for the public	2	18	25	54	1	100
5. Lawyers are mainly interested in making money	1	20	21	52	6	100
6. Lawyers have a good understanding of the problems of the ordinary man	2	16	23	56	3	100
7. Lawyers are more sympathetic than doctors	3	47	36	14	1	100
8. In court no one cares whether one has a fair trial or not	7	53	24	15	1	100
9. The law favours the rich over the poor	4	33	19	38	6	100
10. There is no point in spending money for a lawyer to defend an innocent person	8	53	21	16	1	100
11. Lawyers instinctively take the side of the authorities rather than the ordinary man	4	43	29	22	2	100
12. You can expect to get a fair and sympathetic reception in a solicitor's office	—	6	25	66	2	100
13. When one goes into a solicitor's office one has no idea what it will cost one in the end	—	8	16	68	8	100
14. Judges give the same sentences to the poor as to the rich	5	32	20	41	2	100
15. Lawyers are a tricky lot	2	24	33	38	3	100
16. Lawyers are champions of the poor	5	41	36	16	1	100
17. Courts try to see that one gets fair trial	1	6	14	74	5	100
18. A lawyer will charge all he can	1	22	26	46	5	100
19. Lawyers will use only honest methods to get clients out of trouble	3	23	32	40	2	100
20. It would be nice to have a son who was a lawyer	1	11	25	55	7	100

TABLE I—*contd.*

				Percentages		
		Dis-agree strongly	Dis-agree	No view	Agree	Strongly agree	Total

		Disagree strongly	Disagree	No view	Agree	Strongly agree	Total
21.	When passing sentence the judge would tend to give longer sentences to the poor than to the rich for the same offence	5	41	24	26	4	100
22.	When it comes to advice about legal problems trade union officials are much more approachable than lawyers	3	21	45	27	4	100
23.	The law treats everyone alike	5	32	16	45	2	100
24.	The laws are made by the people and stand for what the people want	5	30	21	41	3	100
25.	For a price lawyers will use every trick in the book to help their clients	2	17	27	49	5	100
26.	Lawyers give the same attention to a poor client as to a rich one	4	36	22	36	1	100
27.	Lawyers often overcharge	—	13	47	36	3	100
28.	The courts are reasonably efficient	1	8	21	67	2	100
29.	The law is out of touch with modern conditions	1	25	29	39	5	100
30.	English judges are the best in the world	2	7	37	48	6	100
31.	The people never get a chance to say what kind of laws they want	5	51	21	22	1	100
32.	Lawyers are people whose main job is to defend criminals	3	49	18	29	1	100
33.	Anyone who pleads not guilty should be represented by a lawyer (not motoring cases)	—	6	21	67	4	100
34.	Keep away from lawyers	4	42	24	27	3	100
35.	The poor usually get the raw end of the stick in legal matters	4	39	21	33	3	100

opinions were expressed in only a small minority of cases. The proportions in the two outer categories of attitude (Disagree Strongly and Agree Strongly) varied from 2 to 10 per cent. In most questions they represented just over 5 per cent of the total. Most respondents either simply agreed or disagreed with the statements made.

The responses to forced-choice statements provide no opportunity for qualification, refinement, or explanation. The interpretation of responses to single statements is open to the objection that it is virtually impossible to frame statements which are unambiguous and open only to one interpretation. It is probable that many of our statements were interpreted in different ways by different respondents. Moreover, the particular way a question or statement is phrased may have an important effect on the response. Slight changes in wording or emphasis may create a different result. Nor are respondents always accurate in expressing their true opinions. Their answers may not reflect their true opinions because they have misread or misheard the question, or because they are simply wanting to get the interview finished, or because they are trying to please.

To achieve a somewhat higher degree of reliability we undertook a more systematic analysis of the material. We were fortunate to be guided in this part of our study by Dr A. P. E. L. Sealy, of the Psychology Department of the London School of Economics.

It is highly unlikely that our respondents had ever consciously thought out answers to the questions or statements we put to them before the interview. In answering questions of this kind a person tends to reflect his general attitude to the topic or subject matter and to answer by reference to that underlying attitude. It was this underlying attitude which we sought to ascertain by statistical analysis of the total responses.

There are two basic methods of approach to the task of attempting to unmask the real attitudes underlying responses to questions and statements of this kind: scaling and factor analysis. In scaling a set of items one tries to discover if a single dimension or attitude can be ascertained which underlies as many of the responses as possible. The dimension is identified simply by ascertaining the correlation between the items in the group. When a Likert-type scaling was carried out on the items in this study, it was found that the scale used only about one third of the total number of items. These items formed a single homogeneous cluster in terms of the attitudes[1] they measured; that is, each item correlated highly with

[1] For the psychologist attitudes can be said to be made up of: *beliefs*, which may be defined as probabilistic understanding of casual relationship between things; *opinions*, which are broader than beliefs and can be said to be made up of a number of beliefs; and *evaluations*, which are believed to be the case but which can be of varying weight in the mind of the person concerned. Together these make up his attitude to the subject matter in question.

the results based on the other items pooled together. But with this type of analysis the items that do not appear on the scale have to be discarded, since it is not known to what attitude dimensions, if any, they are linked. It was felt that this would be wasteful of items which could be used if a factor analysis were applied. In factor analysis the aim is to seek out all the groups of homogeneous items on the basis of the correlations between responses to items. The fact that the groups of items are small make this a more precise tool for measurement.

The method of analysis was to extract a predetermined number of factors and then to rotate them to make a simple structure, built up out of relatively few items, where each item is linked to few and, if possible, only one factor. This provides the sharpest and most unequivocal interpretation possible with the available material. The factors then represent a series of hypothetical entities which makes it possible to account for the observed relationships amongst responses. In the present study the assumption was that factors represent broad patterns of beliefs and attitudes underlying people's reaction to the law and the legal system.

The computer analysis produced two alternative methods of approach—one consisting of four and the other of six groups. The advantage of the six-group analysis was that it accounted for 42 per cent of the common variance as compared with 36 per cent in the case of the analysis based on four factors.[1] Also, with six factors there were fewer items that were included in more than one factor. But we were advised that with six factors some were not strong enough to merit reliance being placed on them. Only four factors, it seemed, were really interpretable and this, therefore, was the analysis we pursued.

The analysis presented here is necessarily tentative. In factoring a set of items it has to be borne in mind that several alternative solutions are possible. If, for instance, 30 factors had been established, the resulting material would be far too complex for analysis. If, on the other hand, we had used only one factor, interpretation would have been by reference to a principle too broad and vague to be meaningful. The four-factor analysis was chosen as what

---

[1] *Common variance* is that which is common between any two or more items or variables. The obverse of common variance is either *specific variance*—e.g. a specific meaning that a question has for a person which it shares with no other question—or *error variance*, which means differences resulting from such things as misunderstanding of the question, failure to mark the appropriate answer, desire to confuse the interviewer, inherent inconsistency, etc. The object of the analysis is to account for as high a proportion of common variance as possible.

seemed to be the best compromise between the aims of convenience and exhaustiveness. The factors are not presented as being very precise, but as approximate clusters of items which were statistically related.

The factor analysis identified four main factors, as set out in Table 2. This table also sets out the correlation coefficients of each question.[1]

TABLE 2 FACTOR ANALYSIS

	Factors			
	I	*II*	*III*	*IV*
Questions in the group				
Factor 1: '*Law is equality*'				
The law treats everyone alike	0·74	—	—	—
Judges give the same sentences to the poor as to the rich	0·68	—	—	—
When passing sentence the judge would tend to give longer sentences to the poor than to the rich	0·59	—	·37	—
The laws are made by the people and stand for what the people want	0·55	—	—	− 30
Lawyers are dishonest	0·54	− 20	·50	—
The law favours the rich over the poor	0·54	—	·39	—
Lawyers have their offices in convenient places	0·49	− 32	—	− 32
Lawyers give the same attention to a poor client as to a rich one	0·49	—	—	− 43
The law is out of touch with modern conditions	0·47	—	—	—
The poor usually get the raw end of the stick in legal matters	0·49	—	·55	—
Factor 2: '*The Legal System Works Well*'				
Courts try to see that one gets a fair trial	33	− 56	—	—
You can expect to get a fair and sympathetic reception in a solicitor's office	—	− 51	—	—
Anyone who pleads not guilty should be represented by a lawyer (not including motoring cases)	—	− 51	—	—
The courts are reasonably efficient	31	− 49	—	—
It would be nice to have a son who was a lawyer	—	− 41	—	—
English judges are the best in the world	24	− 42	—	—

[1] A correlation coefficient expresses whether two variables vary together—whether one increases as the other increases.

TABLE 2—*contd.*

			Factors	
	I	II	III	IV
Factor 3: 'Lawyers are a Tricky Lot'				
A lawyer will charge all he can	—	—	0·60	—
Lawyers instinctively take the side of the authorities rather than of the ordinary man	—	—	0·57	—
Keep away from lawyers	—	—	0·55	—
Lawyers are people whose main job is to defend criminals	—	—	−51	—
Lawyers are a tricky lot	—	—	0·51	—
Lawyers are mainly interested in making money	—	—	−49	—
There is no point in spending money for a lawyer to defend an innocent person	—	—	0·43	—
For a price lawyers will use every trick in the book to help their clients	—	—	44	—
Lawyers often overcharge	—	—	41	−37
Factor 4: 'Lawyers can be Trusted'				
Lawyers charge fair prices	—	—	—	−56
Lawyers help rich and poor alike with equal energy	—	—	—	−54
Lawyers are champions of the poor	—	—	—	−55
Lawyers have a good understanding of the problems of the ordinary man	—	−39	—	−49
Lawyers are more sympathetic than doctors	—	—	—	−47
Lawyers will use only honest methods to get clients out of trouble	—	—	—	−47

There were four statements which did not correlate clearly with any of the factors and which were, therefore, discarded:

'In court no one cares whether one has a fair trial or not'.

'When one goes into a solicitor's office one has no idea what it will cost one in the end.'

'When it comes to advice about legal problems, trade union officials are much more approachable than lawyers.'

'The people never get a chance to say what kind of laws they want.'

Most of the items making up Factor 1 are to do with the fairness of the system, and whether it holds the scales between different sections of the community. We summarized this as 'Law is Equality'.

The theme underlying Factor 2, which consists entirely of positively worded statements, is the competence or efficiency of the legal system, though fairness is also an element in the composition of the group. We have styled this factor 'The Legal System Works Well'.

All the items in Factor 3 concern lawyers and how they do their work. All the statements in the group with one exception expressed negative attitudes and were variations on the theme that 'Lawyers Are a Tricky Lot'. This is the title we gave to this factor.

The items in the last factor grouping consist of reactions to positively worded statements concerned with the perception of lawyers as a force for social support or social change. There were no items in the group that did not seem to belong with the possible exception of 26. We have called the factor 'Lawyers Can be Trusted'.

While Factor 1 is based on items that are worded both positively and negatively, Factors 2, 3, and 4 are based on items which are worded in one direction only. This means that for our purposes Factor 1 is the most reliable because respondents had to react to both favourable and unfavourable statements about the system. Factors 2, 3, and 4 by contrast are weaker because they only test responses to questions phrased in one direction. The effect of this is that some part of the differences between respondents in Factors 2, 3, and 4 may be due to response-tendencies rather than to the nature of the statement itself.

For the purpose of the analysis the response to each item was scored on a scale of 1 to 5 and the scores on all the items in the factor were aggregated. Since some of the items were positive statements ('Lawyers charge fair prices') and some negative ('A lawyer will charge all he can'), the scores on some items had to be reversed so as to make them comparable. Strong disagreement with a positive statement would imply a negative attitude about the system, while, conversely, strong disagreement with a negative statement would imply a positive attitude. The scores on all negative items were reversed (these were: Numbers 3, 8, 9, 10, 11, 13, 15, 18, 21, 22, 25, 27, 29, 31, 34, and 35).

When the scores had all been put on to the same basis we aggregated for each respondent within each factor. We analysed the responses by looking at the distribution of respondents in three categories: the 20 per cent who, by their aggregate scores within each factor, showed themselves most positive about the system, the middle 60 per cent, and the 20 per cent who showed themselves most negative about the system. High scores indicated a positive attitude, low scores a negative attitude. We then correlated the responses to the attitude questions with the income, capital, social class, sex, age of school leaving, education, work state, and marital status of our respondents. We also correlated their responses with their knowledge of legal advice and of legal aid, and of solicitors' firms, as well as whether they had spoken to a firm of solicitors during the previous seven years.

The results were then checked for significance by the chi-squared test.

With an analysis based on four factors and thirteen variables there was a possible total of 52 tables. Of these, 22 were statistically significant. Instead of setting all these out in full we have expressed the results in the form of a correlation coefficient which makes it possible to produce them all except Marital Status in one table. Table 3 shows the four factors and a figure representing the correlation coefficient wherever the result was significant by the chi-squared test. The significance of the correlation coefficient is expressed by an asterisk if significant at the 5 per cent level and by two asterisks if significant at the 1 per cent level. The plus sign indicates correlation between rising income, capital, social class, etc., and more positive feelings about the legal system, while a minus sign shows the opposite: a correlation between rising income, social class, etc., and more negative feelings about the system.

The only variable which could not be summarized in Table 3 was that for marital status—because there is no sequential relationship between the categories of married/single/divorced, etc., as there is in the other groups. Marital status was significant by the chi-squared test on Factors 2, 3, and 4. On Factors 2 and 3 married respondents were relatively more positive and the widowed and divorced more negative. On Factor 4 the position was the reverse: the married were relatively more negative whilst the widowed and divorced were more positive. Single respondents were more positive on Factors 3 and 4 but more negative on Factor 1.

The net impression of this analysis is that in sixteen out of the nineteen significant results presented in Table 3 positive feelings about the system were associated with greater means, education, knowledge, and higher social class. In three instances the results went the other way. A large proportion of the tests showed no significant results at all.

Clearly more research is needed in this area but our results may be said to provide some, though hardly strong, support for the belief that the less knowledge about the system or social or economic advantage one has the more likely it is that one will have a negative attitude to it.

TABLE 3 CORRELATION COEFFICIENT

		Factor 1	Factor 2	Factor 3	Factor 4
1.	Income	—	—	(+) 0·066**	(−) 0·094**
2.	Capital	(+) 0·094**	(+) 0·119**	(+) 0·054*	—
3.	Social Class	(+) 0·057**	—	—	—
4.	Sex*	—	—	—	(+) 0·100**
5.	Working or not†	(+) 0·055*	—	(−) 0·067**	(+) 0·078**
6.	Age of leaving school‡	(+) 0·062*	—	(+) 0·064**	(+) 0·049*
7.	Educational qualification§	—	—	—	—
8.	Knew a firm of solicitors§	—	(+) 0·141**	(+) 0·096**	—
9.	How much do lawyers charge‖	—	(+) 0·144**	(+) 0·086**	—
10.	Spoken to firm of solicitors in past seven years	—	—	—	—
11.	Knew poor can get free or cheap advice in solicitor's firm	—	—	—	—
12.	Had heard of legal aid scheme§	—	(+) 0·069*	(+) 0·061*	—

*The plus sign indicates that males were more significantly more negative about the system than females.

†The plus sign indicates that those who were working were more negative about the legal system than those who were not.

‡The plus sign indicates that those who left school earlier had a more negative attitude than those who left school later.

§The plus sign indicates that knowledge was associated with more positive feelings.

‖The plus sign shows that those who thought lawyers charged more were also more negative about the system.

Index

Accidents (*see Personal injuries*)

Accountants, 149, 153

Affiliation problems, 70, 71, 72, 79, 80, 90, 93, 96, 102, 103, 218, 237

Almoners, 153 (*see also Medical social workers*)

Amalgamated Engineering Union, 59, 86

Bank managers, 146, 149, 150, 153, 225

Bermondsey, 5, 22, 50
Parliamentary constituency of, 3, 17, 48, 233

Bernhard Baron Legal Advisory Service, 18, 34, 232, 234, 239

Bethnal Green,
citizens' advice bureau at, 22, 45
former Metropolitan Borough of, 3, 6
information department at, 50
Parliamentary constituency of, 3, 18, 48, 231

Blackwall, 6

Board of Trade, 148, 151, 153

Bow, 6, 15

Bromley, 6

Brown, R. W., M.P., 48, 84

Camberwell, 5
former Metropolitan Borough of, 3, 50
information centre at, 41, 50

Cambridge House,
family advice centre at, 51
foundation of, 30
legal advice centre at, 17, 22, 30–1, 32, 207, 215, 232, 240
work of, 30–1

Census,
1961, xi
1966, 9, 10, 89

Children's departments, 51, 57, 72, 76, 92, 218

Cambridge House (Southwark), 51, 232
Islington, 51, 233
Tower Hamlets, 232

Citizens' advice bureaux, 37, 38, 39–47, 53, 57, 58, 59, 62, 68, 71, 72, 73' 75, 76, 77, 78, 79, 83, 90, 92, 95– 101, 104, 147, 148, 149, 150, 151, 152, 153, 197, 198, 207, 208, 211, 213, 214, 215, 216, 217, 218, 221, 224, 225, 228, 231, 234, 235, 236, 238, 240
Bethnal Green, 17, 43
Bow Road, 15, 45
Dame Colet House, 17, 43, 44, 45, 231, 240
Denison House, 41
distribution of, 44
facilities at, 44–5
Finsbury, 16, 44, 231, 240
Islington, 16, 19, 41, 43, 44, 70, 231, 240
Jewish Institute, 17, 40, 43, 44, 45, 231, 240
opening hours of, 43
Pilgrim House, 17, 43, 44, 45, 231, 240
policy of, 46
Poplar, 15
Poplar House, 17, 40, 43, 44, 45, 231, 240
public knowledge of, 188–91, 221, 222
St Margaret's House 44, 45, 231, 240
Southwark, 16, 20, 41, 43, 44, 70, 188, 190, 231, 240
Tower Hamlets, 21, 40, 41, 43, 70, 188, 190, 211
Toynbee Hall, 17, 43, 44, 45, 231, 240
training scheme of, 42–3

Civil Service Union, 59

Compulsory purchase order problems, 71, 72, 78, 79, 90, 96
Conservative Party, 15, 49
    candidate for Peckham, 15
        for Southwark, 49, 233
    Peckham, 232
    Stepney, legal advice centre of, 15, 49, 232, 239
Corbett, Mrs F. A., M.P., 48
Courts, 54–6
    county courts, 56, 223, 229
        Bow, 86
        Lambeth, 85
    hearings, 161, 164, 166, 223
    magistrates courts, 54, 85, 233
        Clerkenwell, 85
        North London, 54, 85, 241
        Old Street, 31, 85, 241
        Thames, 31, 54, 85, 241
        Tower Bridge, 85, 241
    petty sessional courts, 55
    police courts, 229
Criminal problems, 71, 72, 73, 78, 79, 80, 82, 90, 93, 95, 96, 102, 167, 179–80, 220, 238
Cubitt Town, 6
Custody of children, 70, 71, 72, 78, 79, 90, 102, 218

Daily Express, 60
Daily Mail, 60, 87
Daily Mirror, 60, 87
Daily Sketch, 60, 87
Dame Colet House
    citizens' advice bureau at, 17, 22, 43, 44, 45, 231, 240
    legal advice centre at, 18, 34, 232
Dealers' associations, 149, 153
Death in the family, 130–3, 149, 157
    (see also Wills and winding up of estates)
Debt collection agencies, 149, 153
Debt problems, 71, 72, 78, 79, 80, 90, 93, 96, 102, 103, 169, 216, 217, 218, 237
    owed debts, 129, 143, 144, 148–9, 153, 154, 155, 156, 157, 158, 162, 163, 164, 169, 181, 219
    taken to court for debt, 129–30, 143, 144, 149, 153, 154, 155, 156, 158, 162, 163, 164, 167, 181, 219, 220

Defective goods (see Faulty goods and services)
Denison House citizens' advice bureau, 41
Divorce Reform Act 1970, 142
Doctors, 151, 207
    general practitioners, 73, 76, 77, 91, 97, 148
    surgeons, 150, 153
Dulwich, 5, 22
    Parliamentary constituency of, 3, 13, 17, 48, 84, 233

Electrical Trades Union, 59
Employment and redundancy problems, 60, 70, 71, 72, 73, 79, 80, 83, 90, 93, 96, 97, 102, 140–1, 143, 144, 151, 153, 154, 155, 156, 158, 162, 164, 181, 186, 216, 217, 218, 219, 220, 237
Epileptic societies, 151
Evans, A., M.P., 48
Eviction,
    attempted, 123–4, 143, 144, 147, 153, 154, 155, 156, 158, 162, 163, 164, 167, 181, 217, 219, 220, 221
    attempts to, 124, 143, 144, 147, 153, 154, 155, 156, 158, 167, 181, 219

Family advice centres, 51, 68, 73
    Cambridge House, 51
    Isle of Dogs, 51, 231
    Islington, 51
    Shadwell, 232
    Southwark, 232
    Tower Hamlets, 51
    Toynbee, 51, 232
Family Planning Association, 62
Family relationship problems, 70, 71, 72, 78, 79, 80, 90, 93, 96, 218
Family Welfare Association, 40, 41–3, 189
Faulty goods and services, 60, 71, 72, 79, 90, 93, 95, 96, 102, 124–6, 143, 144, 148, 153, 154, 155, 156, 157, 158, 168–9, 178, 181, 182, 219, 220
Finsbury, 4
    citizens' advice bureau at, 16, 44, 231, 240
    former Metropolitan Borough of, 3

Finsbury—*cont.*
    Shoreditch and,
        Parliamentary constituency of,
            3, 48, 84, 233
Fletcher, Sir Eric, M.P., 48, 84
Friends Neighbourhood House, 35, 233

General and Municipal Workers' Un-
    ion, 59
Gordon, J., 49
Greater London, 9, 10, 11, 39, 42
Greater London Council, 12, 29, 30, 31,
    32, 40, 45
Greek-Cypriot Brotherhood, 61, 87
Gunter, Rt Hon. R. V., M.P., 47

Heath, Rt Hon. Edward, M.P., x
Hilton, W. S., M.P., 48
Hire purchase problems, 58, 60, 83
    (*see also Instalment arrears*)
Homelessness, 71, 72, 78, 79, 90, 96
Hospitals, 57, 86, 151, 229, 233
House purchase problems, 70, 71, 72,
    79, 90, 93, 96, 124, 143, 144, 148,
    153, 154, 155, 156, 157, 158, 167,
    181, 217, 219
House repair problems, 122, 143, 144,
    146–7, 153, 154, 156, 158, 181,
    217, 219
Houses of Parliament, 48
Housing Act 1957, 167
Housing departments, 76, 92, 147, 218,
    229, 234
(*see also Local authority legal and housing
services*)
    Islington, 52, 69, 231
    Southwark, 52, 69, 233
    Tower Hamlets, 52, 69, 233
Housing problems, 70, 71, 72, 78, 79,
    90, 93, 96, 102, 147

Income tax problems, 71, 72, 73, 78, 79,
    90, 93, 96, 102
Information departments, 50, 73, 218,
    234
    Southwark, 231
        Bermondsey, 50
        Camberwell, 50
    Tower Hamlets, 50
Inner London, 9, 10, 11, 42, 53
Inner London Education Authority, 40

Instalment arrears, 127–8, 143, 144,
    148, 154, 155, 156, 157, 158, 162,
    163, 164, 169, 179, 181, 219 (*see
    also Hire purchase problems*)
Insurance brokers, 149, 150, 153, 216
Insurance problems, 71, 79
Isle of Dogs, 6, 15, 45, 51, 84
Islington, 3, 49, 70, 160, 211, 213, 214,
    231, 242
    advisory services in, 14–23
        adequacy of, 206
    children's department in, 51, 233
    citizens' advice bureaux in, 16, 19,
        41, 43–6, 69, 70, 188, 190, 191,
        208, 240
    elections in, 13
    historical development of, 4
    hospitals in, 57
    housing in, 9–13
    housing department in, 52, 69, 231
    legal advice centres in, 29–36, 69
    legal department in, 36–8, 69
    maternity and child welfare depart-
        ment in, 51, 243
    Members of Parliament for, 16, 48,
        49, 69
    Parliamentary constituencies in, 3
        Islington East, 3, 16, 48, 233
        Islington North, 3, 16, 48, 231
        Islington South-west, 3, 16, 48,
            231
        Shoreditch and Finsbury, 3, 16,
            48, 84, 233
    police in, 56, 85
    population density of, 8
    probation service in, 16, 53, 69, 228,
        232, 240
    rent tribunal in, 55–6, 86
    size of, 7
    social services in, 26–8, 160, 207, 214
    welfare department in, 233
Islington Tenants' and Residents'
    Association, 61, 87

John Hilton Bureau, 60, 87, 216
Juvenile court cases, 142, 143, 144, 152,
    153, 154, 155, 156, 158, 162, 164,
    167, 181, 187, 219

Labour Exchange, 151, 153, 207
Labour party, 13, 47, 207

Landlord and tenant problems, 53, 58, 61, 70, 71, 72, 78, 79, 80, 82, 83, 90, 93, 95, 96, 102, 123-4, 143, 144, 147, 168-9, 218, 237

Law List, 14, 46, 54, 55

Lawrence, Ivan, 49

Law Society, ix, 24, 25

Lawyers (*see Solicitors*)

Leases, 120-21, 143, 144, 146, 153, 154, 155, 156, 158, 167, 217, 219

Legal advice centres, 15, 19-21, 29-36, 57, 62, 68, 70, 72, 73, 74, 75, 76, 77, 83, 91, 92, 93, 97, 98, 101-6, 146, 147, 148, 149, 150, 151, 152, 153, 211, 213, 214, 215, 218, 220, 225, 233, 238

    Bernhard Baron, 18, 34, 232, 234, 239

    Cambridge House, 17, 30-1, 32, 207, 215, 232, 234, 240

    Dame Colet House, 18, 34, 232

    Friends Neighbourhood House, 35, 233

    Islington, 16, 35, 215

    Leysian Mission, 16, 35, 233

    Mary Ward, 29-30, 32, 207, 215, 229, 230, 232, 234, 240

    Poor Man's Lawyer, Islington, 233

    Toynbee Hall, 18, 32-3, 207, 215, 231, 234, 240

    University House, 18, 31-2, 44, 232, 234, 239

Legal Aid and Advice Act 1949, 24

Legal aid and advice scheme, 24-8, 57, 155, 160, 161-4, 207, 222, 224-5, 238

    knowledge of, 194-9, 221

Legal departments, 36-8, 63, 76, 91, 218 (*see also Local authority legal and housing services*)

    Islington, 36-8

    Southwark, 36-8

    Tower Hamlets, 36-8, 231

Leysian Mission, 16, 35, 233

Liberal party, 49, 84-5, 233

Limehouse, 6

Local Authority departments, 15, 16, 17, 18, 49-52, 74, 147, 152, 153, 207, 211, 214, 233 (*see also under Children's, Housing, Information, Legal, Maternity and Child Welfare, Public Health, and Welfare departments*)

Local authority legal and housing services, 68, 70, 72, 73, 74, 75, 76, 77, 92, 93

Local authority social services, 68, 70, 73, 74, 75, 76, 92, 93, 218 (*see also under Children's, Information, Maternity and child welfare, and Welfare departments*)

Local councillors, 61-2, 73, 76, 92

London Council of Social Service, 40, 42, 43

London Government Act 1963, 3

London Regional Citizens' Advice Bureau Advisory Committee, 40

London Transport, 150, 153

Lord Chancellor's Legal Aid Advisory Committee, ix

Magistrates Courts Act 1952, 55

Marriage Guidance Association, 62, 151, 153

Mary Ward Legal Advice Centre, 29-30, 32, 207, 215, 229, 230, 232, 234, 240

Maternity and child welfare clinics, 51, 77, 218

    Islington, 51, 231, 234

Matrimonial problems, 53, 58, 70, 71, 72, 78, 79, 80, 82, 90, 93, 96, 97, 102, 103, 141-2, 143, 144, 151, 153, 156, 158, 162, 163, 164, 167, 169, 181, 218, 219, 220, 222, 237

Medical social workers, 57, 147

Mellish, R., M.P., 84

Members of Parliament, 15, 16, 17, 18, 22, 47-9, 63, 68, 70, 72, 73, 74, 75, 76, 77, 84, 87, 92, 93, 147, 207, 211, 213, 214, 215, 218, 229, 231, 233, 238, 239

Mile End, 6

Millwall, 6

Mikardo, I., M.P., 48, 84

Milner-Holland Report, 12, 123

Ministry of Labour, 74, 76, 92, 104

Ministry of Social Security, 57, 58, 76, 91, 92, 153, 229, 233

Molony Committee on Consumer Protection, 40

National Assistance Board (*see Supplementary Benefits Commission*)

National Board for Prices and Incomes, ix, 216
National Citizens' Advice Bureaux Council, 39, 42, 46
National Union of Furniture and Trade Operatives, 60
Need for legal services, 109–45
Newington, 5
Neighbour problems, 71, 79, 96, 238
News of the World, 60, 87, 216
Newspapers, 60, 87, 228

Old Ford, 6, 15

Parliamentary constituencies,
  Bermondsey, 3, 17, 48, 233
  Bethnal Green, 3, 18, 48, 231
  Dulwich, 3, 13, 17, 48, 84, 233
  Islington East, 3, 16, 48, 233
  Islington North, 3, 16, 48, 231
  Islington South-west, 3, 16, 48, 231
  Peckham, 3, 17, 48, 84, 233
  Poplar, 3, 18, 48, 84, 233
  Shoreditch and Finsbury, 3, 16, 48, 84, 233
  Southwark, 2, 48, 49
  Stepney, 3, 18, 48, 233
Peckham, 5
  Conservative candidate for, 15
  Parliamentary constituency of, 3, 17, 48, 84, 233
People, The, 60, 87
Personal and financial difficulties, 71, 72, 79, 80, 90, 93, 94, 96
Personal injuries, 70, 71, 72, 73, 78, 79, 82, 83, 90, 93, 95, 96, 102, 135–40, 143, 144, 150, 153, 154, 155, 156, 158, 162, 164, 169–78, 181, 183, 216, 218, 219, 220, 237
Pilgrim House citizens' advice bureau, 17, 43, 44, 45, 231, 240
Police, 56–7, 74, 76, 85, 92, 97, 104, 150, 153, 207, 216, 229, 233
Political parties, 47–9, 63, 68, 74, 76, 92, 147, 211, 218, 233
Poplar, 6
  citizens' advice bureau in, 15
  former Metropolitan Borough of, 3
  Parliamentary constituency of, 3, 18, 48, 233
Poplar House citizens' advice bureau, 17, 40, 43, 44, 45, 231, 240

Population in the three boroughs, 8
  decline in, 7
  density per acre, 8
Poor Man's Lawyer, Islington, 233
Prices and Incomes Board (*see National Board for Prices and Incomes*)
Probate Registry, Personal Applications Department, 130, 149
Probation Service, 15, 22, 52–4, 57, 62, 68, 72, 73, 74, 75, 76, 77, 79, 80, 91, 92, 97, 98, 104, 152, 153, 207, 211, 214, 215, 224, 228, 234, 238, 241
  Islington, 16, 53, 69, 228, 232, 240
  Southwark, 17, 53, 69, 232, 240
  Tower Hamlets, 18, 53, 69, 232, 240
Protection from Eviction Act 1964, 36, 167
Psychiatric social workers, 148, 153
Public health departments, 50–1, 76, 92
  Tower Hamlets, 51, 83, 233

Rate rebate problems, 71, 72, 73, 90, 93, 96, 102
Rent Acts, 24, 50, 123, 167
Rent officer service, 15, 24, 36–8, 72, 77, 147, 153, 218, 234
  Islington, 16, 231
  Southwark, 17, 231
  Tower Hamlets, 18, 82, 233
Rent tribunal, 38, 55–6, 83, 86, 147, 168, 233
Repair problems (*see House repair problems*)
Reynolds, G., M.P., 48
Rotherhithe, 22

St Margaret's House citizens' advice bureau, 43, 44, 45, 231, 240
Shadwell, 6, 15, 51, 52
  family advice centre in, 232
Shoreditch and Finsbury,
  Parliamentary constituency of, 3, 16, 48, 84, 233
Silkin, The Hon. S. C., M.P., 48
Social security problems, 60, 71, 72, 73, 79, 80, 90, 93, 94, 95, 96, 140, 143, 144, 150, 153, 154, 155, 156, 157, 158, 162, 164, 181, 185, 218, 219, 220, 238
Society of Conservative Lawyers, ix

Society of Graphical and Allied Trades, 59
Society of Labour Lawyers, ix
Solicitors, 14–15, 24–8, 37, 57, 58, 59, 76, 77, 79, 80–2, 92, 97, 98, 103, 146, 147, 148, 149, 150, 151, 152, 153, 156–60, 207, 211, 213–14, 216, 219, 220, 221, 222, 224, 238
  and legal aid, 24–8, 198–9
  attitudes to, 249–58
  cost of, 200–2, 221
  Islington, 15, 24–8, 160, 207, 213–14
  perceived role of, 203–5, 224
  public image of, 225
  public knowledge and use of, 191–4
  Southwark, 15, 24–8, 82, 160, 191, 208, 213–14
  Tower Hamlets, 15, 24–8, 160, 191, 208, 213–14
Southwark, 3, 211, 213, 228, 242
  advisory services, in, 14–23
    adequacy of, 206
  children's department in, 51, 232
  citizens' advice bureaux in, 16, 20, 41, 43, 44, 69, 70, 188, 190, 231, 240
  historical development of, 5–6
  housing in, 9–13
  housing department in, 52, 69, 233
  information department in, 50, 231
  legal advice centres in, 29–36, 69
  legal department in, 36–8, 69, 233
  Members of Parliament for, 17, 48, 49, 67
  Parliamentary constituencies in, 3
    Bermondsey, 3, 17, 48, 233
    Southwark, 3, 48, 49
    Peckham, 3, 17, 48, 84, 233
    Dulwich, 3, 13, 17, 48, 84, 233
  police in, 56, 85
  population density of, 8
  probation service in, 17, 53, 69, 232, 240
  rent tribunal in, 55–6
  size of, 7
  social services in, 69
  solicitors in, 15, 26–8, 82, 160, 191, 208, 213–14
  welfare department in, 52, 231
Spitalfields, 6
Stepney, 6

Conservative party in, 15, 49, 232, 239
  former Metropolitan Borough of, 3
  Parliamentary constituency of, 3, 18, 48, 233
Sunday Mirror, 60, 87
Supplementary benefits
  claims, 78, 140
  commission, 25, 207
Surveyors, 147, 153

Tower Hamlets, 3, 22, 49, 213, 224, 228, 242
  advisory services in, 14–23
    adequacy of, 206
  children's department in, 51, 232
  citizens' advice bureaux in, 21, 40, 41, 43, 70, 188, 190, 211
  historical development of, 6–7
  housing in, 9–13
  housing department in, 52, 69, 83, 233
  legal advice centres in, 29–36, 69
  legal department in, 36–8, 69, 70, 231
  Members of Parliament for, 48, 49, 69
  Parliamentary constituencies in, 3
    Bethnal Green, 3, 18, 48, 231
    Poplar, 3, 18, 48, 233
    Stepney, 3, 18, 48, 233
  police in, 56
  population density of, 8
  probation service in, 53, 69, 232, 240
  public health department in, 51, 83, 233
  rent officer in, 82
  rent tribunal in, 55–6
  size of, 7
  social services in, 69
  solicitors in, 15, 26–8, 160, 191, 208, 213–14
  welfare department in, 52, 231
Town Halls (see Local authority departments)
Toynbee Hall
  citizens' advice bureau at, 17, 22, 43, 44, 45, 231, 240
  family advice centre at, 51, 232
  legal advice centre at, 18, 32–3, 207, 215, 231, 234, 240
Trade Unions, 58–60, 76, 86, 92, 150, 153, 207, 216, 217, 227, 233

Transport and General Workers Union, 59, 86

University House legal advice centre, 18, 31, 32, 44, 232, 234, 239

Voluntary agencies, 76, 91, 92, 97

Walworth, 5
Wapping, 6, 51

Welfare departments, 52, 72, 76, 92, 207, 218
  Islington, 233
  Southwark, 52, 231
  Tower Hamlets, 52, 231
  Whitechapel, 6
Wills and winding up of estates, 71, 72, 73, 79, 90, 96, 102, 130–5, 143, 144, 149–50, 153, 154, 155, 156, 157, 158, 183, 216, 219, 237

B6